K-ON! 4

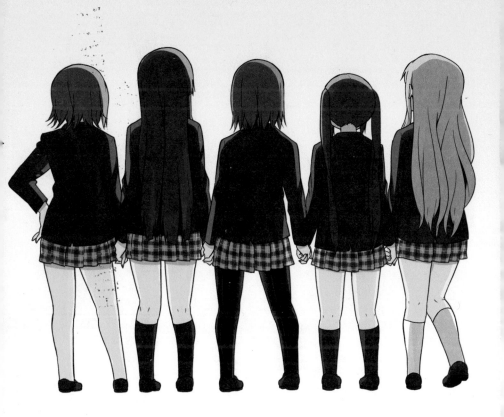

PRESENTED BY
kakifly

C H A R A C T E R S

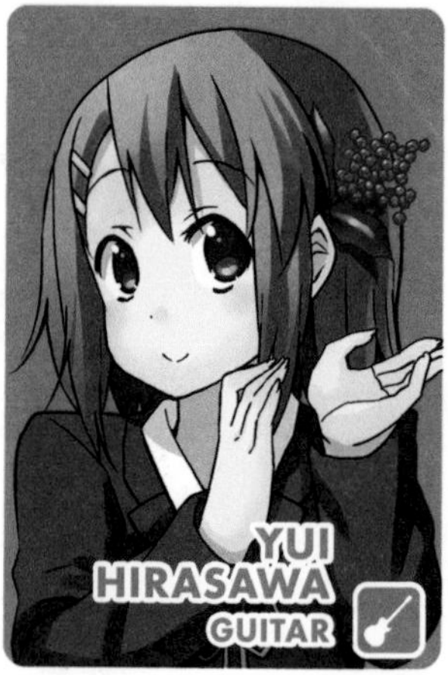
YUI
HIRASAWA
GUITAR

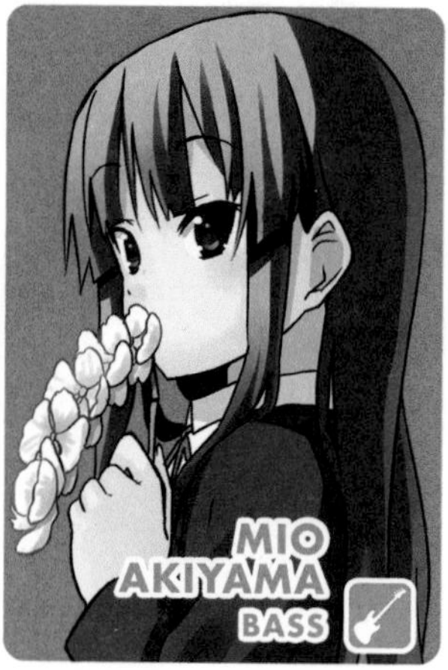
MIO
AKIYAMA
BASS

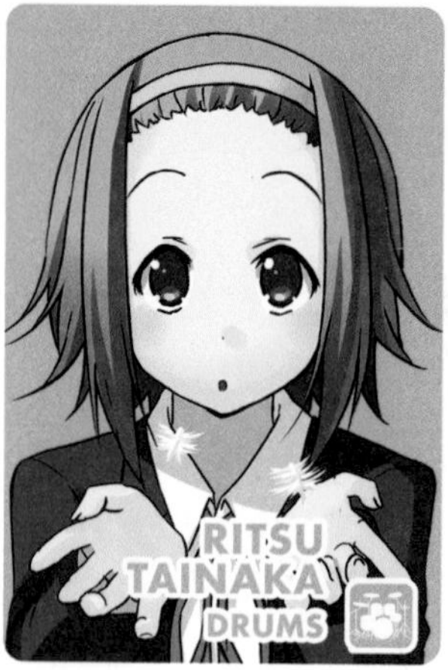
RITSU
TAINAKA
DRUMS

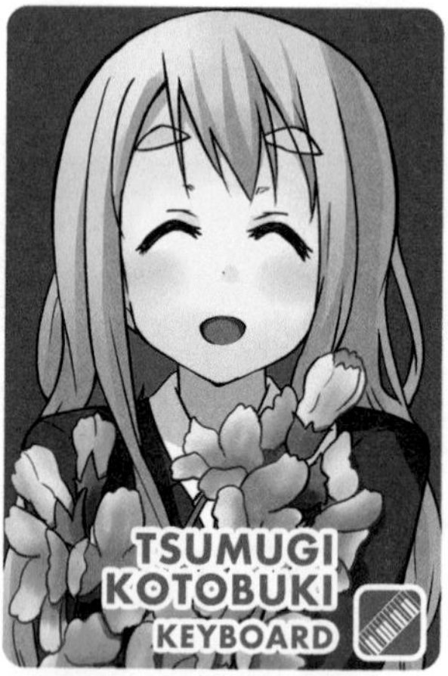
TSUMUGI
KOTOBUKI
KEYBOARD

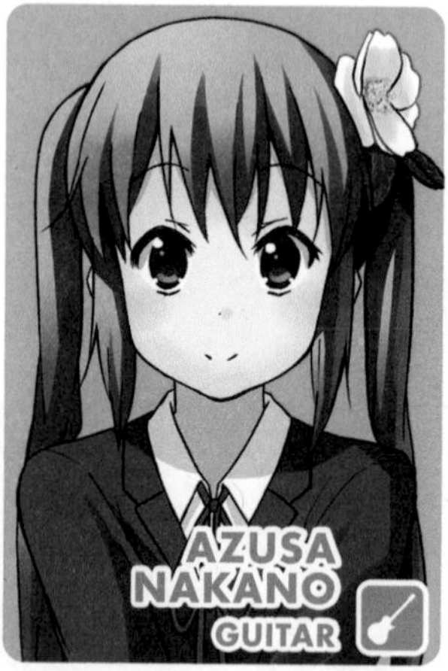
AZUSA
NAKANO
GUITAR

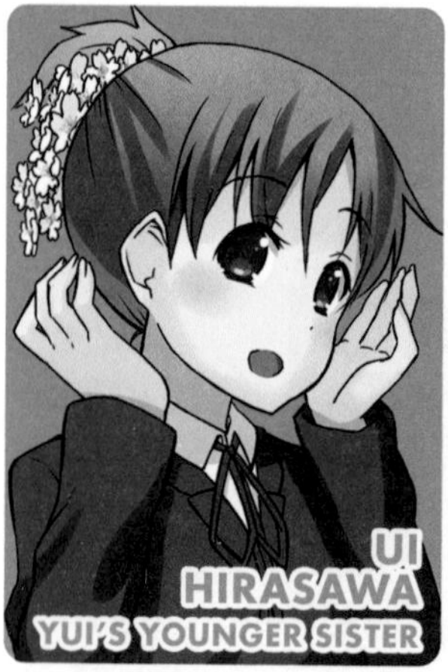
UI
HIRASAWA
YUI'S YOUNGER SISTER

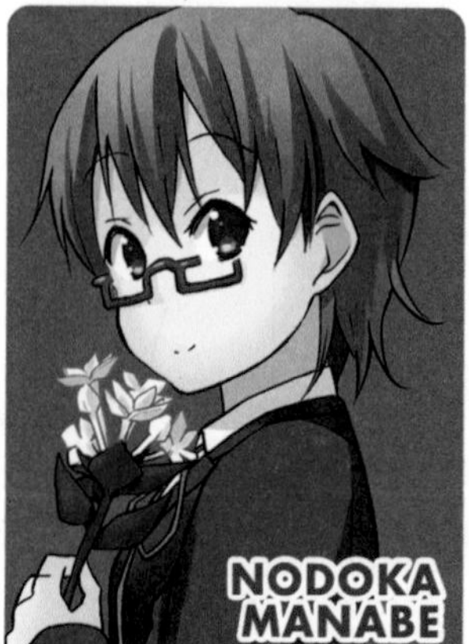
NODOKA
MANABE
YUI'S FRIEND

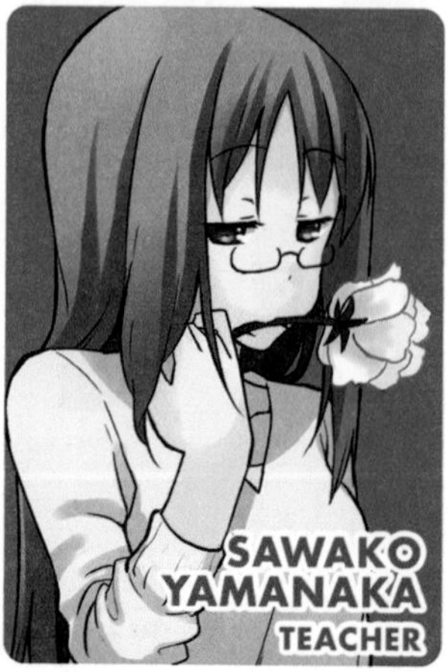
SAWAKO
YAMANAKA
TEACHER

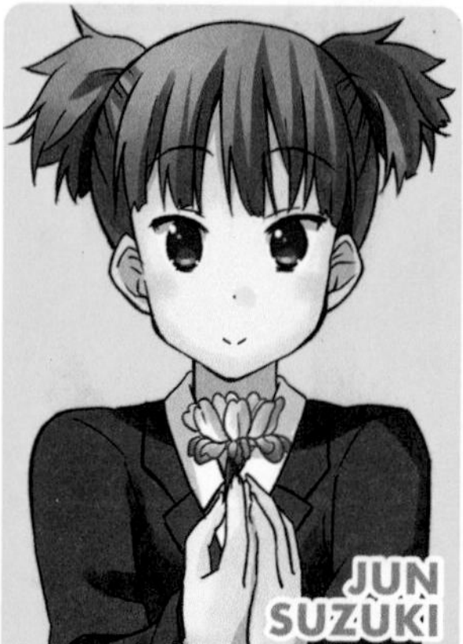
JUN
SUZUKI
UI AND AZUSA'S FRIEND

K-ON! CHARACTER INTRO kakifly

HOUBUNSHA MANGA TIME KR COMICS

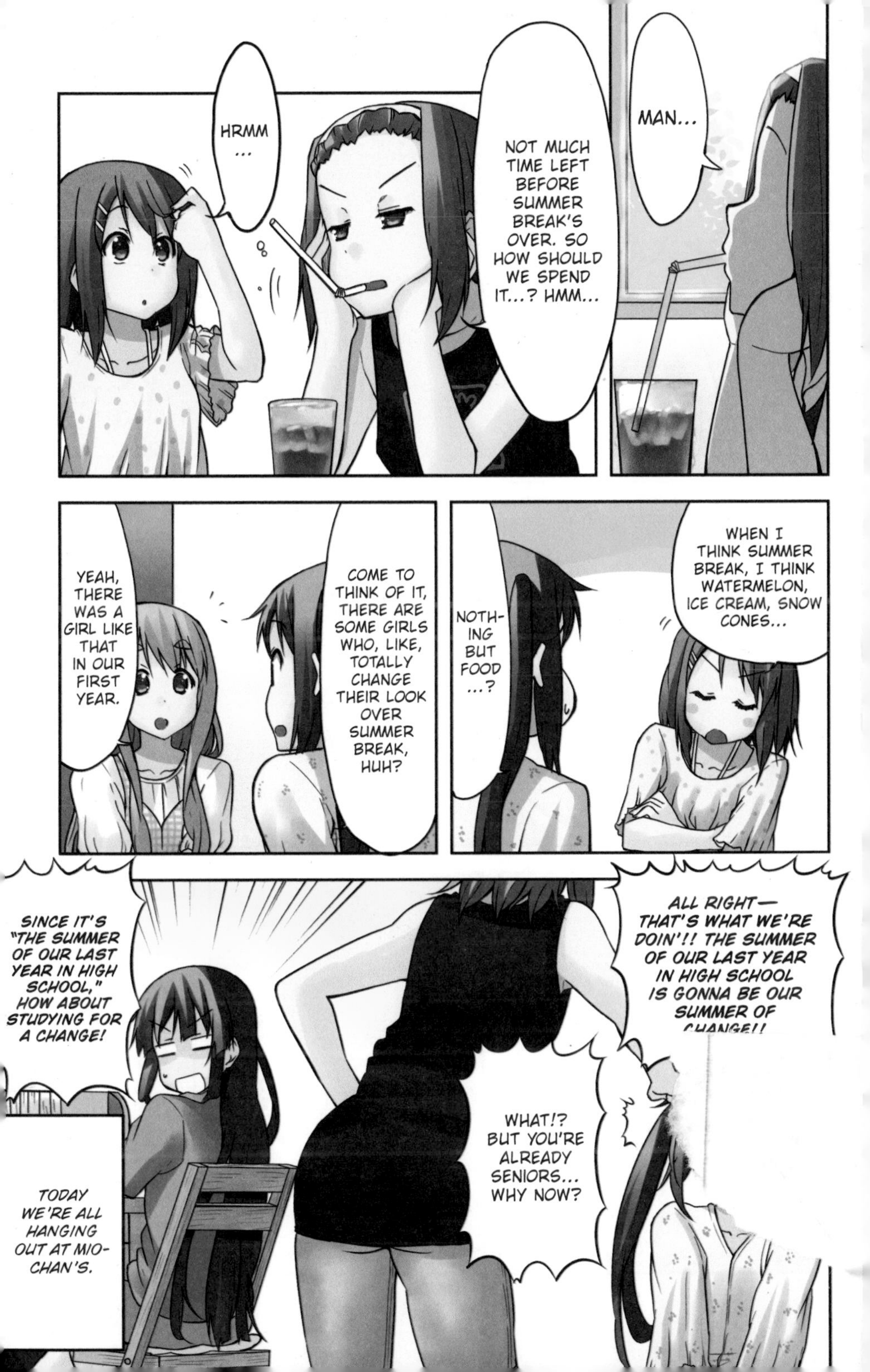
MAN...
NOT MUCH TIME LEFT BEFORE SUMMER BREAK'S OVER. SO HOW SHOULD WE SPEND IT...? HMM...
HRMM ...
WHEN I THINK SUMMER BREAK, I THINK WATERMELON, ICE CREAM, SNOW CONES...
NOTHING BUT FOOD ...?
COME TO THINK OF IT, THERE ARE SOME GIRLS WHO, LIKE, TOTALLY CHANGE THEIR LOOK OVER SUMMER BREAK, HUH?
YEAH, THERE WAS A GIRL LIKE THAT IN OUR FIRST YEAR.
ALL RIGHT—THAT'S WHAT WE'RE DOIN'!! THE SUMMER OF OUR LAST YEAR IN HIGH SCHOOL IS GONNA BE OUR SUMMER OF CHANGE!!
SINCE IT'S "THE SUMMER OF OUR LAST YEAR IN HIGH SCHOOL," HOW ABOUT STUDYING FOR A CHANGE!
WHAT!? BUT YOU'RE ALREADY SENIORS... WHY NOW?
TODAY WE'RE ALL HANGING OUT AT MIO-CHAN'S.

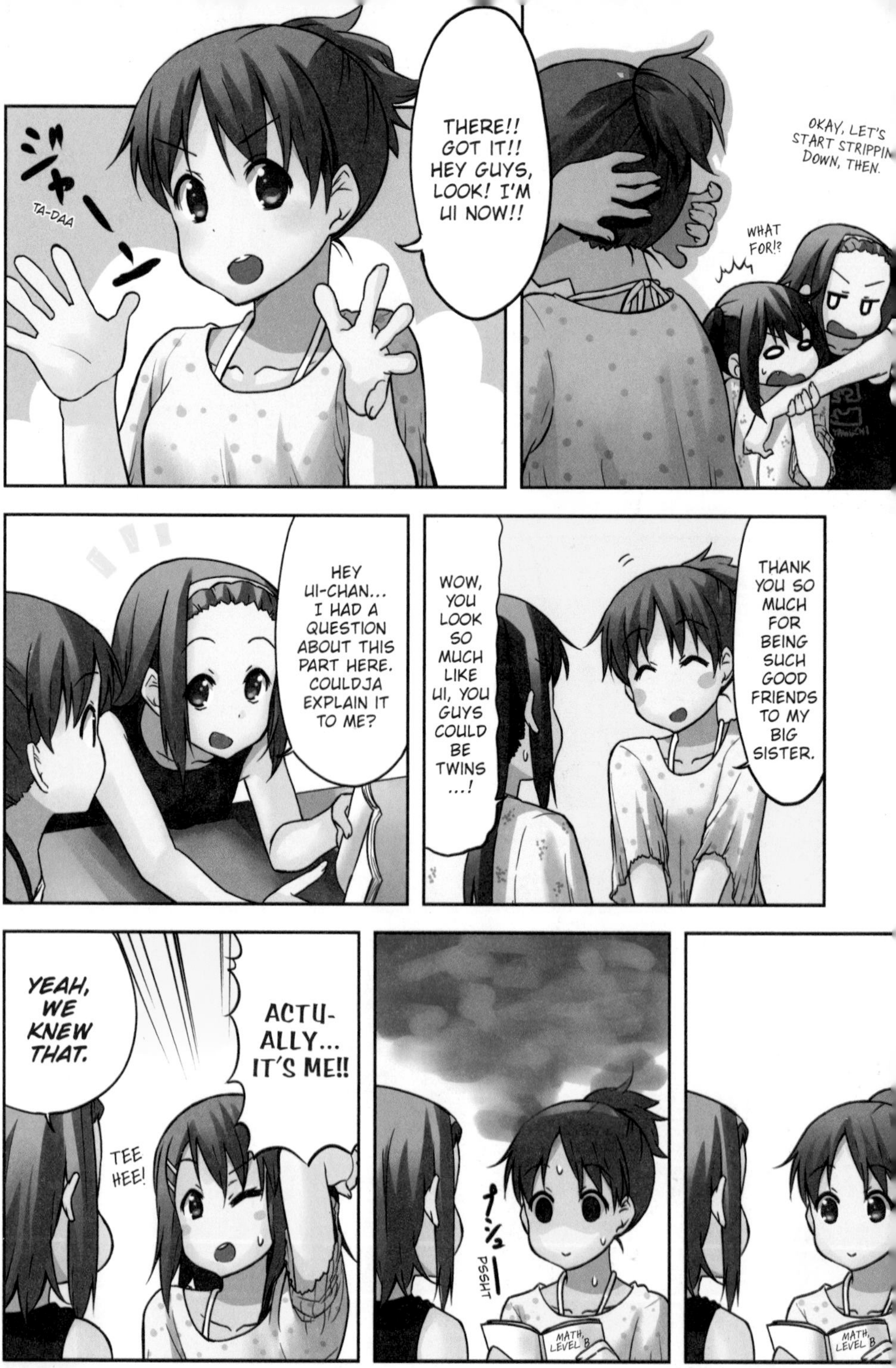
TA-DAA
THERE!! GOT IT!! HEY GUYS, LOOK! I'M UI NOW!!
OKAY, LET'S START STRIPPIN DOWN, THEN.
WHAT FOR!?
HEY UI-CHAN... I HAD A QUESTION ABOUT THIS PART HERE. COULDJA EXPLAIN IT TO ME?
THANK YOU SO MUCH FOR BEING SUCH GOOD FRIENDS TO MY BIG SISTER.
WOW, YOU LOOK SO MUCH LIKE UI, YOU GUYS COULD BE TWINS...!
ACTU-ALLY... IT'S ME!!
YEAH, WE KNEW THAT.
TEE HEE!
PSSHT
MATH, LEVEL B
MATH, LEVEL B

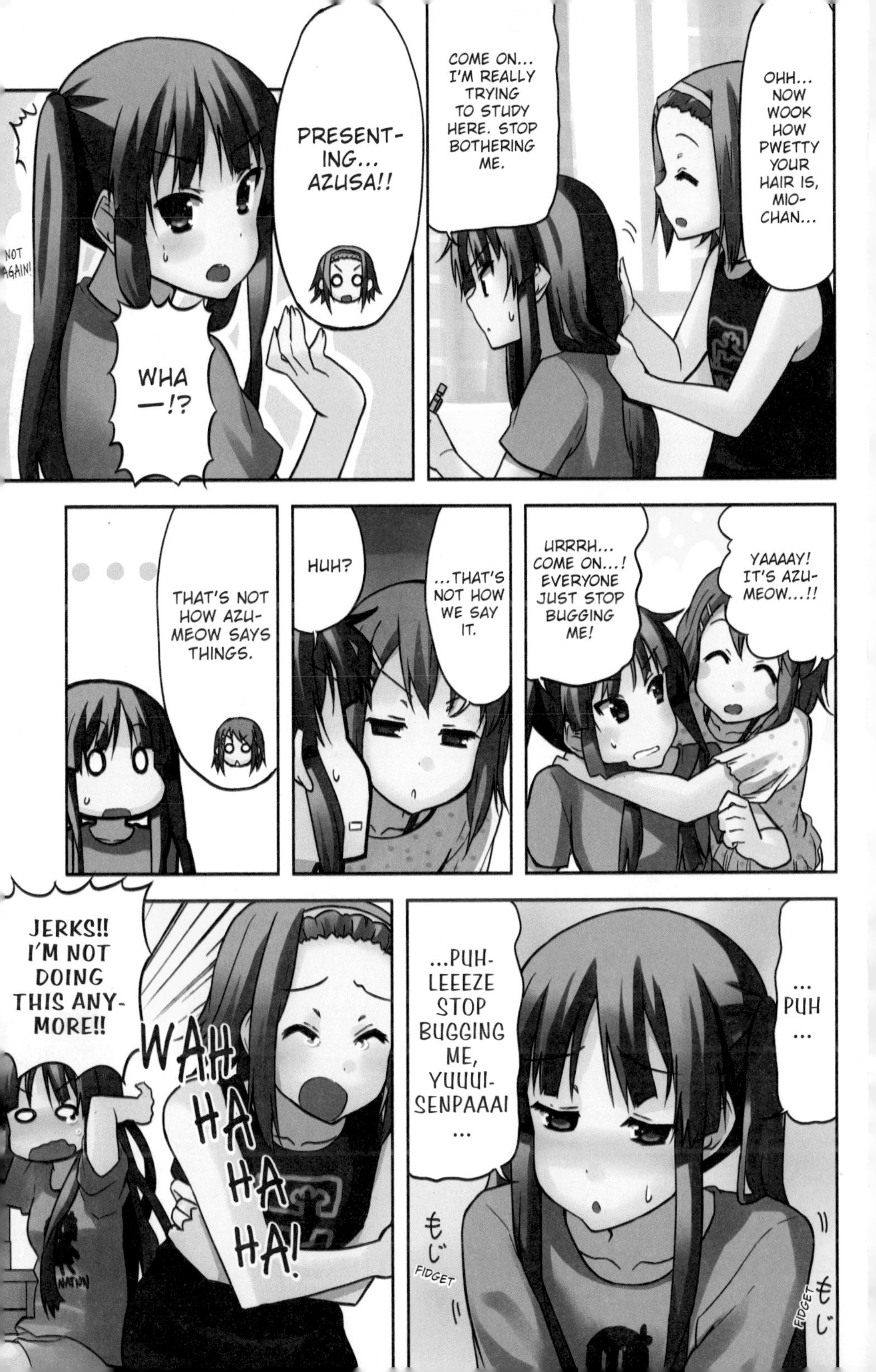

OHH... NOW WOOK HOW PWETTY YOUR HAIR IS, MIO-CHAN...
COME ON... I'M REALLY TRYING TO STUDY HERE. STOP BOTHERING ME.
PRESENT-ING... AZUSA!!
WHA—!?
NOT AGAIN!
YAAAAY! IT'S AZU-MEOW...!!
URRRH... COME ON...! EVERYONE JUST STOP BUGGING ME!
...THAT'S NOT HOW WE SAY IT.
HUH?
THAT'S NOT HOW AZU-MEOW SAYS THINGS.
...
... PUH ...
...PUH-LEEEZE STOP BUGGING ME, YUUUI-SENPAAAI ...
もじ FIDGET
もじ FIDGET
WAH HA HA HA HA!
JERKS!! I'M NOT DOING THIS ANY-MORE!!

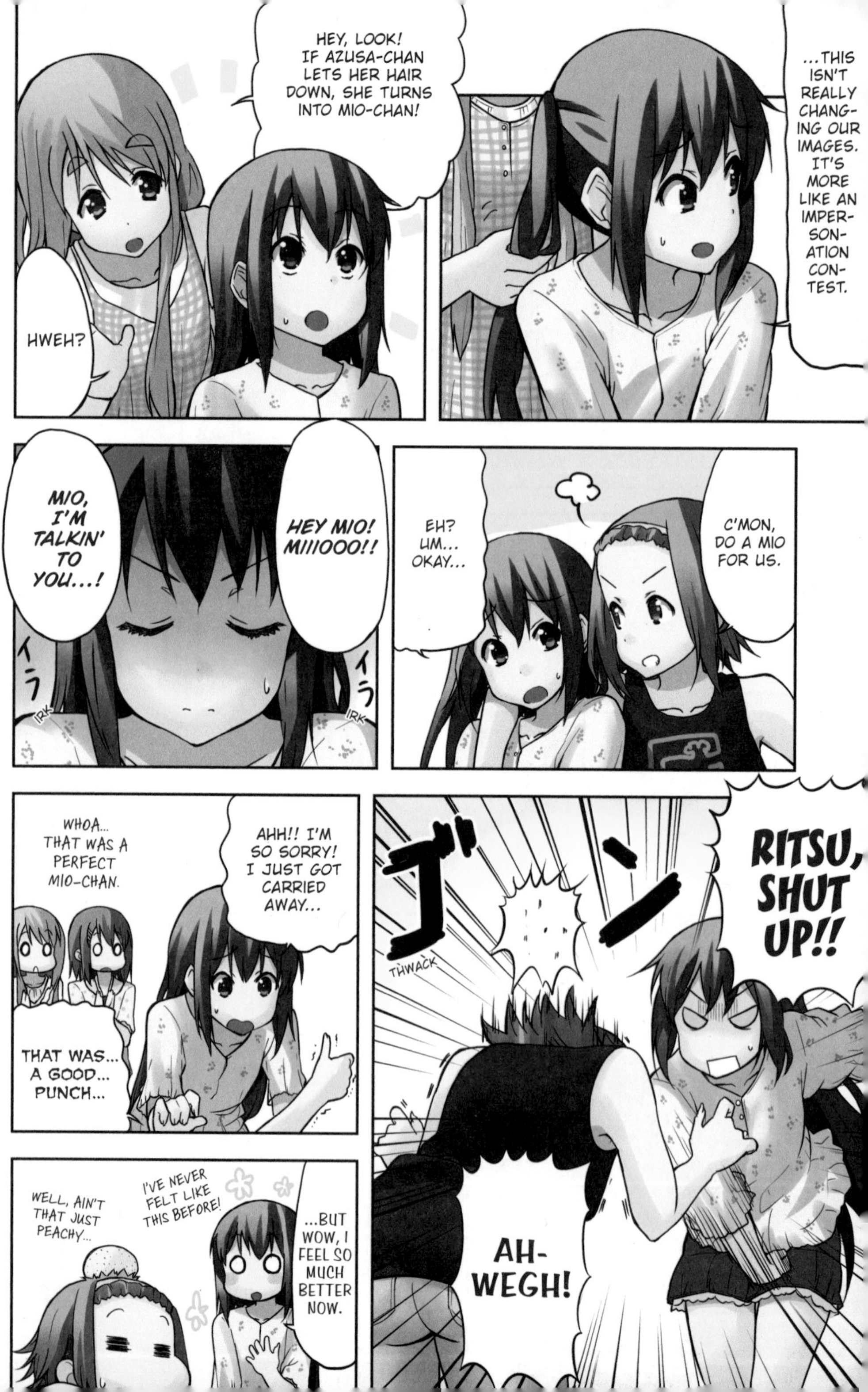
...THIS ISN'T REALLY CHANGING OUR IMAGES. IT'S MORE LIKE AN IMPERSONATION CONTEST.
HEY, LOOK! IF AZUSA-CHAN LETS HER HAIR DOWN, SHE TURNS INTO MIO-CHAN!
HWEH?
C'MON, DO A MIO FOR US.
EH? UM... OKAY...
HEY MIO! MIIIOOO!!
MIO, I'M TALKIN' TO YOU...!
イラ
IRK
イラ
IRK
RITSU, SHUT UP!!
THWACK
AH-WEGH!
AHH!! I'M SO SORRY! I JUST GOT CARRIED AWAY...
WHOA... THAT WAS A PERFECT MIO-CHAN.
THAT WAS... A GOOD... PUNCH...
...BUT WOW, I FEEL SO MUCH BETTER NOW.
I'VE NEVER FELT LIKE THIS BEFORE!
WELL, AIN'T THAT JUST PEACHY...

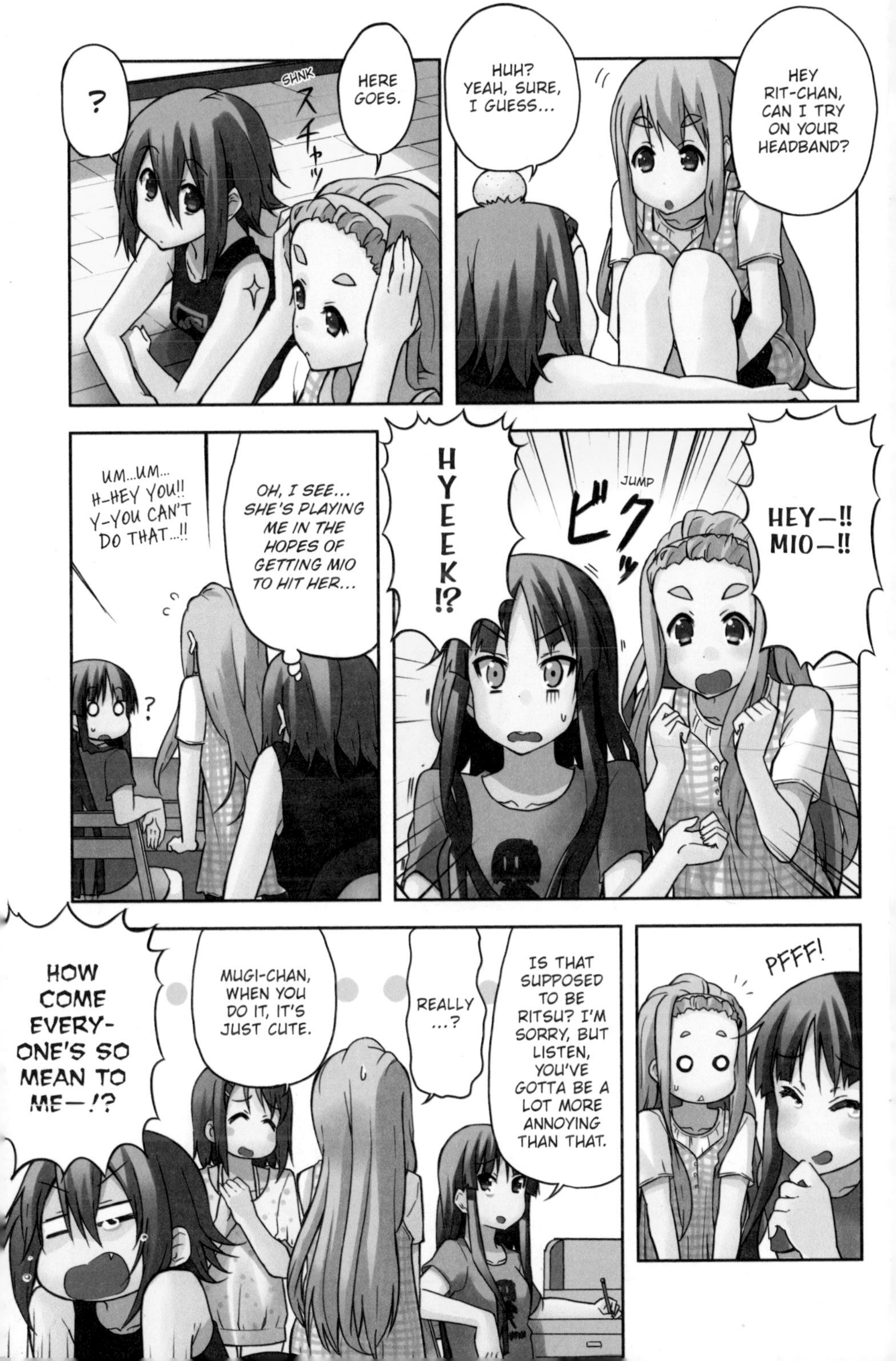
HEY RIT-CHAN, CAN I TRY ON YOUR HEADBAND?
HUH? YEAH, SURE, I GUESS...
HERE GOES.
SHNK
スチャッ
?
HEY—!! MIO—!!
JUMP
ビクッ
HYEEK!?
OH, I SEE... SHE'S PLAYING ME IN THE HOPES OF GETTING MIO TO HIT HER...
UM...UM... H-HEY YOU!! Y-YOU CAN'T DO THAT...!!
?
PFFF!
IS THAT SUPPOSED TO BE RITSU? I'M SORRY, BUT LISTEN, YOU'VE GOTTA BE A LOT MORE ANNOYING THAN THAT.
REALLY ...?
MUGI-CHAN, WHEN YOU DO IT, IT'S JUST CUTE.
HOW COME EVERY-ONE'S SO MEAN TO ME—!?

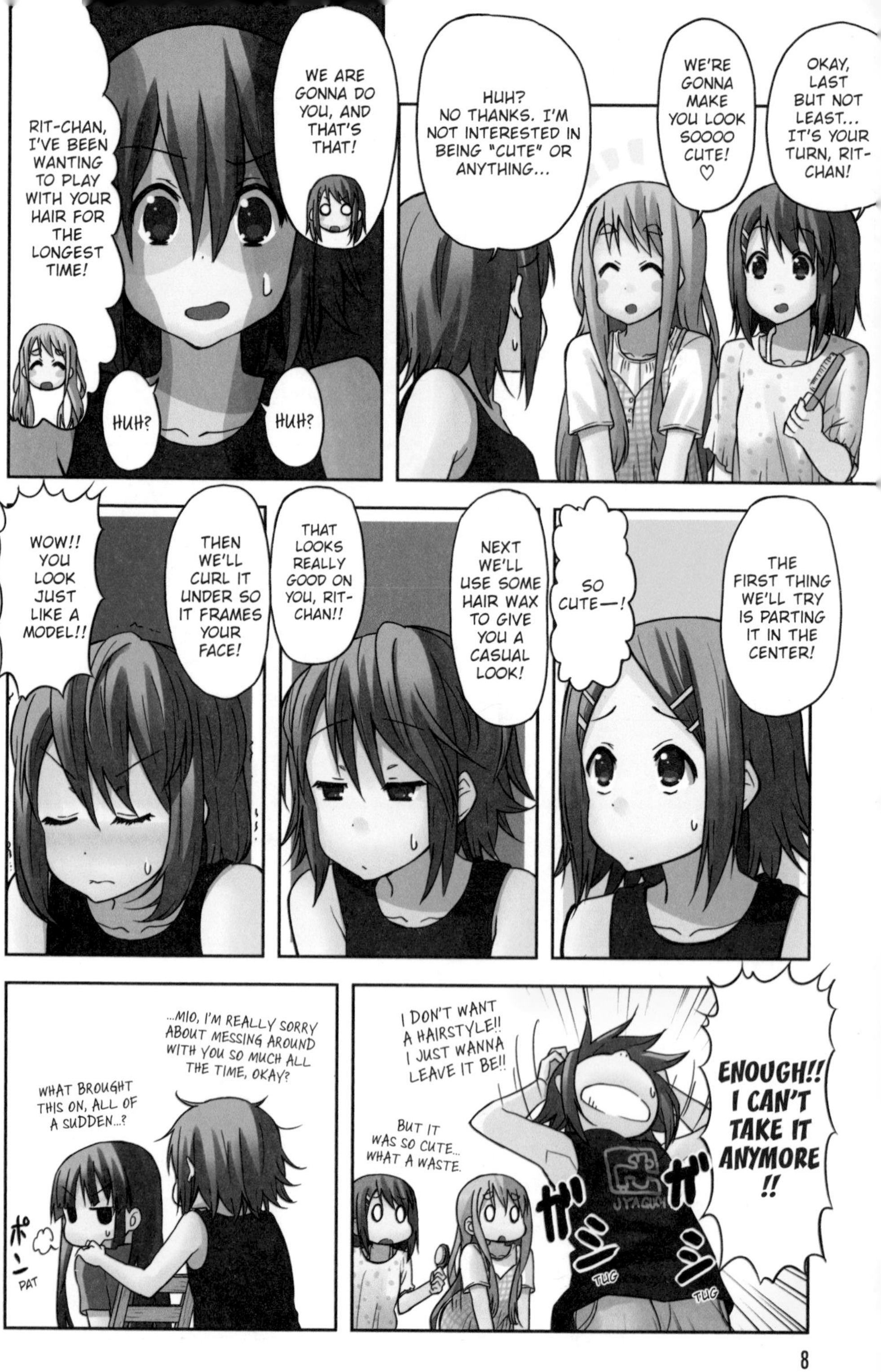
OKAY, LAST BUT NOT LEAST... IT'S YOUR TURN, RIT-CHAN!
WE'RE GONNA MAKE YOU LOOK SOOOO CUTE! ♡
HUH? NO THANKS. I'M NOT INTERESTED IN BEING "CUTE" OR ANYTHING...
WE ARE GONNA DO YOU, AND THAT'S THAT!
RIT-CHAN, I'VE BEEN WANTING TO PLAY WITH YOUR HAIR FOR THE LONGEST TIME!
HUH?
HUH?
THE FIRST THING WE'LL TRY IS PARTING IT IN THE CENTER!
SO CUTE—!
NEXT WE'LL USE SOME HAIR WAX TO GIVE YOU A CASUAL LOOK!
THAT LOOKS REALLY GOOD ON YOU, RIT-CHAN!!
THEN WE'LL CURL IT UNDER SO IT FRAMES YOUR FACE!
WOW!! YOU LOOK JUST LIKE A MODEL!!
ENOUGH!! I CAN'T TAKE IT ANYMORE!!
I DON'T WANT A HAIRSTYLE!! I JUST WANNA LEAVE IT BE!!
BUT IT WAS SO CUTE... WHAT A WASTE.
TUG
TUG
...MIO, I'M REALLY SORRY ABOUT MESSING AROUND WITH YOU SO MUCH ALL THE TIME, OKAY?
WHAT BROUGHT THIS ON, ALL OF A SUDDEN...?
PAT

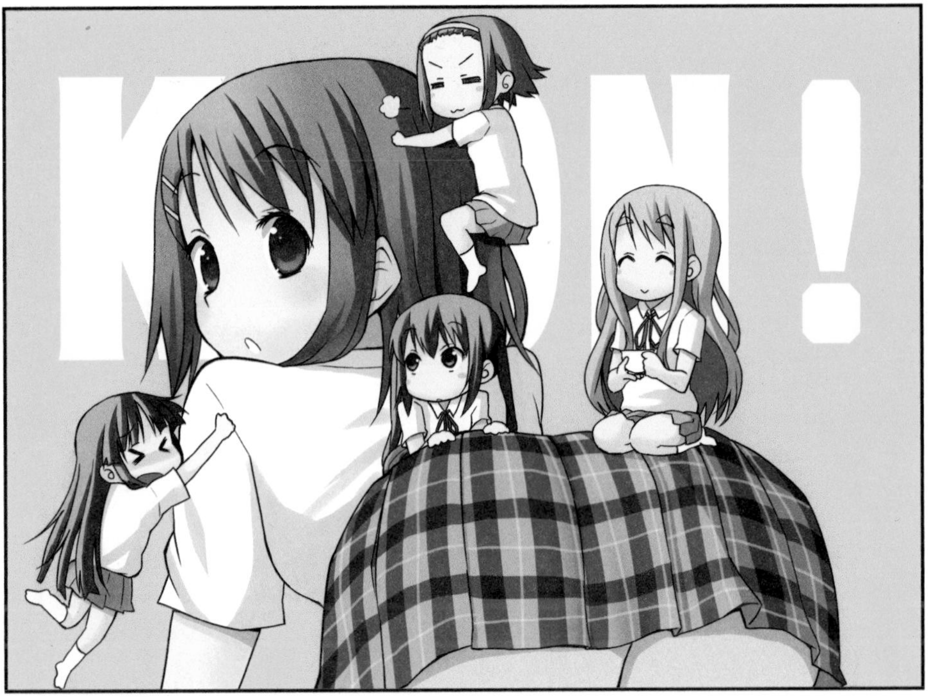

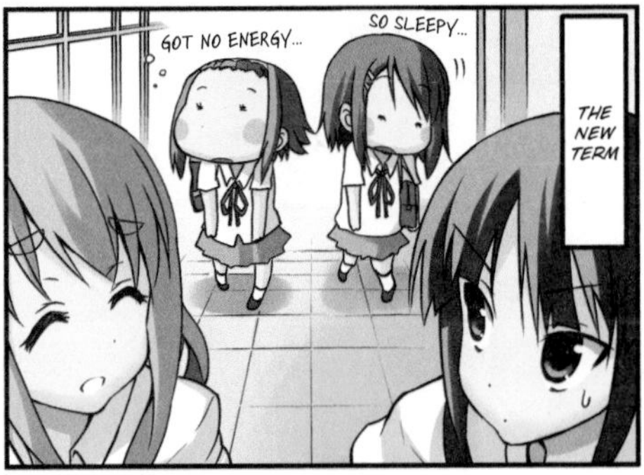
THE NEW TERM
GOT NO ENERGY...
SO SLEEPY...

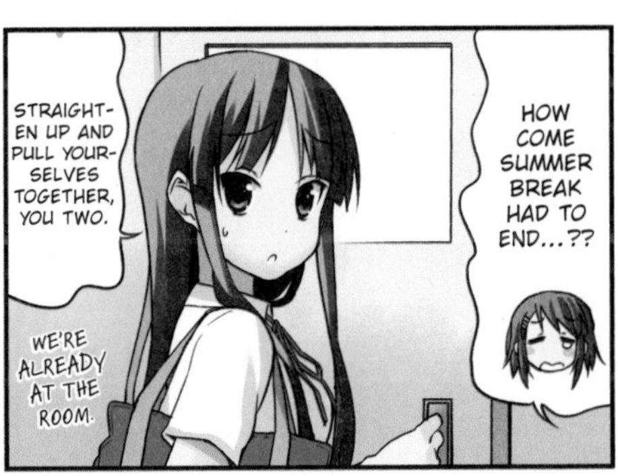
HOW COME SUMMER BREAK HAD TO END...??
STRAIGHT-EN UP AND PULL YOUR-SELVES TOGETHER, YOU TWO.
WE'RE ALREADY AT THE ROOM.

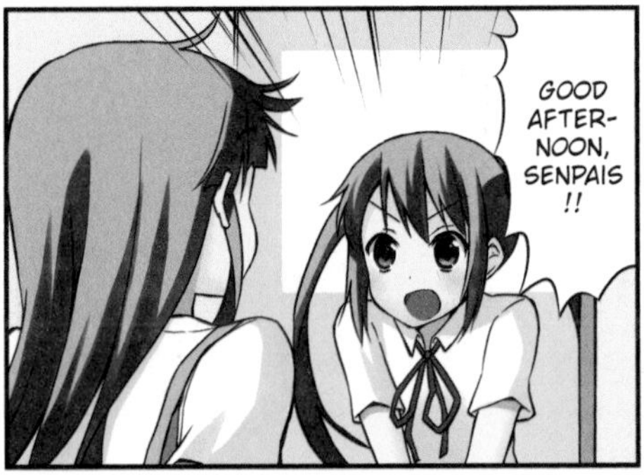
GOOD AFTER-NOON, SENPAIS !!

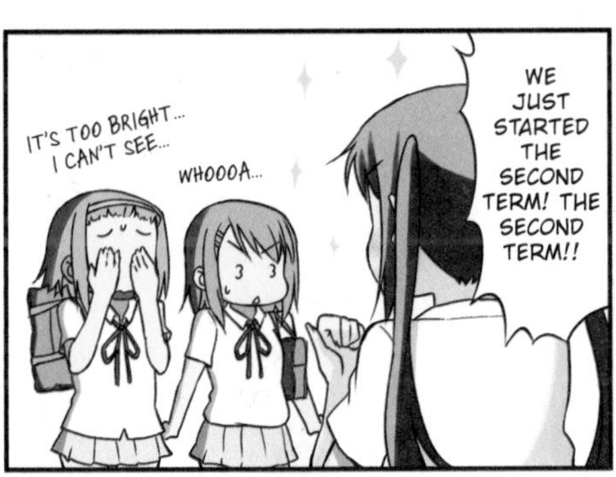
WE JUST STARTED THE SECOND TERM! THE SECOND TERM!!
IT'S TOO BRIGHT... I CAN'T SEE...
WHOOOA...

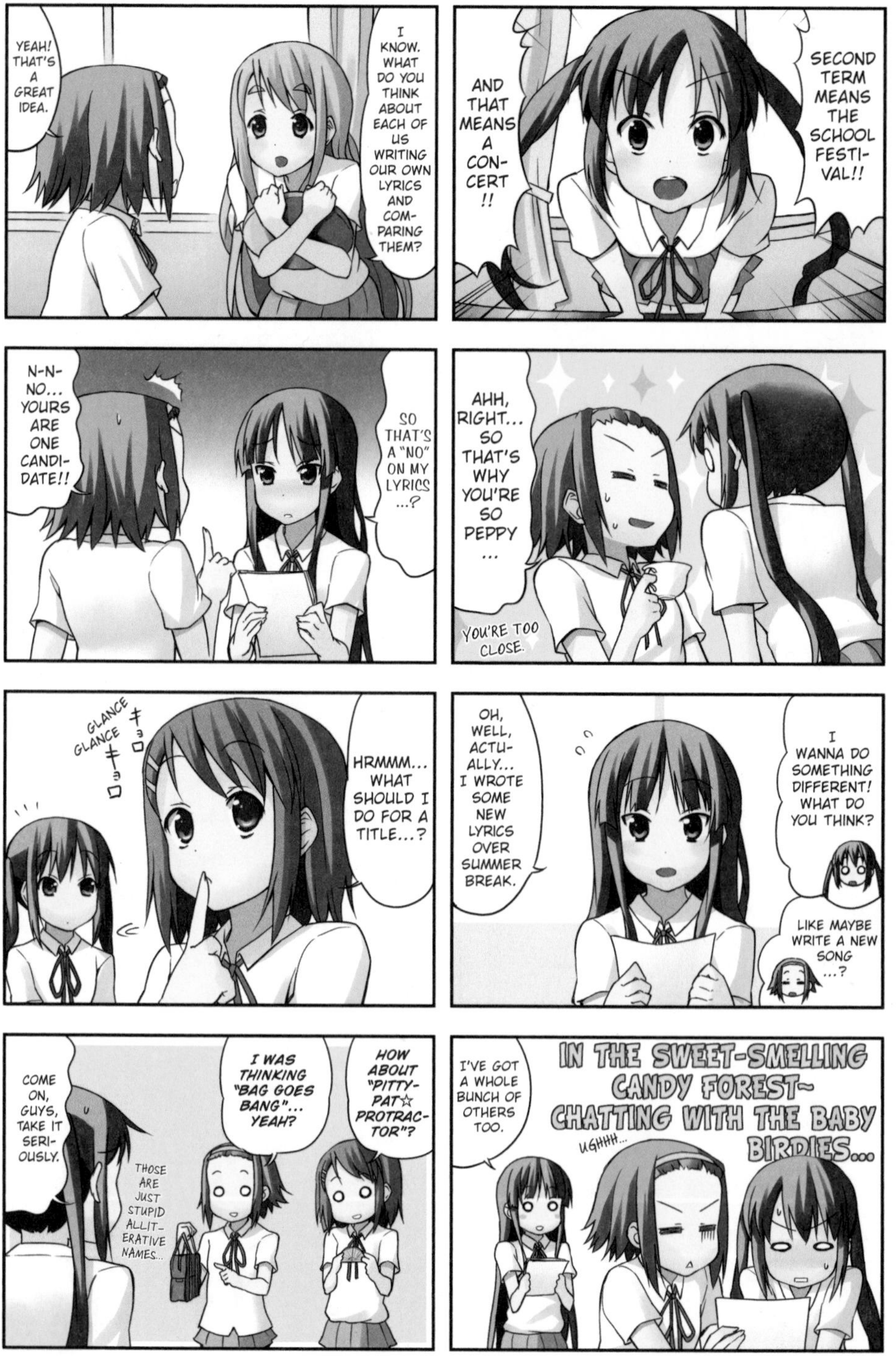
SECOND TERM MEANS THE SCHOOL FESTIVAL!!
AND THAT MEANS A CONCERT!!
AHH, RIGHT... SO THAT'S WHY YOU'RE SO PEPPY...
YOU'RE TOO CLOSE.
I WANNA DO SOMETHING DIFFERENT! WHAT DO YOU THINK?
LIKE MAYBE WRITE A NEW SONG ...?
OH, WELL, ACTUALLY... I WROTE SOME NEW LYRICS OVER SUMMER BREAK.
IN THE SWEET-SMELLING CANDY FOREST~ CHATTING WITH THE BABY BIRDIES...
I'VE GOT A WHOLE BUNCH OF OTHERS TOO.
UGHHH...
I KNOW. WHAT DO YOU THINK ABOUT EACH OF US WRITING OUR OWN LYRICS AND COMPARING THEM?
YEAH! THAT'S A GREAT IDEA.
SO THAT'S A "NO" ON MY LYRICS ...?
N-N-NO... YOURS ARE ONE CANDIDATE!!
HRMMM... WHAT SHOULD I DO FOR A TITLE...?
GLANCE キョロ
GLANCE キョロ
HOW ABOUT "PITTY-PAT☆ PROTRACTOR"?
I WAS THINKING "BAG GOES BANG"... YEAH?
COME ON, GUYS, TAKE IT SERIOUSLY.
THOSE ARE JUST STUPID ALLITERATIVE NAMES...

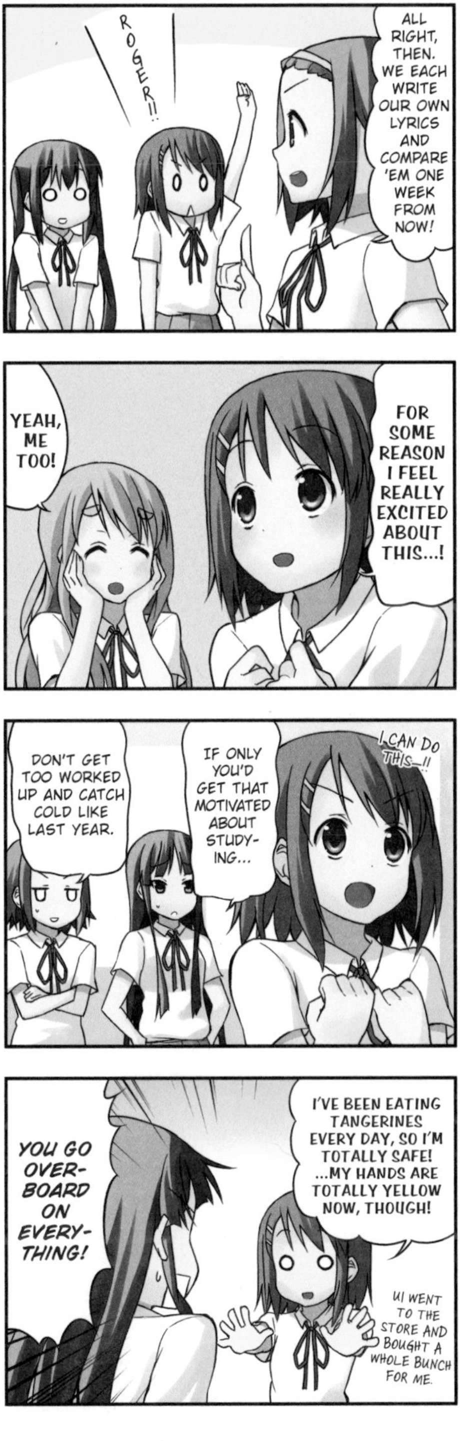
ALL RIGHT, THEN. WE EACH WRITE OUR OWN LYRICS AND COMPARE 'EM ONE WEEK FROM NOW!
ROGER!!
FOR SOME REASON I FEEL REALLY EXCITED ABOUT THIS...!
YEAH, ME TOO!
I CAN DO THIS...!!
IF ONLY YOU'D GET THAT MOTIVATED ABOUT STUDYING...
DON'T GET TOO WORKED UP AND CATCH COLD LIKE LAST YEAR.
I'VE BEEN EATING TANGERINES EVERY DAY, SO I'M TOTALLY SAFE! ...MY HANDS ARE TOTALLY YELLOW NOW, THOUGH!
YOU GO OVERBOARD ON EVERYTHING!
UI WENT TO THE STORE AND BOUGHT A WHOLE BUNCH FOR ME.
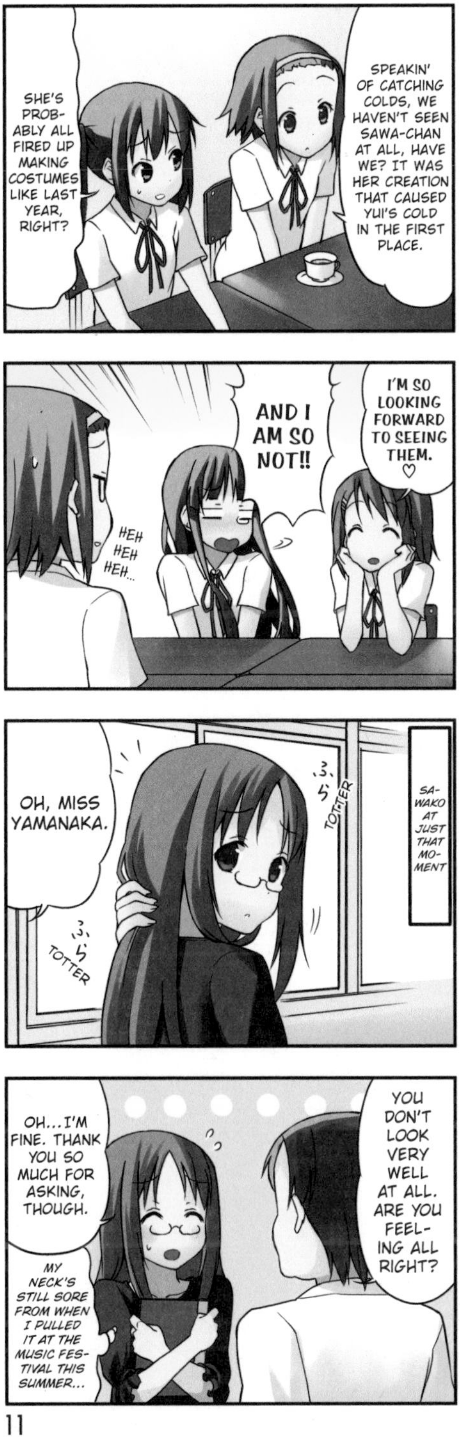
SPEAKIN' OF CATCHING COLDS, WE HAVEN'T SEEN SAWA-CHAN AT ALL, HAVE WE? IT WAS HER CREATION THAT CAUSED YUI'S COLD IN THE FIRST PLACE.
SHE'S PROBABLY ALL FIRED UP MAKING COSTUMES LIKE LAST YEAR, RIGHT?
I'M SO LOOKING FORWARD TO SEEING THEM. ♡
AND I AM SO NOT!!
HEH HEH HEH...
SAWAKO AT JUST THAT MOMENT
TOTTER
OH, MISS YAMANAKA.
TOTTER
YOU DON'T LOOK VERY WELL AT ALL. ARE YOU FEELING ALL RIGHT?
OH... I'M FINE. THANK YOU SO MUCH FOR ASKING, THOUGH.
MY NECK'S STILL SORE FROM WHEN I PULLED IT AT THE MUSIC FESTIVAL THIS SUMMER...

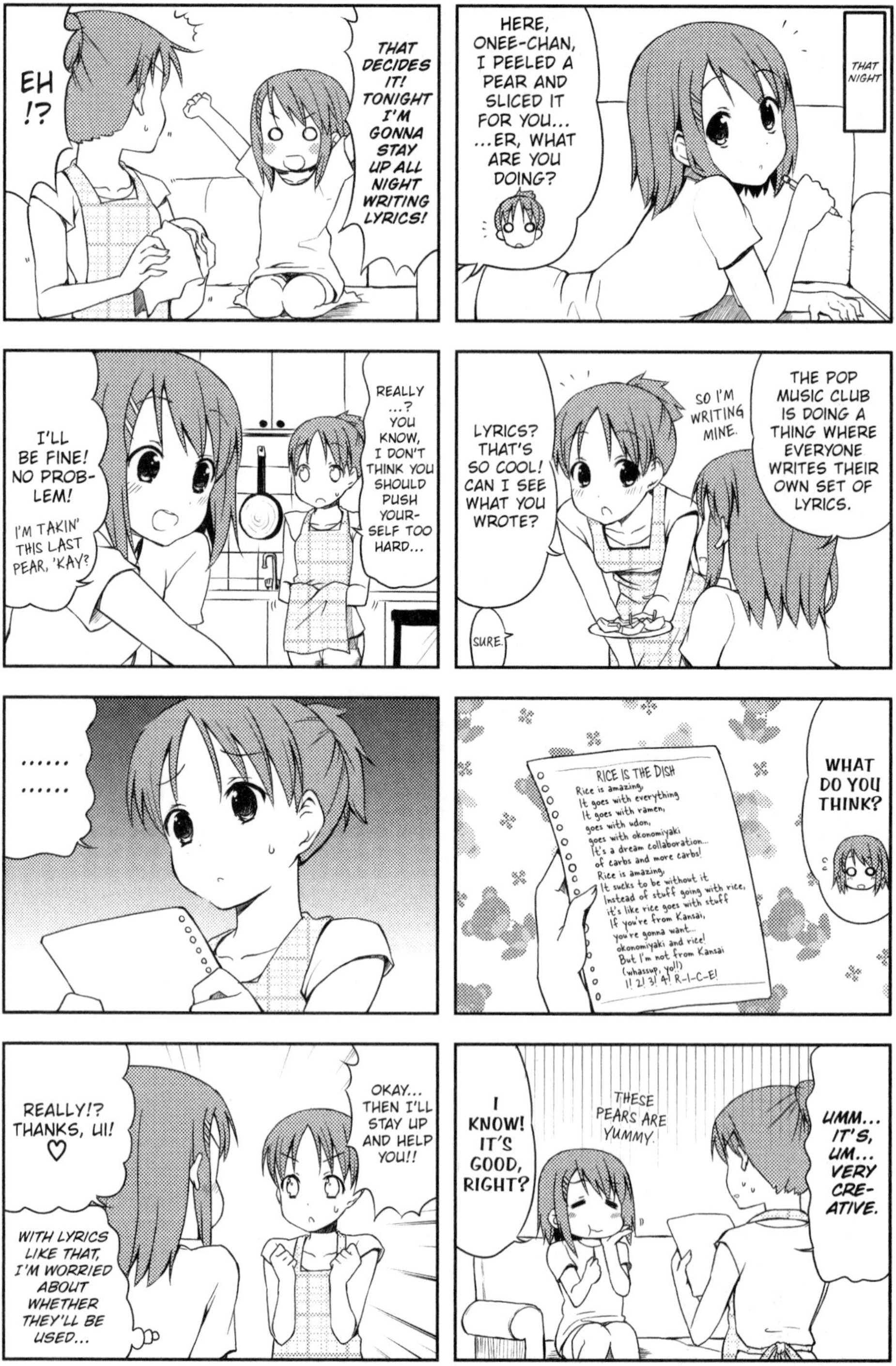
THAT NIGHT
HERE, ONEE-CHAN, I PEELED A PEAR AND SLICED IT FOR YOU... ...ER, WHAT ARE YOU DOING?
THE POP MUSIC CLUB IS DOING A THING WHERE EVERYONE WRITES THEIR OWN SET OF LYRICS.
SO I'M WRITING MINE.
LYRICS? THAT'S SO COOL! CAN I SEE WHAT YOU WROTE?
SURE.
WHAT DO YOU THINK?
RICE IS THE DISH
Rice is amazing,
It goes with everything
It goes with ramen,
goes with udon,
goes with okonomiyaki
It's a dream collaboration...
of carbs and more carbs!
Rice is amazing,
It sucks to be without it
Instead of stuff going with rice,
it's like rice goes with stuff
If you're from Kansai,
you're gonna want...
okonomiyaki and rice!
But I'm not from Kansai
(whassup, yo!!)
1! 2! 3! 4! R-I-C-E!
UMM... IT'S, UM... VERY CRE-ATIVE.
I KNOW! IT'S GOOD, RIGHT?
THESE PEARS ARE YUMMY.
THAT DECIDES IT! TONIGHT I'M GONNA STAY UP ALL NIGHT WRITING LYRICS!
EH !?
REALLY ...? YOU KNOW, I DON'T THINK YOU SHOULD PUSH YOUR-SELF TOO HARD...
I'LL BE FINE! NO PROB-LEM!
I'M TAKIN' THIS LAST PEAR, 'KAY?
....
OKAY... THEN I'LL STAY UP AND HELP YOU!!
REALLY!? THANKS, UI! ♡
WITH LYRICS LIKE THAT, I'M WORRIED ABOUT WHETHER THEY'LL BE USED...

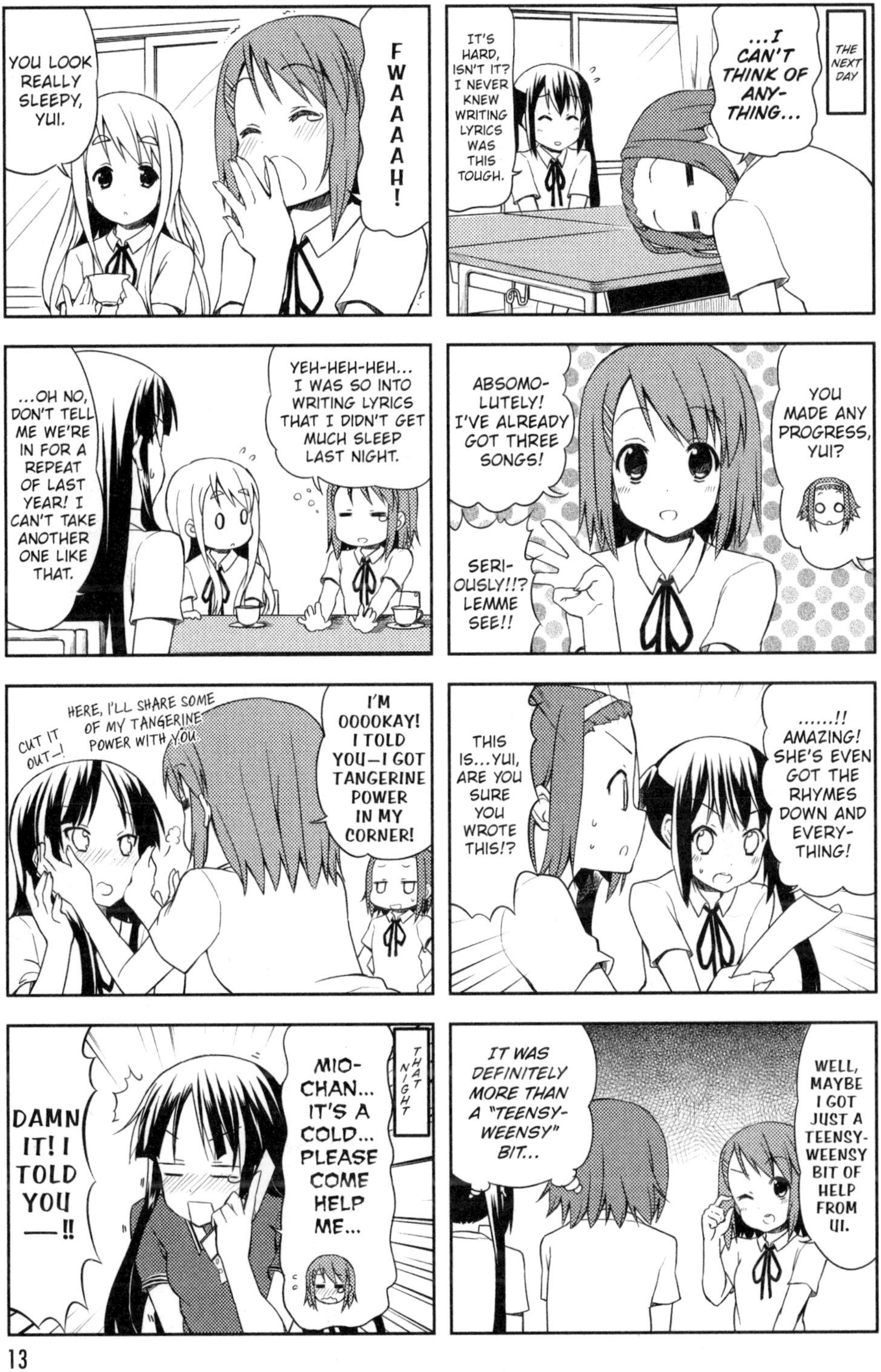
THE NEXT DAY
...I CAN'T THINK OF ANYTHING...
IT'S HARD, ISN'T IT? I NEVER KNEW WRITING LYRICS WAS THIS TOUGH.
YOU MADE ANY PROGRESS, YUI?
ABSOMOLUTELY! I'VE ALREADY GOT THREE SONGS!
SERIOUSLY!!? LEMME SEE!!
......!! AMAZING! SHE'S EVEN GOT THE RHYMES DOWN AND EVERYTHING!
THIS IS...YUI, ARE YOU SURE YOU WROTE THIS!?
WELL, MAYBE I GOT JUST A TEENSY-WEENSY BIT OF HELP FROM UI.
IT WAS DEFINITELY MORE THAN A "TEENSY-WEENSY" BIT...
FWAAAAAH!
YOU LOOK REALLY SLEEPY, YUI.
YEH-HEH-HEH... I WAS SO INTO WRITING LYRICS THAT I DIDN'T GET MUCH SLEEP LAST NIGHT.
...OH NO, DON'T TELL ME WE'RE IN FOR A REPEAT OF LAST YEAR! I CAN'T TAKE ANOTHER ONE LIKE THAT.
I'M OOOOKAY! I TOLD YOU—I GOT TANGERINE POWER IN MY CORNER!
HERE, I'LL SHARE SOME OF MY TANGERINE POWER WITH YOU.
CUT IT OUT—!
THAT NIGHT
MIO-CHAN... IT'S A COLD... PLEASE COME HELP ME...
DAMN IT! I TOLD YOU—!!

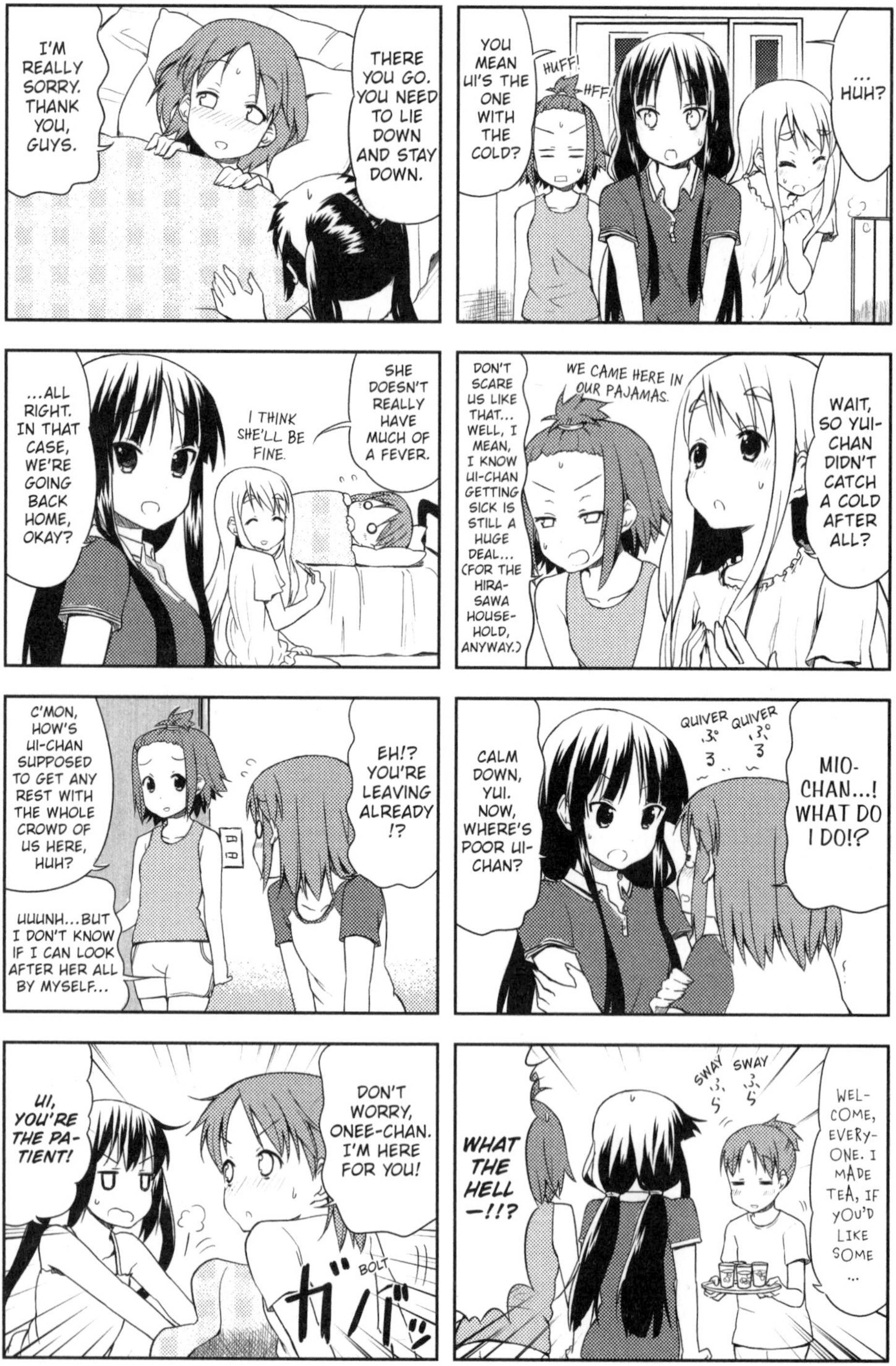
...HUH?
HUFF!
HFF!
YOU MEAN UI'S THE ONE WITH THE COLD?
WAIT, SO YUI-CHAN DIDN'T CATCH A COLD AFTER ALL?
WE CAME HERE IN OUR PAJAMAS.
DON'T SCARE US LIKE THAT... WELL, I MEAN, I KNOW UI-CHAN GETTING SICK IS STILL A HUGE DEAL... (FOR THE HIRASAWA HOUSEHOLD, ANYWAY.)
MIO-CHAN...! WHAT DO I DO!?
QUIVER QUIVER
CALM DOWN, YUI. NOW, WHERE'S POOR UI-CHAN?
WEL-COME, EVERY-ONE. I MADE TEA, IF YOU'D LIKE SOME...
SWAY SWAY
WHAT THE HELL—!!?
THERE YOU GO. YOU NEED TO LIE DOWN AND STAY DOWN.
I'M REALLY SORRY. THANK YOU, GUYS.
SHE DOESN'T REALLY HAVE MUCH OF A FEVER.
I THINK SHE'LL BE FINE.
...ALL RIGHT. IN THAT CASE, WE'RE GOING BACK HOME, OKAY?
EH!? YOU'RE LEAVING ALREADY!?
C'MON, HOW'S UI-CHAN SUPPOSED TO GET ANY REST WITH THE WHOLE CROWD OF US HERE, HUH?
UUUNH...BUT I DON'T KNOW IF I CAN LOOK AFTER HER ALL BY MYSELF...
DON'T WORRY, ONEE-CHAN. I'M HERE FOR YOU!
BOLT
ガバッ
UI, YOU'RE THE PATIENT!

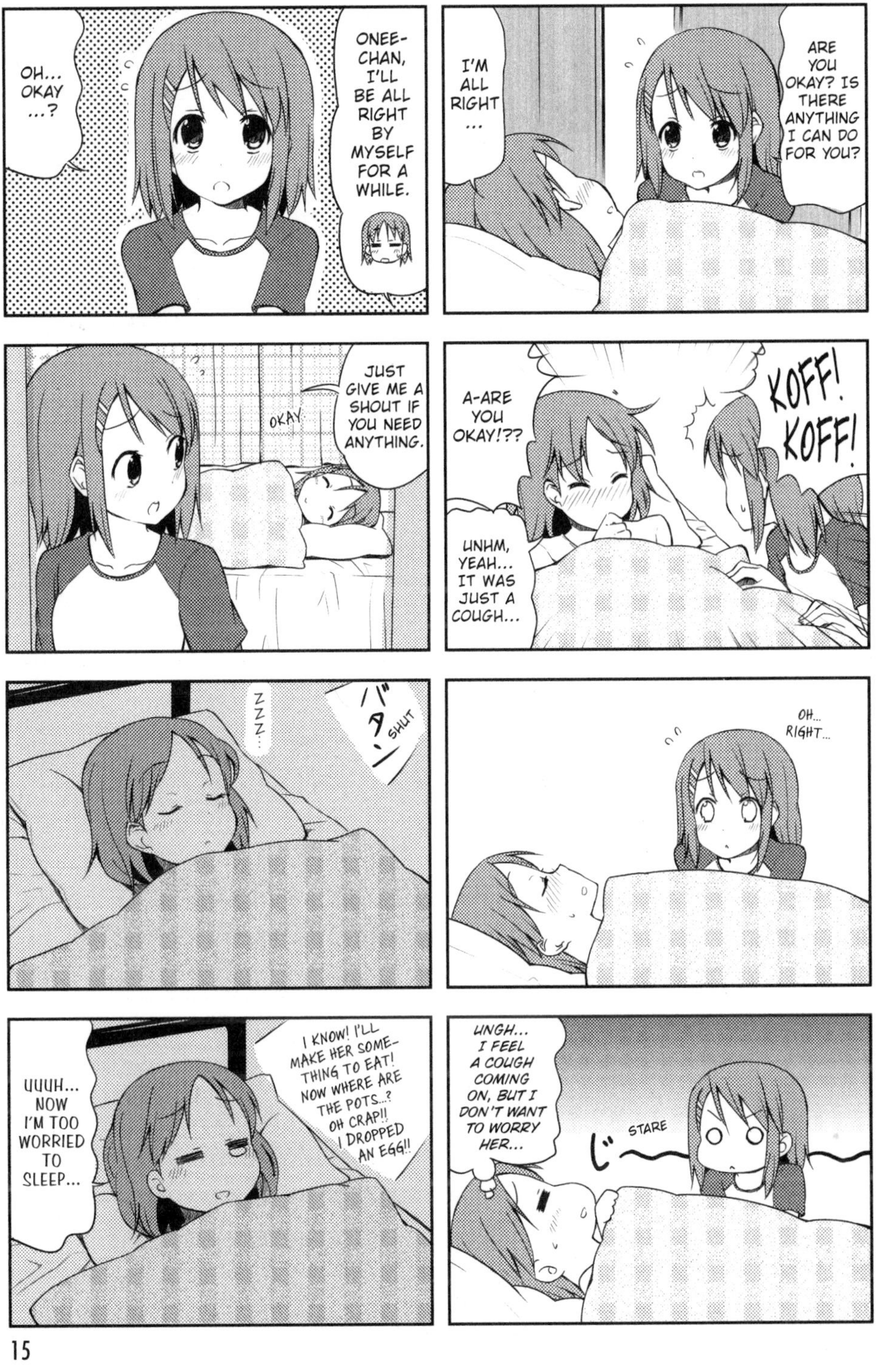
ARE YOU OKAY? IS THERE ANYTHING I CAN DO FOR YOU?
I'M ALL RIGHT...
KOFF! KOFF!
A-ARE YOU OKAY!??
UNHM, YEAH... IT WAS JUST A COUGH...
OH... RIGHT...
UNGH... I FEEL A COUGH COMING ON, BUT I DON'T WANT TO WORRY HER...
STARE
ONEE-CHAN, I'LL BE ALL RIGHT BY MYSELF FOR A WHILE.
OH... OKAY...?
JUST GIVE ME A SHOUT IF YOU NEED ANYTHING.
OKAY
SHUT
ZZZ...
I KNOW! I'LL MAKE HER SOME-THING TO EAT! NOW WHERE ARE THE POTS...? OH CRAP!! I DROPPED AN EGG!!
UUUH... NOW I'M TOO WORRIED TO SLEEP...

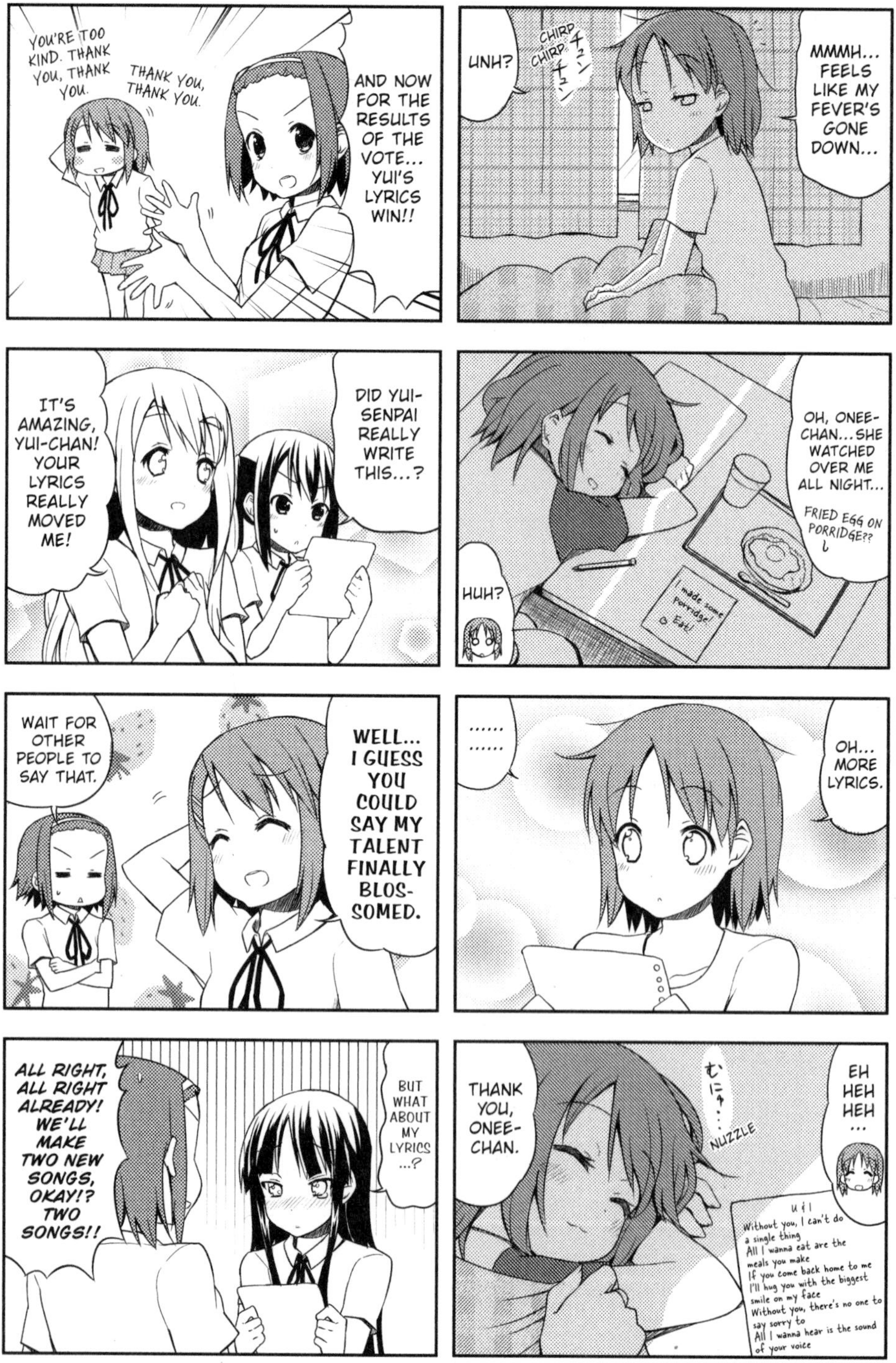
MMMH... FEELS LIKE MY FEVER'S GONE DOWN...
CHIRP CHIRP チュン チュン
UNH?
OH, ONEE-CHAN... SHE WATCHED OVER ME ALL NIGHT...
FRIED EGG ON PORRIDGE??
I made some porridge! Eat!
HUH?
OH... MORE LYRICS.
......
......
EH HEH HEH ...
むにゃ... NUZZLE
THANK YOU, ONEE-CHAN.
U & I
Without you, I can't do a single thing
All I wanna eat are the meals you make
If you come back home to me
I'll hug you with the biggest smile on my face
Without you, there's no one to say sorry to
All I wanna hear is the sound of your voice
AND NOW FOR THE RESULTS OF THE VOTE... YUI'S LYRICS WIN!!
THANK YOU, THANK YOU.
YOU'RE TOO KIND. THANK YOU, THANK YOU.
DID YUI-SENPAI REALLY WRITE THIS...?
IT'S AMAZING, YUI-CHAN! YOUR LYRICS REALLY MOVED ME!
WELL... I GUESS YOU COULD SAY MY TALENT FINALLY BLOSSOMED.
WAIT FOR OTHER PEOPLE TO SAY THAT.
BUT WHAT ABOUT MY LYRICS...?
ALL RIGHT, ALL RIGHT ALREADY! WE'LL MAKE TWO NEW SONGS, OKAY!? TWO SONGS!!

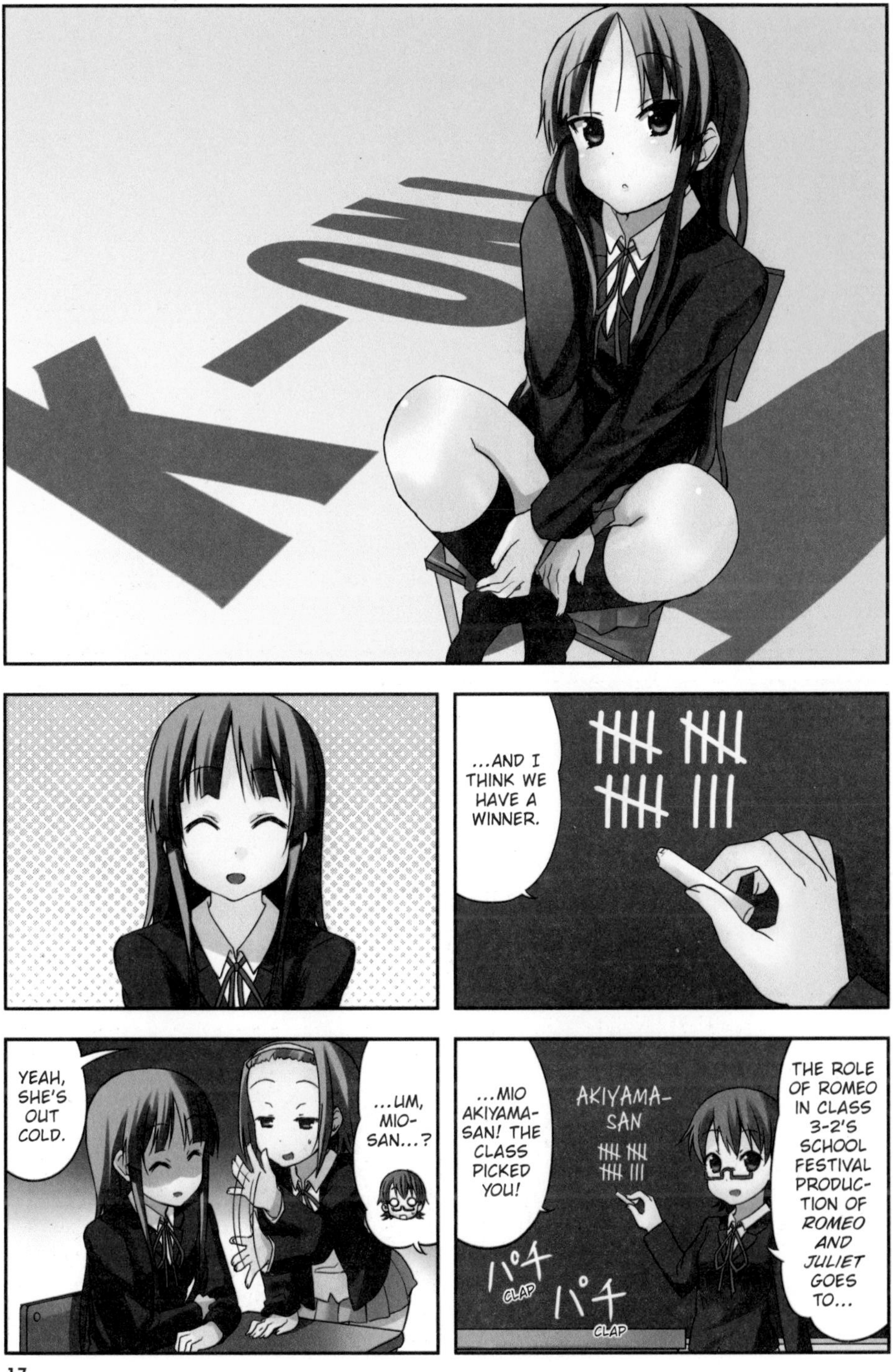
K-ON
...AND I THINK WE HAVE A WINNER.
THE ROLE OF ROMEO IN CLASS 3-2'S SCHOOL FESTIVAL PRODUCTION OF *ROMEO AND JULIET* GOES TO...
AKIYAMA-SAN
...MIO AKIYAMA-SAN! THE CLASS PICKED YOU!
パチ
CLAP
パチ
CLAP
...UM, MIO-SAN...?
YEAH, SHE'S OUT COLD.

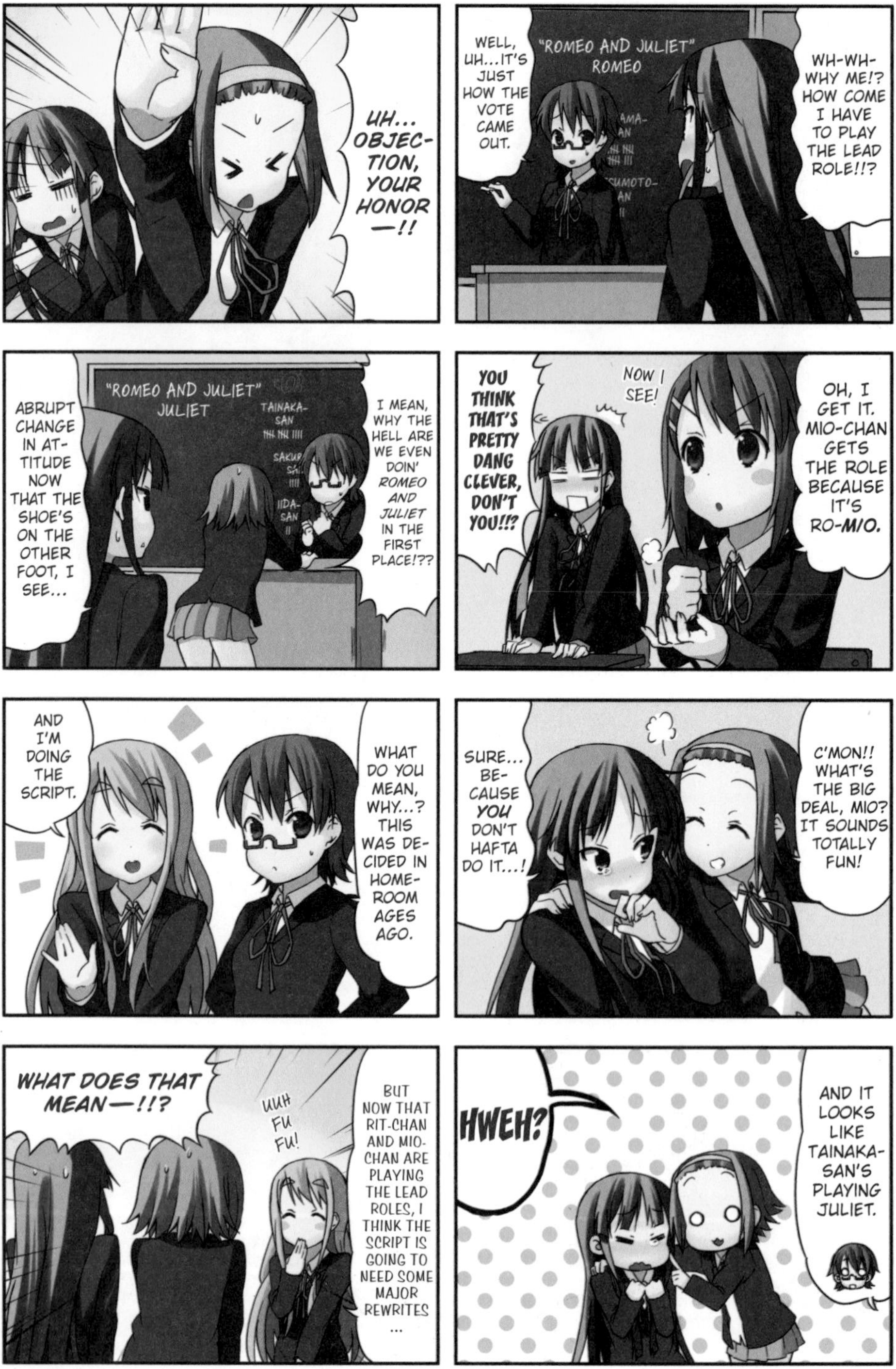
WH-WH-WHY ME!? HOW COME I HAVE TO PLAY THE LEAD ROLE!!?
"ROMEO AND JULIET"
ROMEO
WELL, UH...IT'S JUST HOW THE VOTE CAME OUT.
OH, I GET IT. MIO-CHAN GETS THE ROLE BECAUSE IT'S RO-*MIO.*
NOW I SEE!
YOU THINK THAT'S PRETTY DANG CLEVER, DON'T YOU!!?
C'MON!! WHAT'S THE BIG DEAL, MIO? IT SOUNDS TOTALLY FUN!
SURE... BE-CAUSE ***YOU*** DON'T HAFTA DO IT...!
AND IT LOOKS LIKE TAINAKA-SAN'S PLAYING JULIET.
HWEH?
UH... OBJECTION, YOUR HONOR—!!
I MEAN, WHY THE HELL ARE WE EVEN DOIN' *ROMEO AND JULIET* IN THE FIRST PLACE!??
"ROMEO AND JULIET"
JULIET
TAINAKA-SAN
IIDA-SAN
ABRUPT CHANGE IN ATTITUDE NOW THAT THE SHOE'S ON THE OTHER FOOT, I SEE...
WHAT DO YOU MEAN, WHY...? THIS WAS DECIDED IN HOMEROOM AGES AGO.
AND I'M DOING THE SCRIPT.
BUT NOW THAT RIT-CHAN AND MIO-CHAN ARE PLAYING THE LEAD ROLES, I THINK THE SCRIPT IS GOING TO NEED SOME MAJOR REWRITES...
UUH FU FU!
WHAT DOES THAT MEAN—!!?

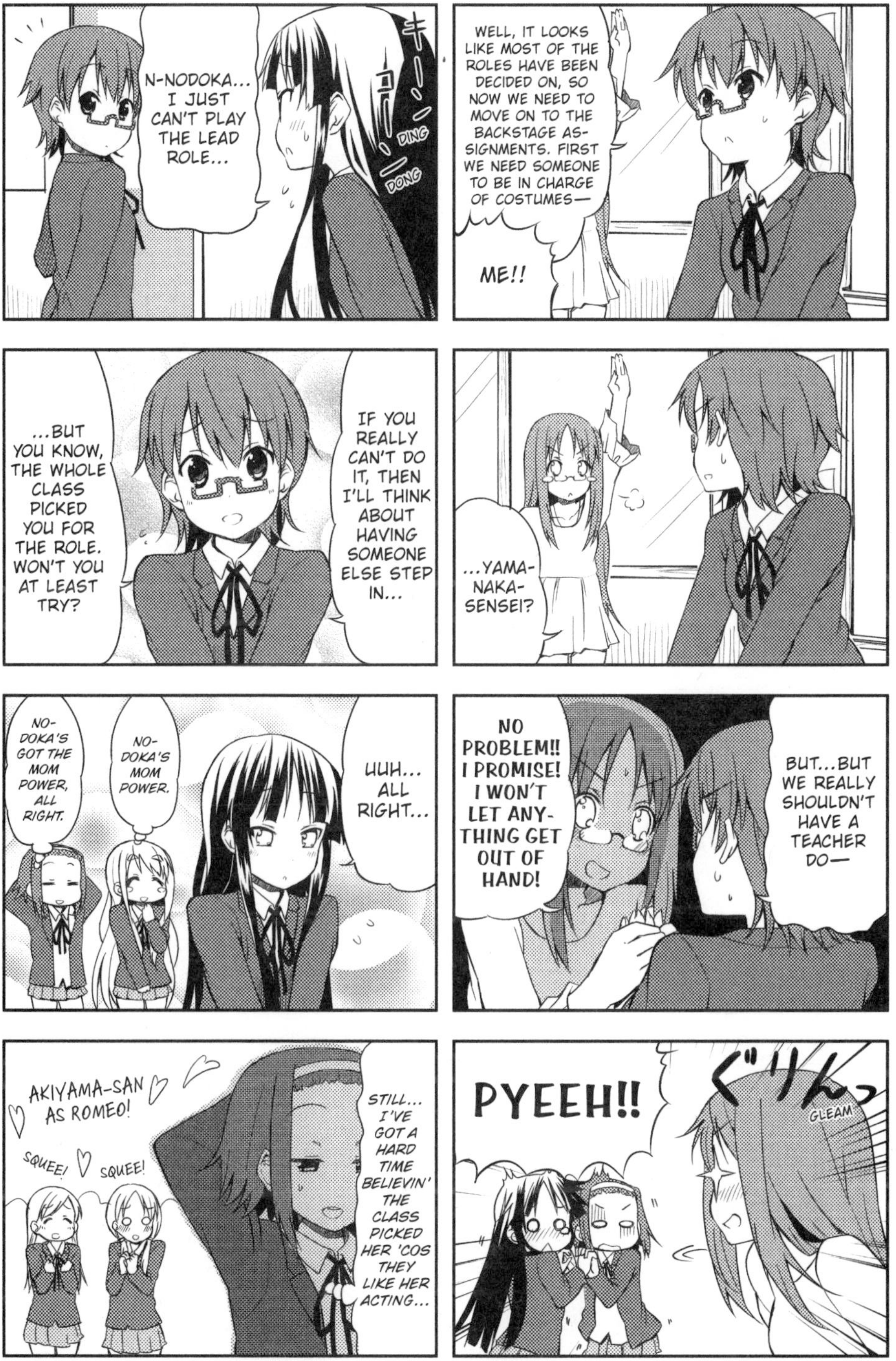
WELL, IT LOOKS LIKE MOST OF THE ROLES HAVE BEEN DECIDED ON, SO NOW WE NEED TO MOVE ON TO THE BACKSTAGE AS-SIGNMENTS. FIRST WE NEED SOMEONE TO BE IN CHARGE OF COSTUMES—
ME!!
...YAMA-NAKA-SENSEI?
BUT...BUT WE REALLY SHOULDN'T HAVE A TEACHER DO—
NO PROBLEM!! I PROMISE! I WON'T LET ANY-THING GET OUT OF HAND!
ぐりんっ
GLEAM
PYEEH!!
キーンコーン
DING
DONG
N-NODOKA... I JUST CAN'T PLAY THE LEAD ROLE...
IF YOU REALLY CAN'T DO IT, THEN I'LL THINK ABOUT HAVING SOMEONE ELSE STEP IN...
...BUT YOU KNOW, THE WHOLE CLASS PICKED YOU FOR THE ROLE. WON'T YOU AT LEAST TRY?
UUH... ALL RIGHT...
NO-DOKA'S MOM POWER.
NO-DOKA'S GOT THE MOM POWER, ALL RIGHT.
STILL... I'VE GOT A HARD TIME BELIEVIN' THE CLASS PICKED HER 'COS THEY LIKE HER ACTING...
AKIYAMA-SAN AS ROMEO!
SQUEE!
SQUEE!

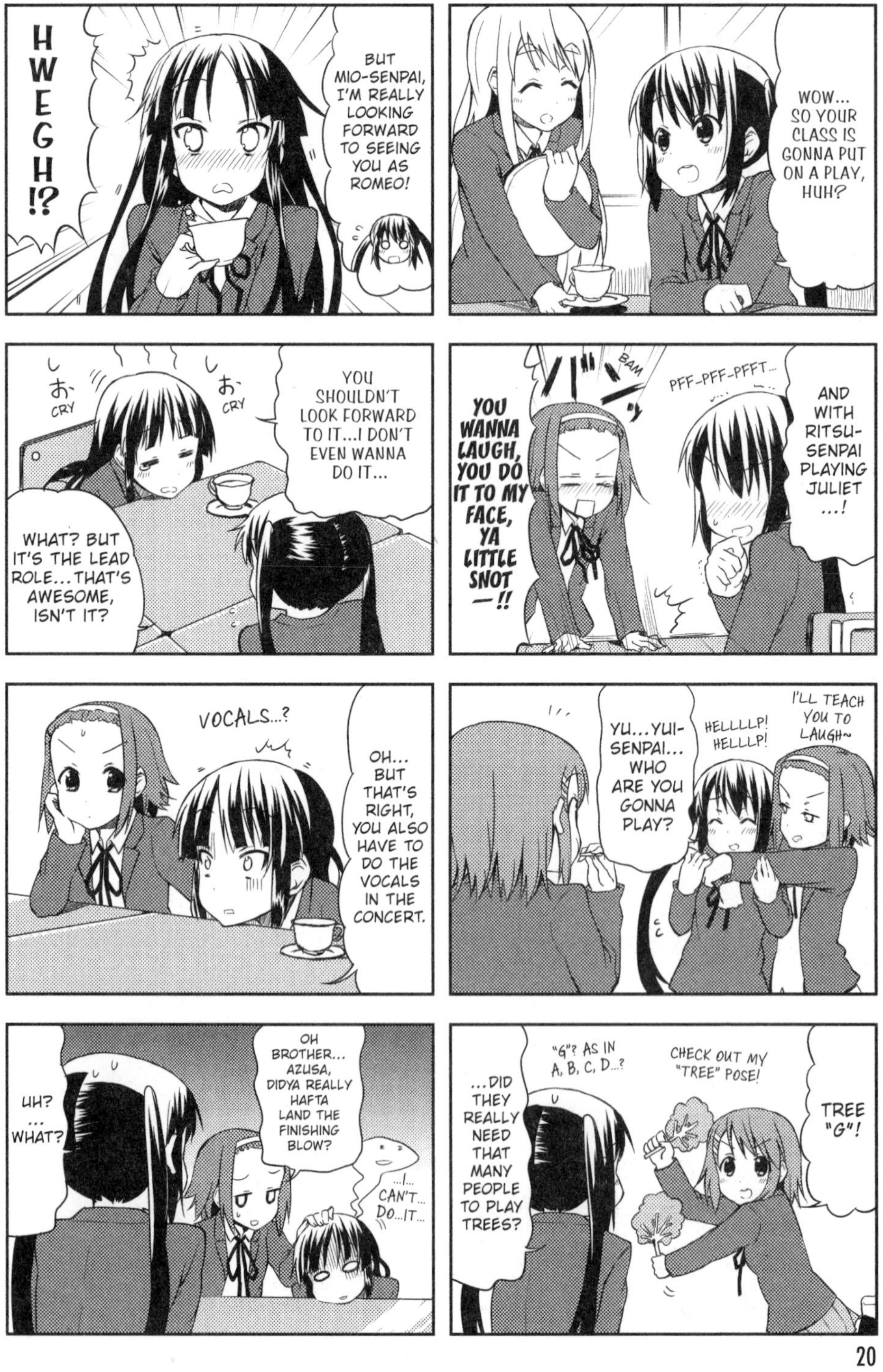
WOW... SO YOUR CLASS IS GONNA PUT ON A PLAY, HUH?
AND WITH RITSU-SENPAI PLAYING JULIET...!
PFF-PFF-PFFT...
BAM
YOU WANNA LAUGH, YOU DO IT TO MY FACE, YA LITTLE SNOT—!!
I'LL TEACH YOU TO LAUGH~
HELLLLP! HELLLP!
YU...YUI-SENPAI... WHO ARE YOU GONNA PLAY?
TREE "G"!
CHECK OUT MY "TREE" POSE!
"G"? AS IN A, B, C, D...?
...DID THEY REALLY NEED THAT MANY PEOPLE TO PLAY TREES?
BUT MIO-SENPAI, I'M REALLY LOOKING FORWARD TO SEEING YOU AS ROMEO!
HWEGH!?
YOU SHOULDN'T LOOK FORWARD TO IT...I DON'T EVEN WANNA DO IT...
しお CRY
しお CRY
WHAT? BUT IT'S THE LEAD ROLE...THAT'S AWESOME, ISN'T IT?
OH... BUT THAT'S RIGHT, YOU ALSO HAVE TO DO THE VOCALS IN THE CONCERT.
VOCALS...?
OH BROTHER... AZUSA, DIDYA REALLY HAFTA LAND THE FINISHING BLOW?
...I... CAN'T... DO...IT...
UH? ...WHAT?

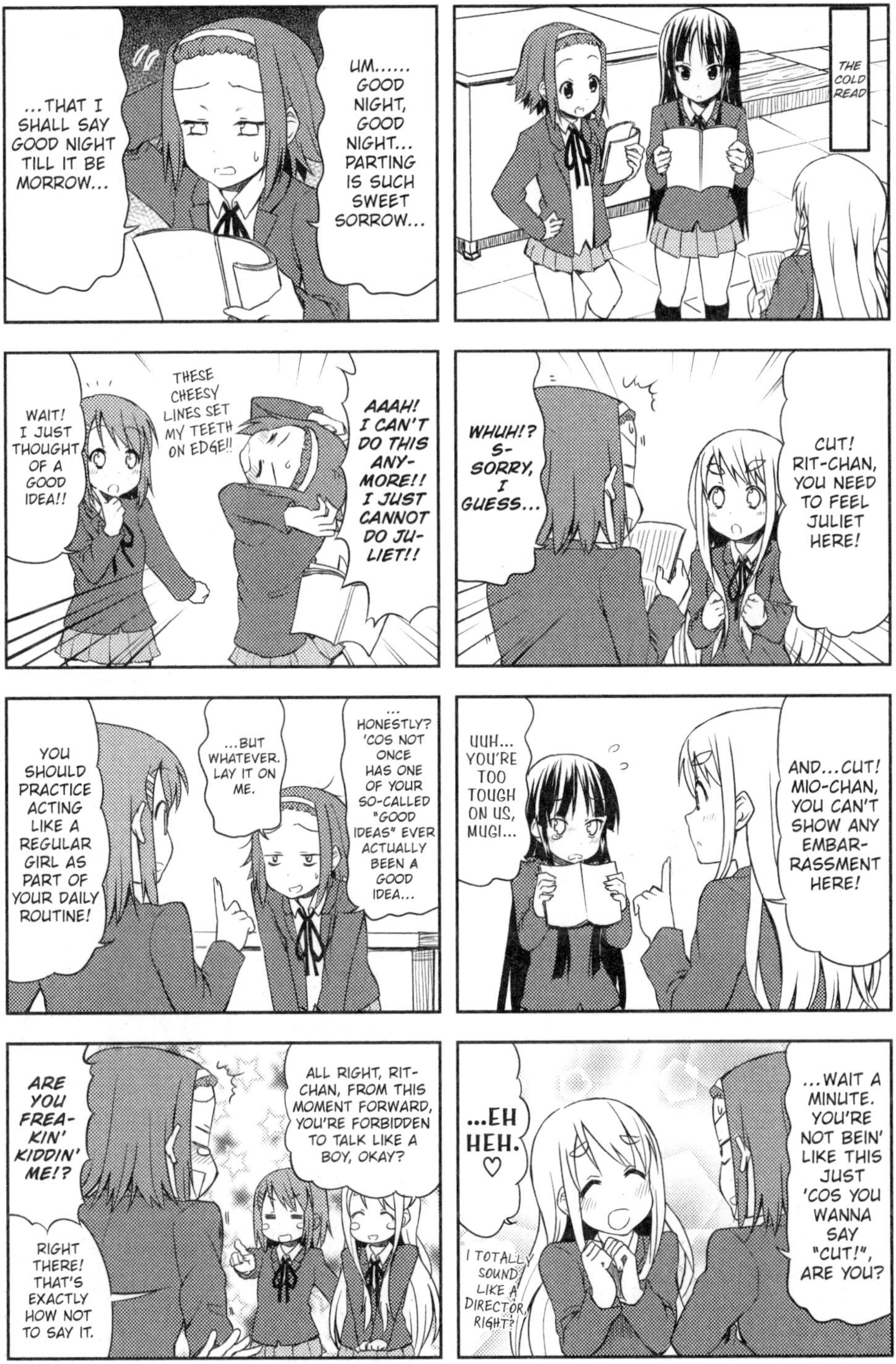
THE COLD READ
CUT! RIT-CHAN, YOU NEED TO FEEL JULIET HERE!
WHUH!? S-SORRY, I GUESS...
AND...CUT! MIO-CHAN, YOU CAN'T SHOW ANY EMBARRASSMENT HERE!
UUH... YOU'RE TOO TOUGH ON US, MUGI...
...WAIT A MINUTE. YOU'RE NOT BEIN' LIKE THIS JUST 'COS YOU WANNA SAY "CUT!", ARE YOU?
...EH HEH. ♡
I TOTALLY SOUND LIKE A DIRECTOR, RIGHT?
UM...... GOOD NIGHT, GOOD NIGHT... PARTING IS SUCH SWEET SORROW...
...THAT I SHALL SAY GOOD NIGHT TILL IT BE MORROW...
AAAH! I CAN'T DO THIS ANYMORE!! I JUST CANNOT DO JULIET!!
THESE CHEESY LINES SET MY TEETH ON EDGE!!
WAIT! I JUST THOUGHT OF A GOOD IDEA!!
...HONESTLY? 'COS NOT ONCE HAS ONE OF YOUR SO-CALLED "GOOD IDEAS" EVER ACTUALLY BEEN A GOOD IDEA...
...BUT WHATEVER. LAY IT ON ME.
YOU SHOULD PRACTICE ACTING LIKE A REGULAR GIRL AS PART OF YOUR DAILY ROUTINE!
ALL RIGHT, RIT-CHAN, FROM THIS MOMENT FORWARD, YOU'RE FORBIDDEN TO TALK LIKE A BOY, OKAY?
ARE YOU FREAKIN' KIDDIN' ME!?
RIGHT THERE! THAT'S EXACTLY HOW NOT TO SAY IT.

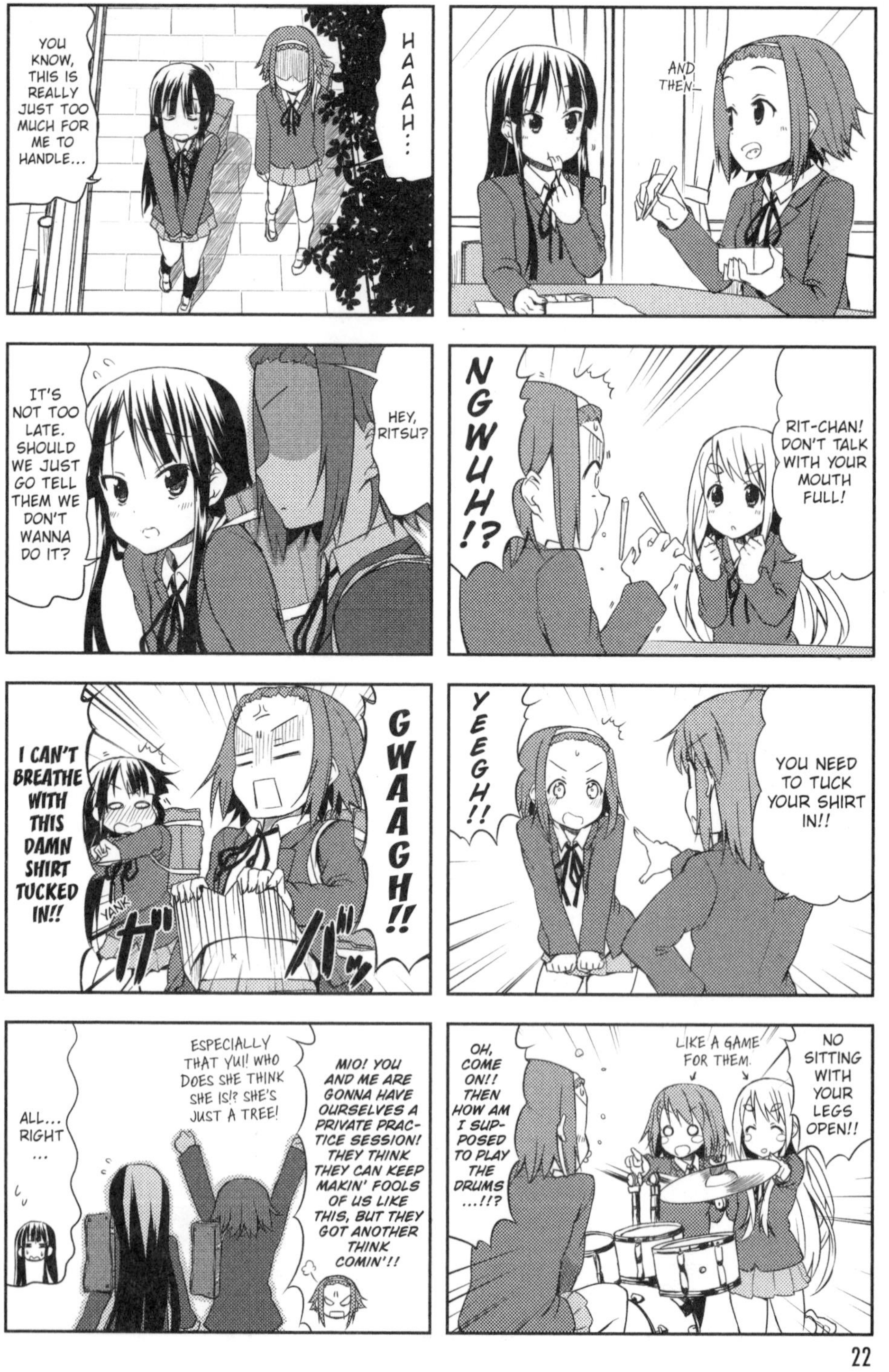
AND THEN—
RIT-CHAN! DON'T TALK WITH YOUR MOUTH FULL!
NGWUH!?
YOU NEED TO TUCK YOUR SHIRT IN!!
YEEGH!!
NO SITTING WITH YOUR LEGS OPEN!!
LIKE A GAME FOR THEM.
OH, COME ON!! THEN HOW AM I SUP-POSED TO PLAY THE DRUMS ...!!?
HAAAAH...
YOU KNOW, THIS IS REALLY JUST TOO MUCH FOR ME TO HANDLE...
HEY, RITSU?
IT'S NOT TOO LATE. SHOULD WE JUST GO TELL THEM WE DON'T WANNA DO IT?
GWAAAGH!!
I CAN'T BREATHE WITH THIS DAMN SHIRT TUCKED IN!!
YANK
MIO! YOU AND ME ARE GONNA HAVE OURSELVES A PRIVATE PRAC-TICE SESSION! THEY THINK THEY CAN KEEP MAKIN' FOOLS OF US LIKE THIS, BUT THEY GOT ANOTHER THINK COMIN'!!
ESPECIALLY THAT YUI! WHO DOES SHE THINK SHE IS!? SHE'S JUST A TREE!
ALL... RIGHT ...

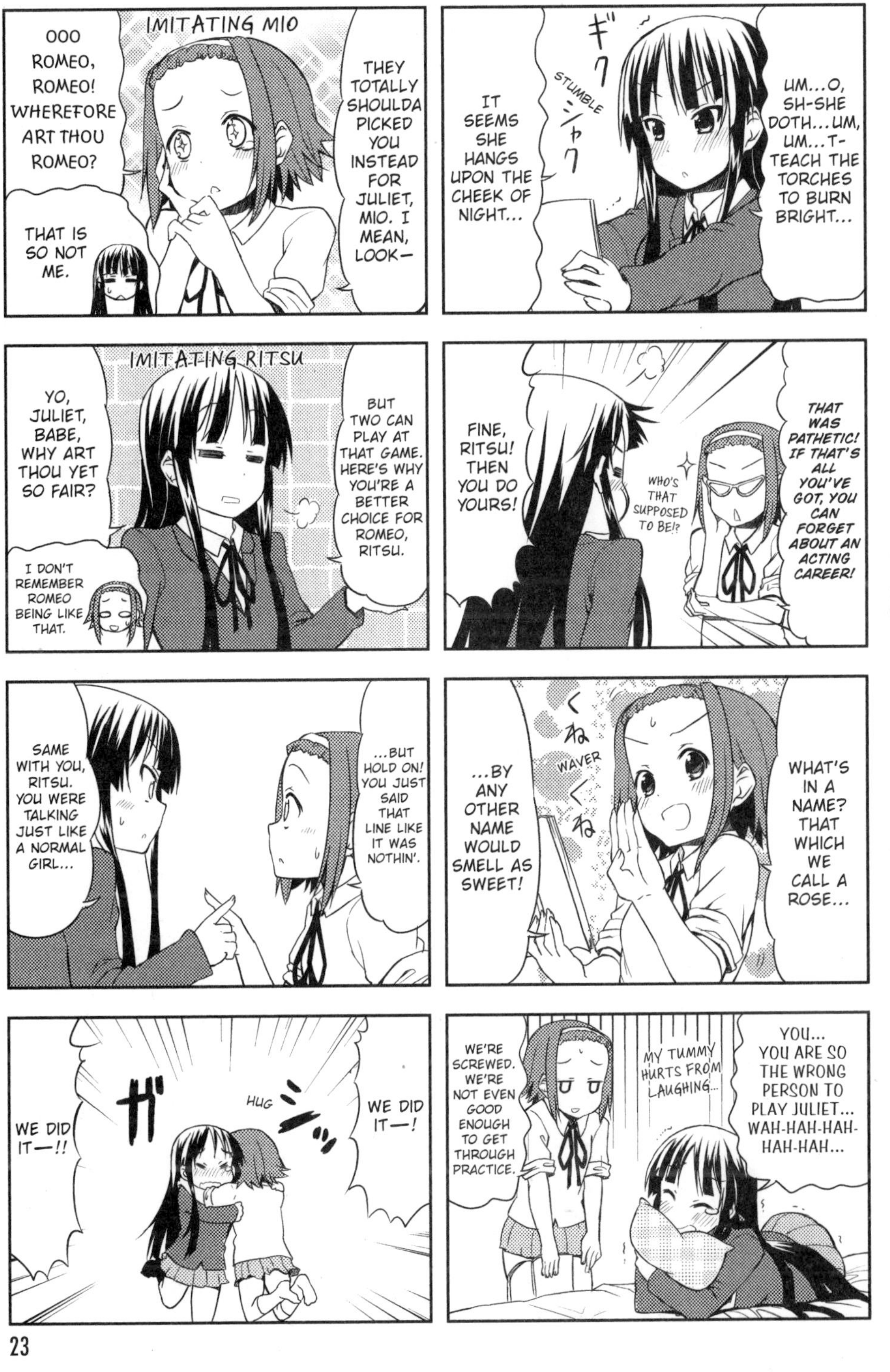
UM...O, SH-SHE DOTH...UM, UM...T-TEACH THE TORCHES TO BURN BRIGHT...
ギク
STUMBLE
シャク
IT SEEMS SHE HANGS UPON THE CHEEK OF NIGHT...
THAT WAS PATHETIC! IF THAT'S ALL YOU'VE GOT, YOU CAN FORGET ABOUT AN ACTING CAREER!
WHO'S THAT SUPPOSED TO BE!?
FINE, RITSU! THEN YOU DO YOURS!
WHAT'S IN A NAME? THAT WHICH WE CALL A ROSE...
くね
WAVER
くね
...BY ANY OTHER NAME WOULD SMELL AS SWEET!
YOU... YOU ARE SO THE WRONG PERSON TO PLAY JULIET... WAH-HAH-HAH-HAH-HAH...
MY TUMMY HURTS FROM LAUGHING...
WE'RE SCREWED. WE'RE NOT EVEN GOOD ENOUGH TO GET THROUGH PRACTICE.
THEY TOTALLY SHOULDA PICKED YOU INSTEAD FOR JULIET, MIO. I MEAN, LOOK—
IMITATING MIO
OOO ROMEO, ROMEO! WHEREFORE ART THOU ROMEO?
THAT IS SO NOT ME.
BUT TWO CAN PLAY AT THAT GAME. HERE'S WHY YOU'RE A BETTER CHOICE FOR ROMEO, RITSU.
IMITATING RITSU
YO, JULIET, BABE, WHY ART THOU YET SO FAIR?
I DON'T REMEMBER ROMEO BEING LIKE THAT.
...BUT HOLD ON! YOU JUST SAID THAT LINE LIKE IT WAS NOTHIN'.
SAME WITH YOU, RITSU. YOU WERE TALKING JUST LIKE A NORMAL GIRL...
WE DID IT—!
ガ
シ
HUG
WE DID IT—!!

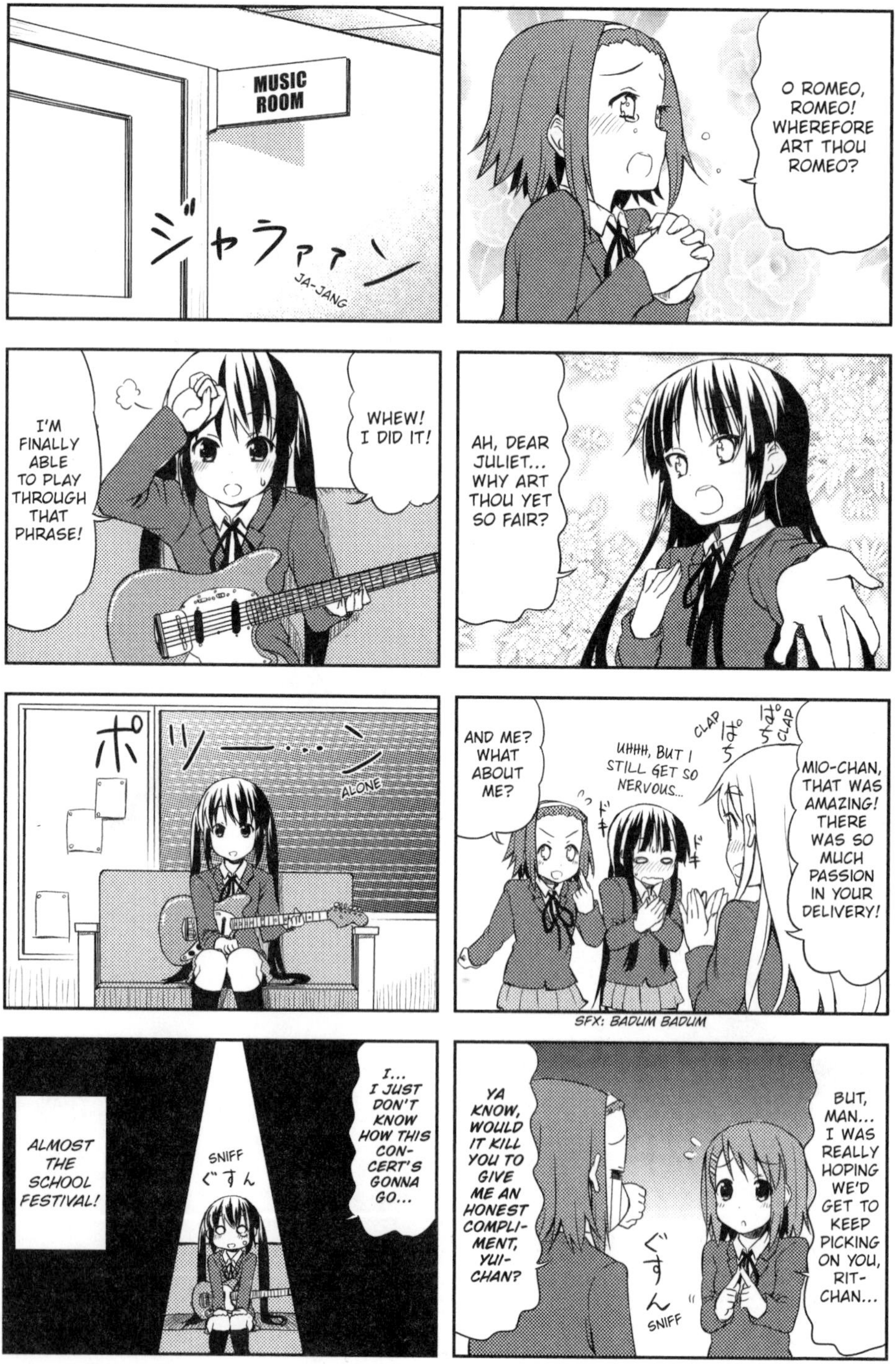
O ROMEO, ROMEO! WHEREFORE ART THOU ROMEO?
AH, DEAR JULIET... WHY ART THOU YET SO FAIR?
ぱち CLAP
ぱち CLAP
MIO-CHAN, THAT WAS AMAZING! THERE WAS SO MUCH PASSION IN YOUR DELIVERY!
ドキ
ドキ
UHHH, BUT I STILL GET SO NERVOUS...
AND ME? WHAT ABOUT ME?
SFX: BADUM BADUM
BUT, MAN... I WAS REALLY HOPING WE'D GET TO KEEP PICKING ON YOU, RIT-CHAN...
ぐすん
SNIFF
YA KNOW, WOULD IT KILL YOU TO GIVE ME AN HONEST COMPLIMENT, YUI-CHAN?
MUSIC ROOM
ジャラァァン
JA-JANG
WHEW! I DID IT!
I'M FINALLY ABLE TO PLAY THROUGH THAT PHRASE!
ポツー…ン
ALONE
I... I JUST DON'T KNOW HOW THIS CONCERT'S GONNA GO...
SNIFF
ぐすん
ALMOST THE SCHOOL FESTIVAL!

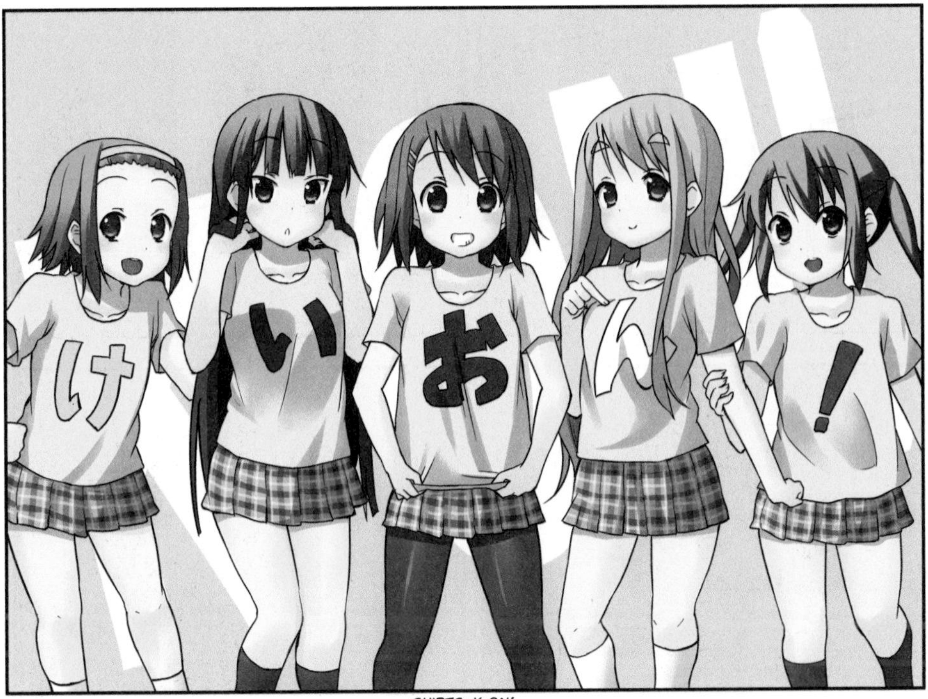
け
い
お
ん
!

SHIRTS: K-ON!

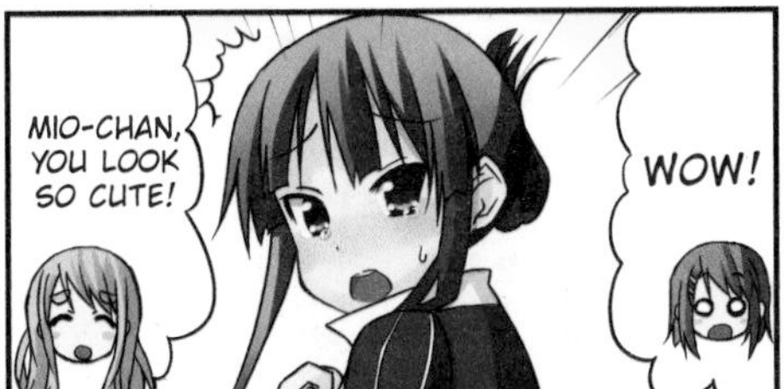
WOW!
MIO-CHAN, YOU LOOK SO CUTE!
EEK!

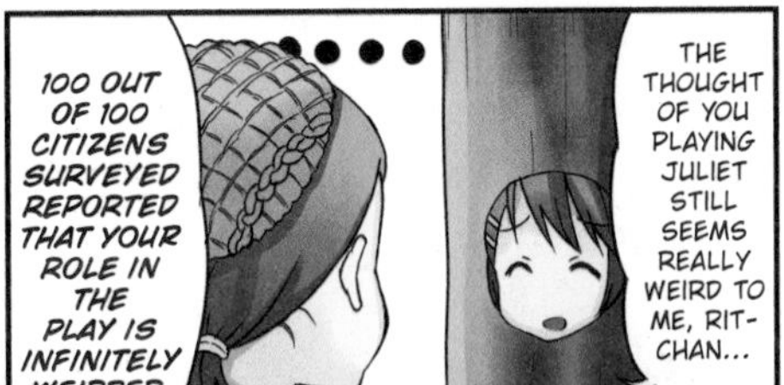
THE THOUGHT OF YOU PLAYING JULIET STILL SEEMS REALLY WEIRD TO ME, RIT-CHAN...
....
100 OUT OF 100 CITIZENS SURVEYED REPORTED THAT YOUR ROLE IN THE PLAY IS INFINITELY WEIRDER.

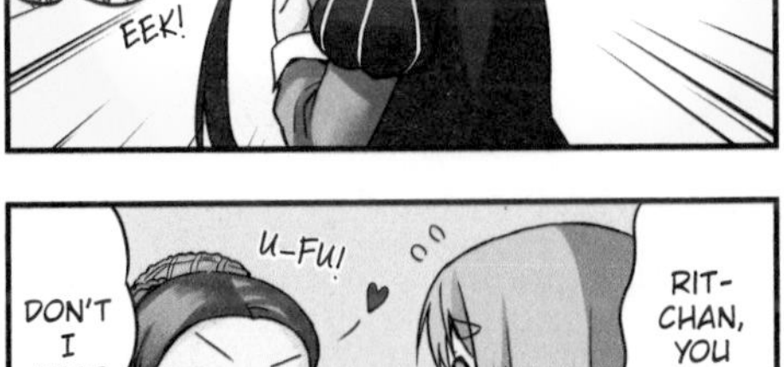
RIT-CHAN, YOU LOOK REALLY CUTE TOO! ♡
U-FU!
DON'T I JUST.

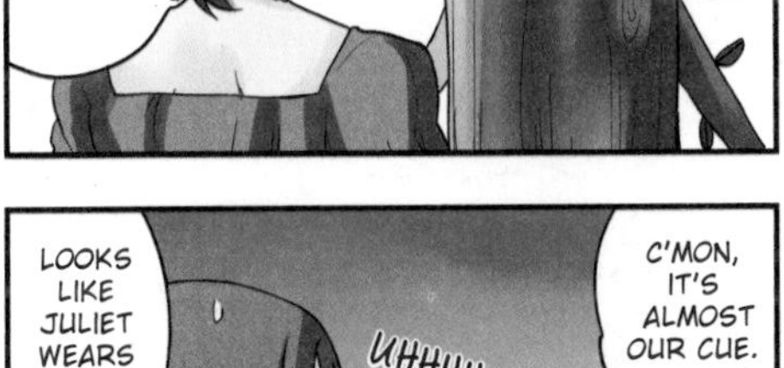
C'MON, IT'S ALMOST OUR CUE.
UHHHH...
LOOKS LIKE JULIET WEARS THE PANTS IN THIS RELATIONSHIP.

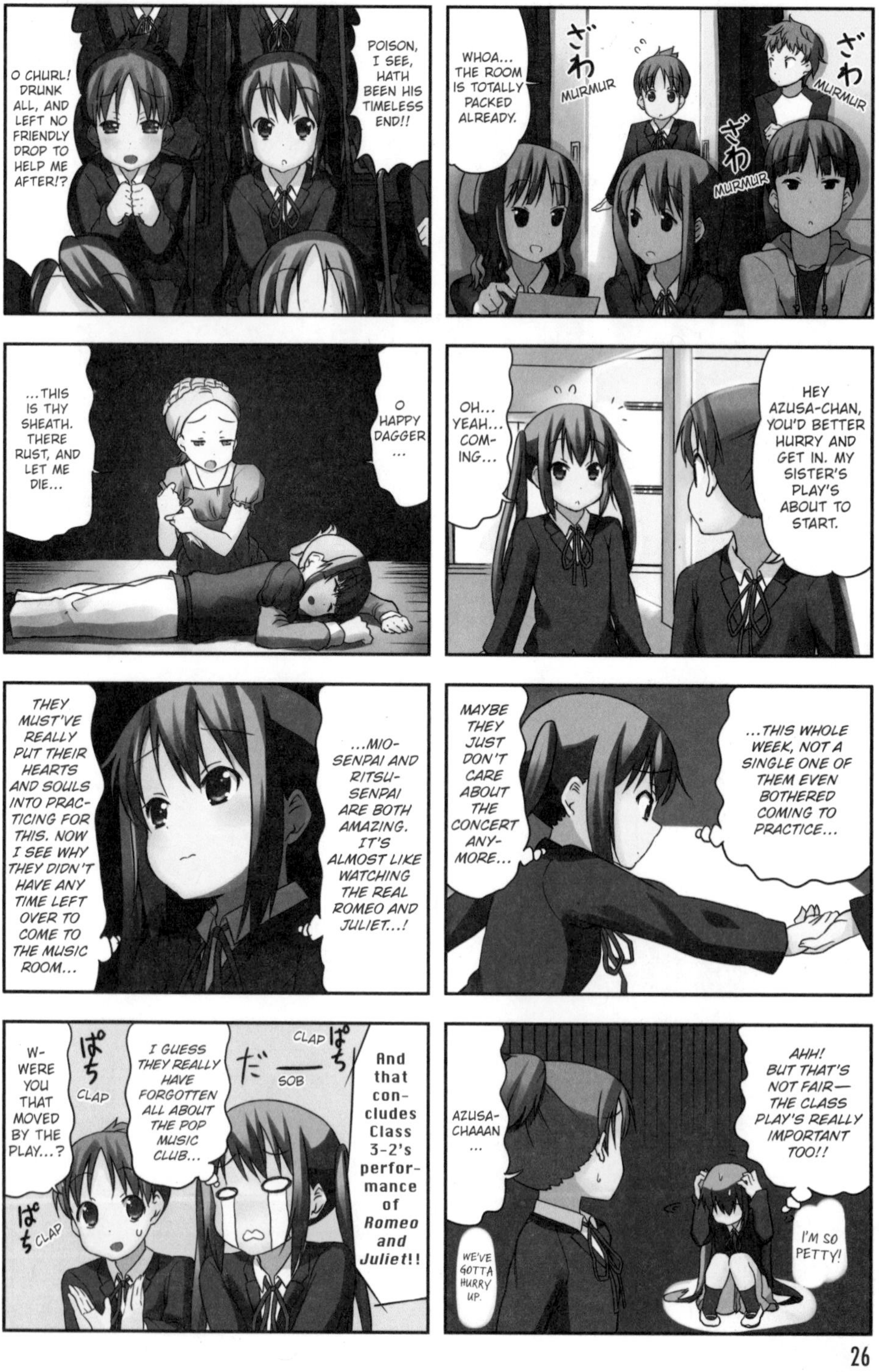

ざわ
MURMUR
ざわ
MURMUR
ざわ
MURMUR
WHOA... THE ROOM IS TOTALLY PACKED ALREADY.
HEY AZUSA-CHAN, YOU'D BETTER HURRY AND GET IN. MY SISTER'S PLAY'S ABOUT TO START.
OH... YEAH... COMING...
...THIS WHOLE WEEK, NOT A SINGLE ONE OF THEM EVEN BOTHERED COMING TO PRACTICE...
MAYBE THEY JUST DON'T CARE ABOUT THE CONCERT ANYMORE...
AHH! BUT THAT'S NOT FAIR— THE CLASS PLAY'S REALLY IMPORTANT TOO!!
I'M SO PETTY!
AZUSA-CHAAAN...
WE'VE GOTTA HURRY UP.
POISON, I SEE, HATH BEEN HIS TIMELESS END!!
O CHURL! DRUNK ALL, AND LEFT NO FRIENDLY DROP TO HELP ME AFTER!?
O HAPPY DAGGER...
...THIS IS THY SHEATH. THERE RUST, AND LET ME DIE...
...MIO-SENPAI AND RITSU-SENPAI ARE BOTH AMAZING. IT'S ALMOST LIKE WATCHING THE REAL ROMEO AND JULIET...!
THEY MUST'VE REALLY PUT THEIR HEARTS AND SOULS INTO PRACTICING FOR THIS. NOW I SEE WHY THEY DIDN'T HAVE ANY TIME LEFT OVER TO COME TO THE MUSIC ROOM...
And that concludes Class 3-2's performance of *Romeo and Juliet*!!
ぱち
CLAP
だー
SOB
I GUESS THEY REALLY HAVE FORGOTTEN ALL ABOUT THE POP MUSIC CLUB...
ぱち
CLAP
W-WERE YOU THAT MOVED BY THE PLAY...?
ぱち
CLAP

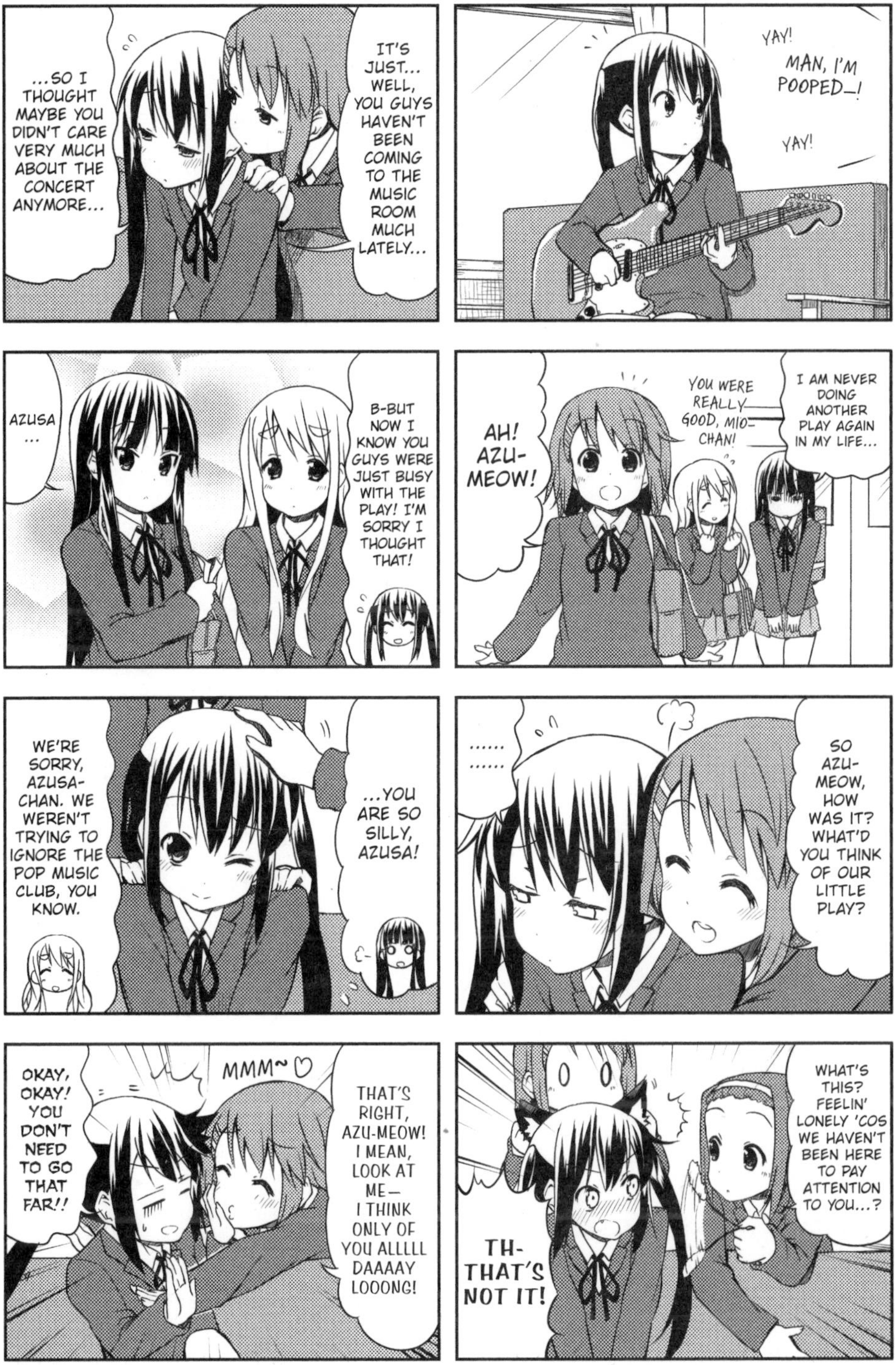

YAY!
MAN, I'M POOPED—!
YAY!
I AM NEVER DOING ANOTHER PLAY AGAIN IN MY LIFE...
YOU WERE REALLY GOOD, MIO-CHAN!
AH! AZU-MEOW!
SO AZU-MEOW, HOW WAS IT? WHAT'D YOU THINK OF OUR LITTLE PLAY?
....
WHAT'S THIS? FEELIN' LONELY 'COS WE HAVEN'T BEEN HERE TO PAY ATTENTION TO YOU...?
TH-THAT'S NOT IT!
IT'S JUST... WELL, YOU GUYS HAVEN'T BEEN COMING TO THE MUSIC ROOM MUCH LATELY...
...SO I THOUGHT MAYBE YOU DIDN'T CARE VERY MUCH ABOUT THE CONCERT ANYMORE...
B-BUT NOW I KNOW YOU GUYS WERE JUST BUSY WITH THE PLAY! I'M SORRY I THOUGHT THAT!
AZUSA ...
...YOU ARE SO SILLY, AZUSA!
WE'RE SORRY, AZUSA-CHAN. WE WEREN'T TRYING TO IGNORE THE POP MUSIC CLUB, YOU KNOW.
THAT'S RIGHT, AZU-MEOW! I MEAN, LOOK AT ME— I THINK ONLY OF YOU ALLLLL DAAAAY LOOONG!
MMM~♡
OKAY, OKAY! YOU DON'T NEED TO GO THAT FAR!!

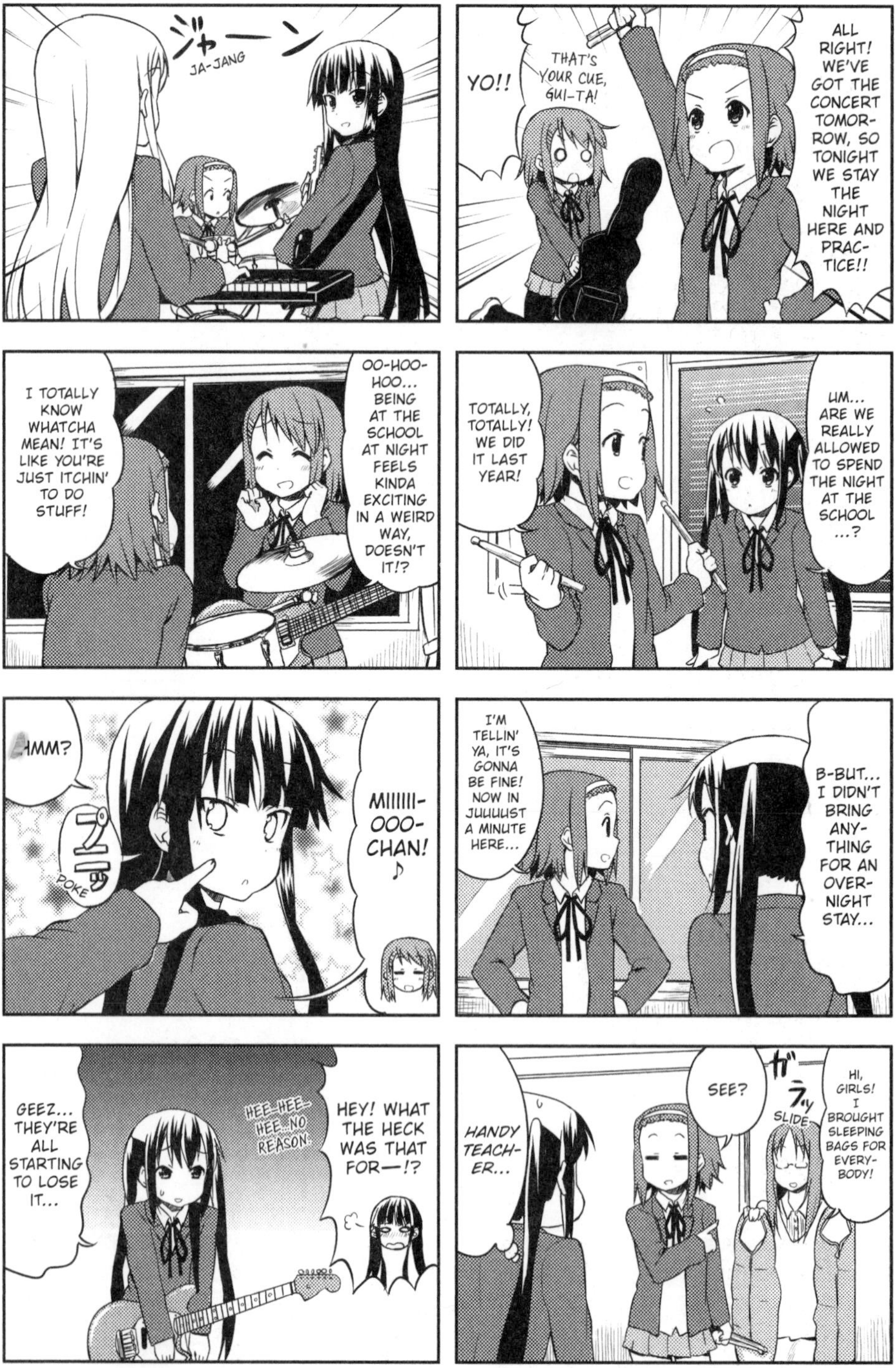
ALL RIGHT! WE'VE GOT THE CONCERT TOMORROW, SO TONIGHT WE STAY THE NIGHT HERE AND PRACTICE!!
THAT'S YOUR CUE, GUI-TA!
YO!!
UM... ARE WE REALLY ALLOWED TO SPEND THE NIGHT AT THE SCHOOL...?
TOTALLY, TOTALLY! WE DID IT LAST YEAR!
B-BUT... I DIDN'T BRING ANYTHING FOR AN OVERNIGHT STAY...
I'M TELLIN' YA, IT'S GONNA BE FINE! NOW IN JUUUUST A MINUTE HERE...
HI, GIRLS! I BROUGHT SLEEPING BAGS FOR EVERYBODY!
ガラッ
SLIDE
SEE?
HANDY TEACHER...
ジャーン
JA-JANG
OO-HOO-HOO... BEING AT THE SCHOOL AT NIGHT FEELS KINDA EXCITING IN A WEIRD WAY, DOESN'T IT!?
I TOTALLY KNOW WHATCHA MEAN! IT'S LIKE YOU'RE JUST ITCHIN' TO DO STUFF!
MIIIIII-OOO-CHAN! ♪
HMM?
プニッ
POKE
HEY! WHAT THE HECK WAS THAT FOR—!?
HEE HEE HEE. NO REASON.
GEEZ... THEY'RE ALL STARTING TO LOSE IT...

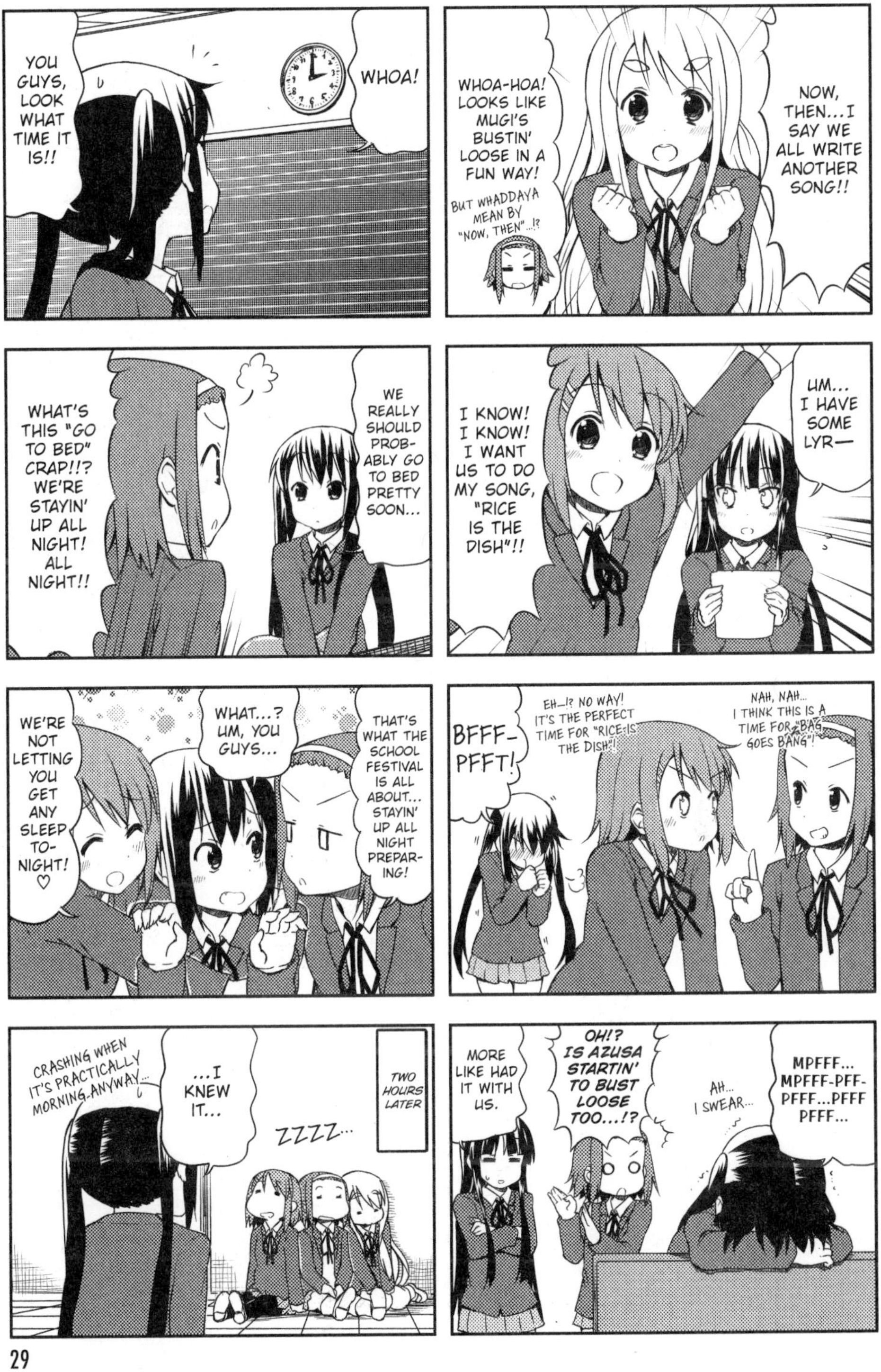

NOW, THEN... I SAY WE ALL WRITE ANOTHER SONG!!
WHOA-HOA! LOOKS LIKE MUGI'S BUSTIN' LOOSE IN A FUN WAY!
BUT WHADDAYA MEAN BY "NOW, THEN"...!?
UM... I HAVE SOME LYR—
I KNOW! I KNOW! I WANT US TO DO MY SONG, "RICE IS THE DISH"!!
NAH, NAH... I THINK THIS IS A TIME FOR "BAG GOES BANG"!
EH—!? NO WAY! IT'S THE PERFECT TIME FOR "RICE IS THE DISH"!
BFFF-PFFT!
MPFFF... MPFFF-PFF-PFFF...PFFF PFFF...
AH... I SWEAR...
OH!? IS AZUSA STARTIN' TO BUST LOOSE TOO...!?
MORE LIKE HAD IT WITH US.
WHOA!
YOU GUYS, LOOK WHAT TIME IT IS!!
WE REALLY SHOULD PROBABLY GO TO BED PRETTY SOON...
WHAT'S THIS "GO TO BED" CRAP!!? WE'RE STAYIN' UP ALL NIGHT! ALL NIGHT!!
THAT'S WHAT THE SCHOOL FESTIVAL IS ALL ABOUT... STAYIN' UP ALL NIGHT PREPARING!
WHAT...? UM, YOU GUYS...
WE'RE NOT LETTING YOU GET ANY SLEEP TONIGHT! ♡
TWO HOURS LATER
ZZZZ...
...I KNEW IT...
CRASHING WHEN IT'S PRACTICALLY MORNING ANYWAY...

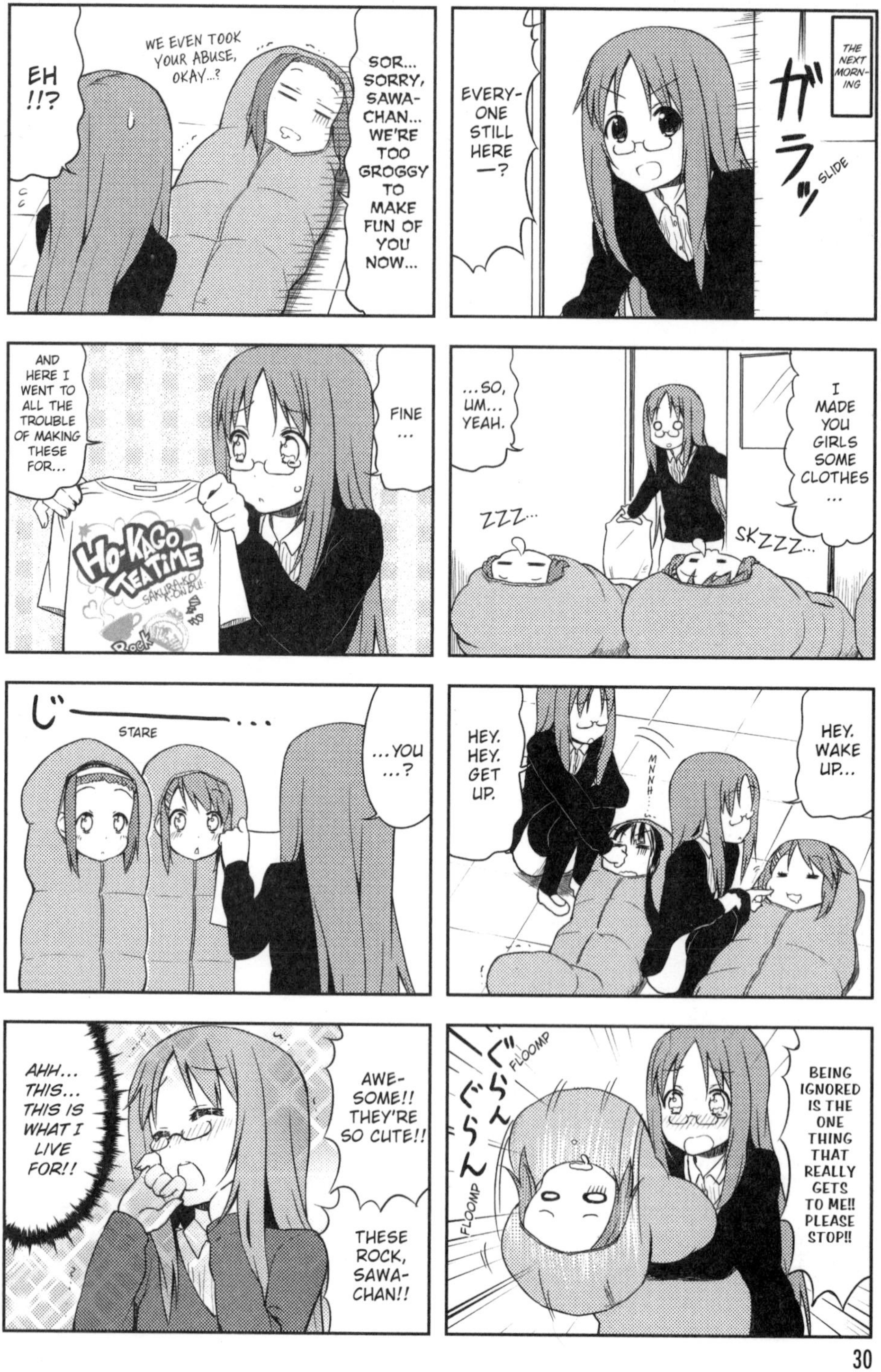
THE NEXT MORNING
ガラッ
SLIDE
EVERY-ONE STILL HERE—?
SOR... SORRY, SAWA-CHAN... WE'RE TOO GROGGY TO MAKE FUN OF YOU NOW...
WE EVEN TOOK YOUR ABUSE, OKAY...?
EH !!?
I MADE YOU GIRLS SOME CLOTHES ...
...SO, UM... YEAH.
ZZZ...
SKZZZ...
FINE ...
AND HERE I WENT TO ALL THE TROUBLE OF MAKING THESE FOR...
HO-KAGO TEA TIME
HEY. WAKE UP...
MNNH...
HEY. HEY. GET UP.
...YOU ...?
じ———...
STARE
BEING IGNORED IS THE ONE THING THAT REALLY GETS TO ME!! PLEASE STOP!!
ぐらん ぐらん
FLOOMP
FLOOMP
AWE-SOME!! THEY'RE SO CUTE!!
THESE ROCK, SAWA-CHAN!!
AHH... THIS... THIS IS WHAT I LIVE FOR!!

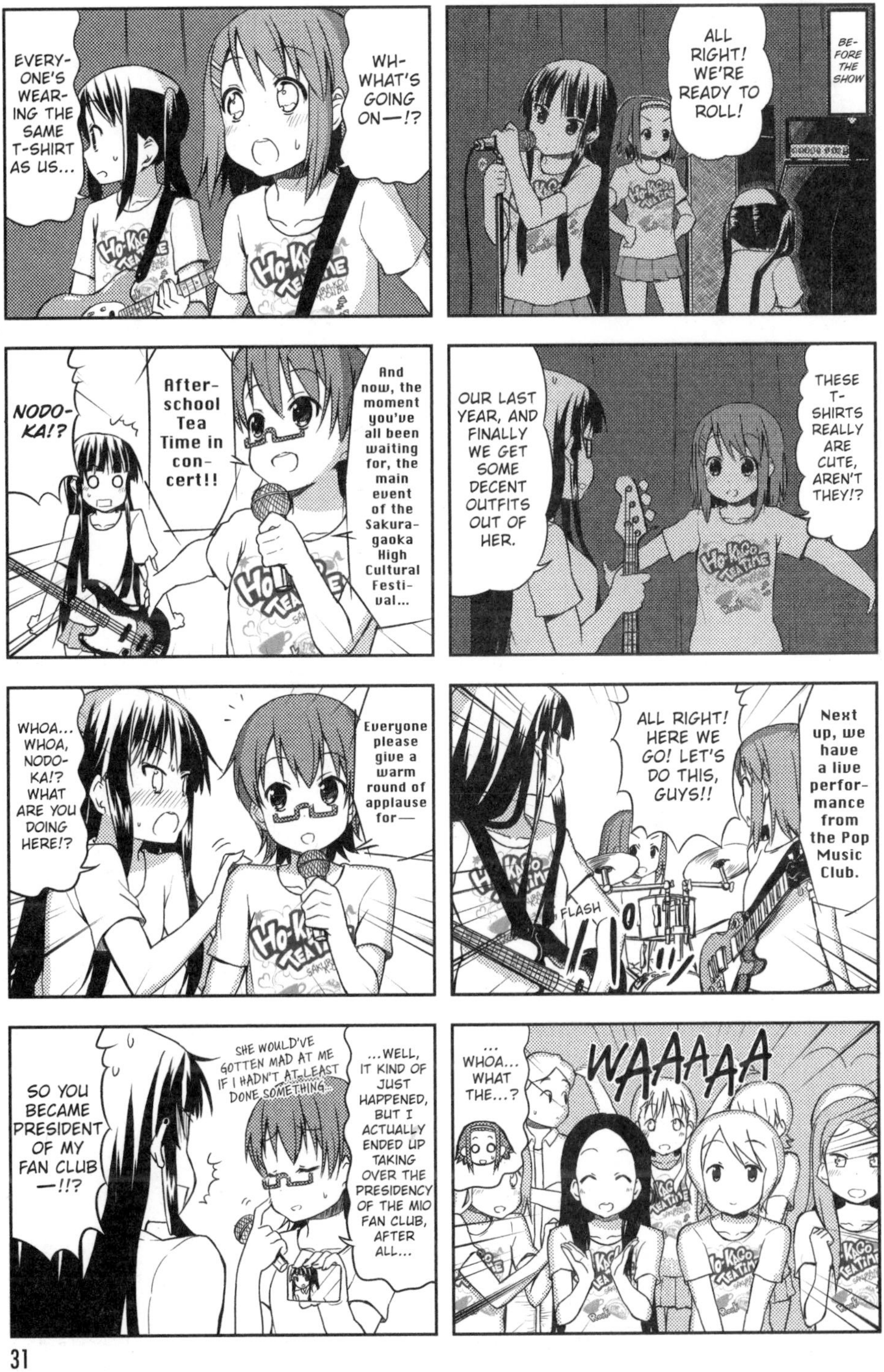
BEFORE THE SHOW
ALL RIGHT! WE'RE READY TO ROLL!
THESE T-SHIRTS REALLY ARE CUTE, AREN'T THEY!?
OUR LAST YEAR, AND FINALLY WE GET SOME DECENT OUTFITS OUT OF HER.
Next up, we have a live performance from the Pop Music Club.
ALL RIGHT! HERE WE GO! LET'S DO THIS, GUYS!!
FLASH
WAAAAA
...WHOA... WHAT THE...?
WH-WHAT'S GOING ON—!?
EVERYONE'S WEARING THE SAME T-SHIRT AS US...
And now, the moment you've all been waiting for, the main event of the Sakuragaoka High Cultural Festival...
After-school Tea Time in concert!!
NODOKA!?
Everyone please give a warm round of applause for—
WHOA... WHOA, NODOKA!? WHAT ARE YOU DOING HERE!?
...WELL, IT KIND OF JUST HAPPENED, BUT I ACTUALLY ENDED UP TAKING OVER THE PRESIDENCY OF THE MIO FAN CLUB, AFTER ALL...
SHE WOULD'VE GOTTEN MAD AT ME IF I HADN'T AT LEAST DONE SOMETHING...
SO YOU BECAME PRESIDENT OF MY FAN CLUB—!!?

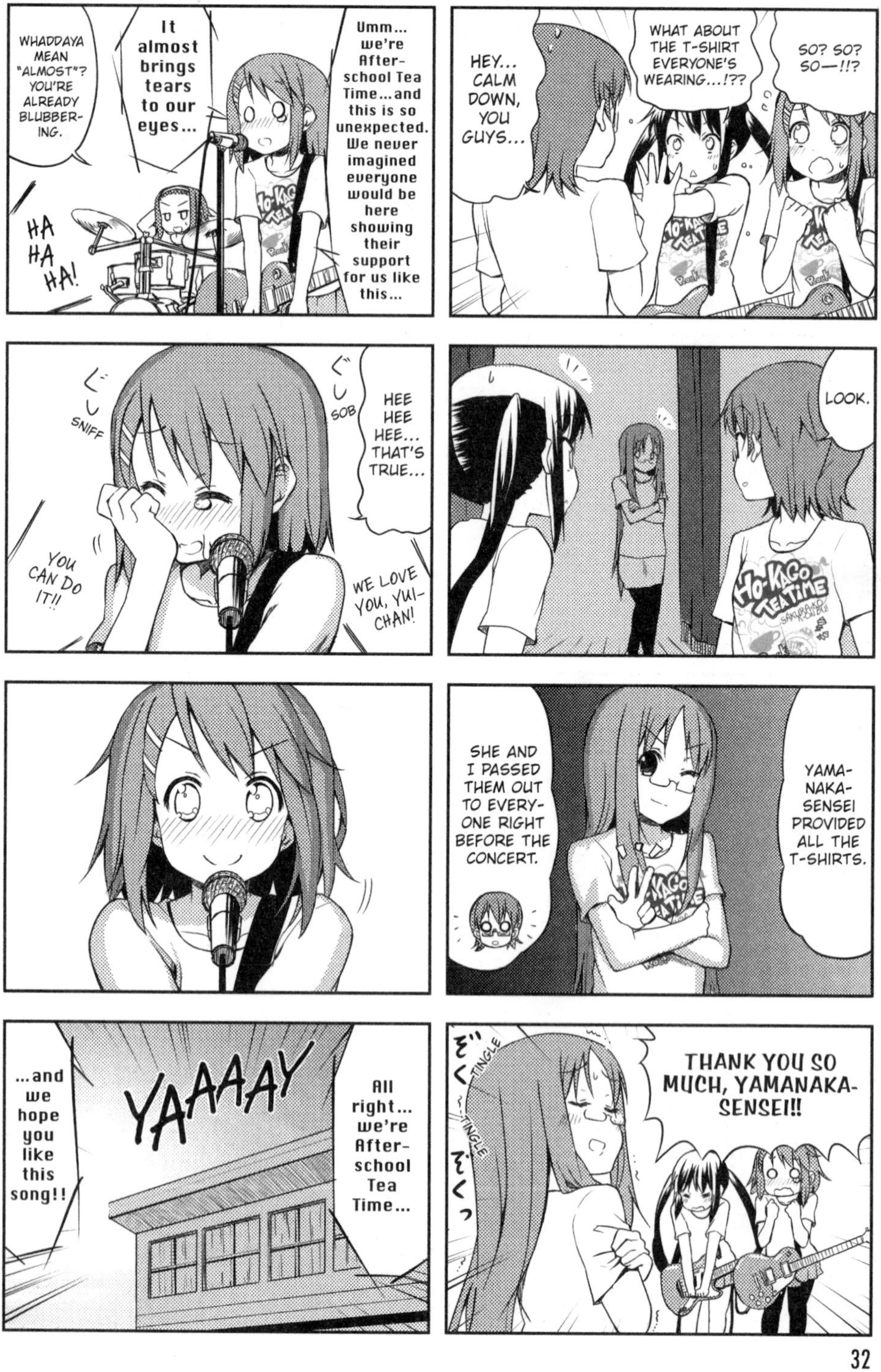
SO? SO? SO—!!?
WHAT ABOUT THE T-SHIRT EVERYONE'S WEARING...!??
HEY... CALM DOWN, YOU GUYS...
LOOK.
YAMA-NAKA-SENSEI PROVIDED ALL THE T-SHIRTS.
SHE AND I PASSED THEM OUT TO EVERY-ONE RIGHT BEFORE THE CONCERT.
THANK YOU SO MUCH, YAMANAKA-SENSEI!!
ぞくっ TINGLE
ぞくっ TINGLE
Umm... we're After-school Tea Time...and this is so unexpected. We never imagined everyone would be here showing their support for us like this...
It almost brings tears to our eyes...
WHADDAYA MEAN "ALMOST"? YOU'RE ALREADY BLUBBER-ING.
HA HA HA!
ぐし SOB
HEE HEE HEE... THAT'S TRUE...
WE LOVE YOU, YUI-CHAN!
ぐし SNIFF
YOU CAN DO IT!!
All right... we're After-school Tea Time...
YAAAAY
...and we hope you like this song!!

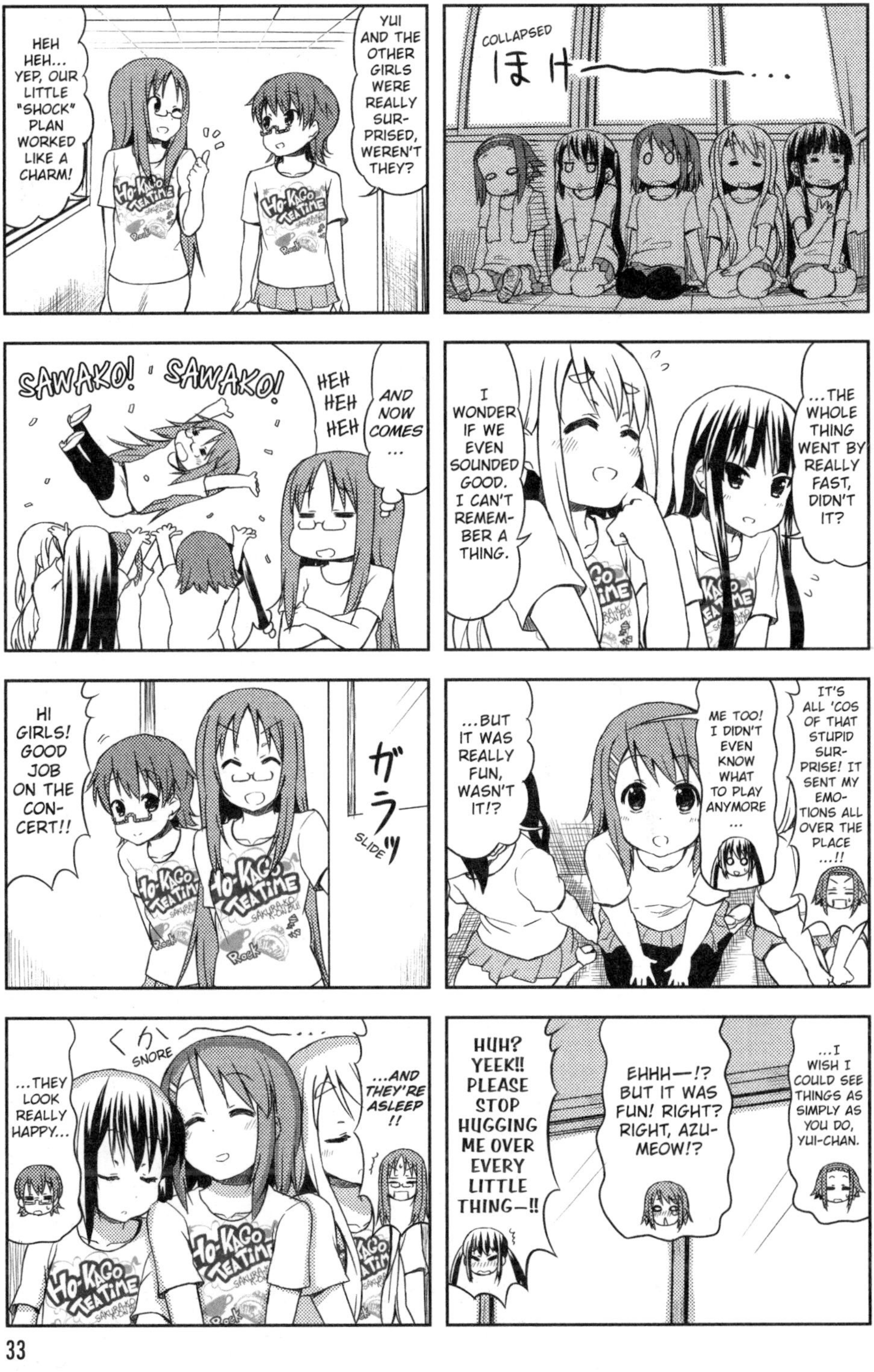
COLLAPSED
ほけー———…
…THE WHOLE THING WENT BY REALLY FAST, DIDN'T IT?
I WONDER IF WE EVEN SOUNDED GOOD. I CAN'T REMEMBER A THING.
IT'S ALL 'COS OF THAT STUPID SURPRISE! IT SENT MY EMOTIONS ALL OVER THE PLACE …!!
ME TOO! I DIDN'T EVEN KNOW WHAT TO PLAY ANYMORE …
…BUT IT WAS REALLY FUN, WASN'T IT!?
…I WISH I COULD SEE THINGS AS SIMPLY AS YOU DO, YUI-CHAN.
EHHH—!? BUT IT WAS FUN! RIGHT? RIGHT, AZU-MEOW!?
HUH? YEEK!! PLEASE STOP HUGGING ME OVER EVERY LITTLE THING—!!
YUI AND THE OTHER GIRLS WERE REALLY SUR-PRISED, WEREN'T THEY?
HEH HEH… YEP, OUR LITTLE "SHOCK" PLAN WORKED LIKE A CHARM!
AND NOW COMES …
HEH HEH HEH
SAWAKO! SAWAKO!
ガラッ
SLIDE
HI GIRLS! GOOD JOB ON THE CON-CERT!!
…AND THEY'RE ASLEEP !!
くかー——…
SNORE
…THEY LOOK REALLY HAPPY…

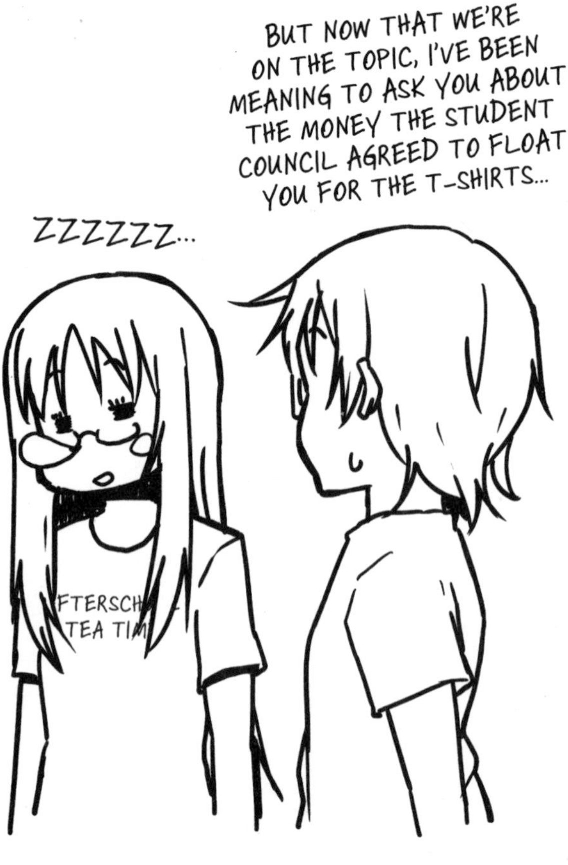
BUT NOW THAT WE'RE ON THE TOPIC, I'VE BEEN MEANING TO ASK YOU ABOUT THE MONEY THE STUDENT COUNCIL AGREED TO FLOAT YOU FOR THE T-SHIRTS...
ZZZZZZ...

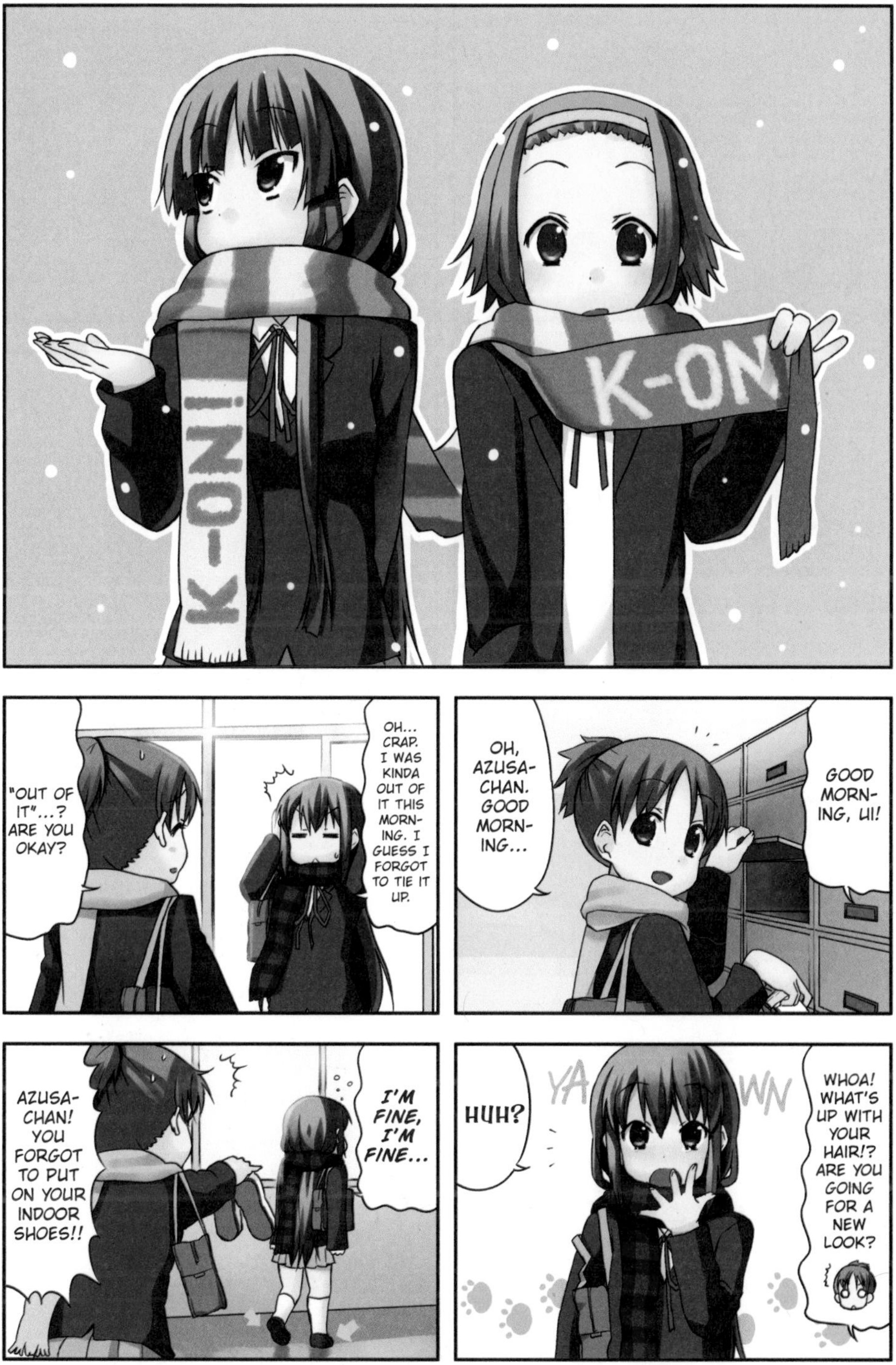
K-ON!
K-ON
GOOD MORNING, UI!
OH, AZUSA-CHAN. GOOD MORNING...
WHOA! WHAT'S UP WITH YOUR HAIR!? ARE YOU GOING FOR A NEW LOOK?
YAWN
HUH?
OH... CRAP. I WAS KINDA OUT OF IT THIS MORNING. I GUESS I FORGOT TO TIE IT UP.
"OUT OF IT"...? ARE YOU OKAY?
I'M FINE, I'M FINE...
AZUSA-CHAN! YOU FORGOT TO PUT ON YOUR INDOOR SHOES!!

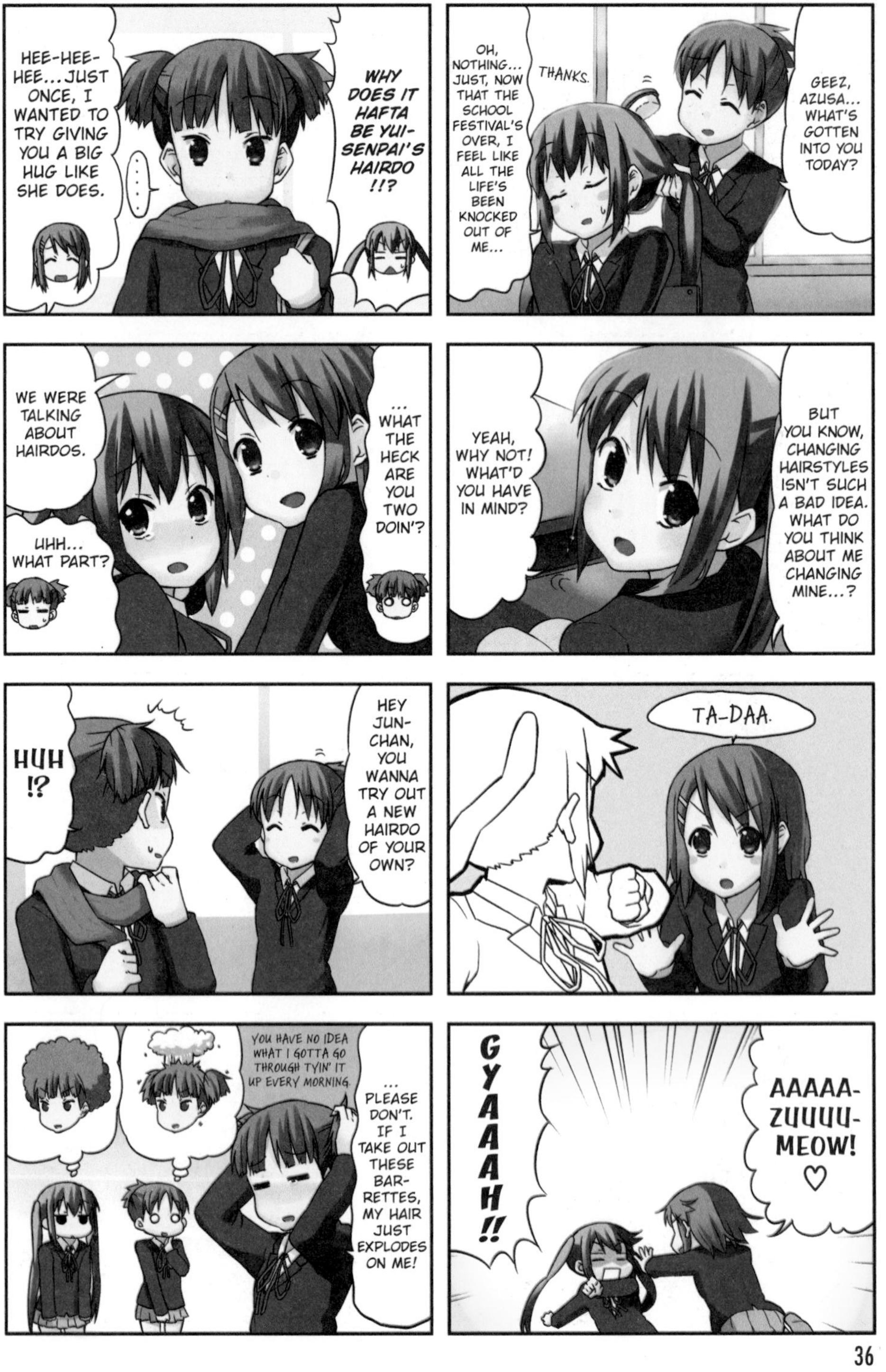
GEEZ, AZUSA... WHAT'S GOTTEN INTO YOU TODAY?
THANKS.
OH, NOTHING... JUST, NOW THAT THE SCHOOL FESTIVAL'S OVER, I FEEL LIKE ALL THE LIFE'S BEEN KNOCKED OUT OF ME...
BUT YOU KNOW, CHANGING HAIRSTYLES ISN'T SUCH A BAD IDEA. WHAT DO YOU THINK ABOUT ME CHANGING MINE...?
YEAH, WHY NOT! WHAT'D YOU HAVE IN MIND?
TA-DAA.
AAAAA-ZUUUU-MEOW! ♡
GYAAAAH!!
WHY DOES IT HAFTA BE YUI-SENPAI'S HAIRDO !!?
HEE-HEE-HEE... JUST ONCE, I WANTED TO TRY GIVING YOU A BIG HUG LIKE SHE DOES.
......
...WHAT THE HECK ARE YOU TWO DOIN'?
WE WERE TALKING ABOUT HAIRDOS.
UHH... WHAT PART?
HEY JUN-CHAN, YOU WANNA TRY OUT A NEW HAIRDO OF YOUR OWN?
HUH !?
...PLEASE DON'T. IF I TAKE OUT THESE BARRETTES, MY HAIR JUST EXPLODES ON ME!
YOU HAVE NO IDEA WHAT I GOTTA GO THROUGH TYIN' IT UP EVERY MORNING.

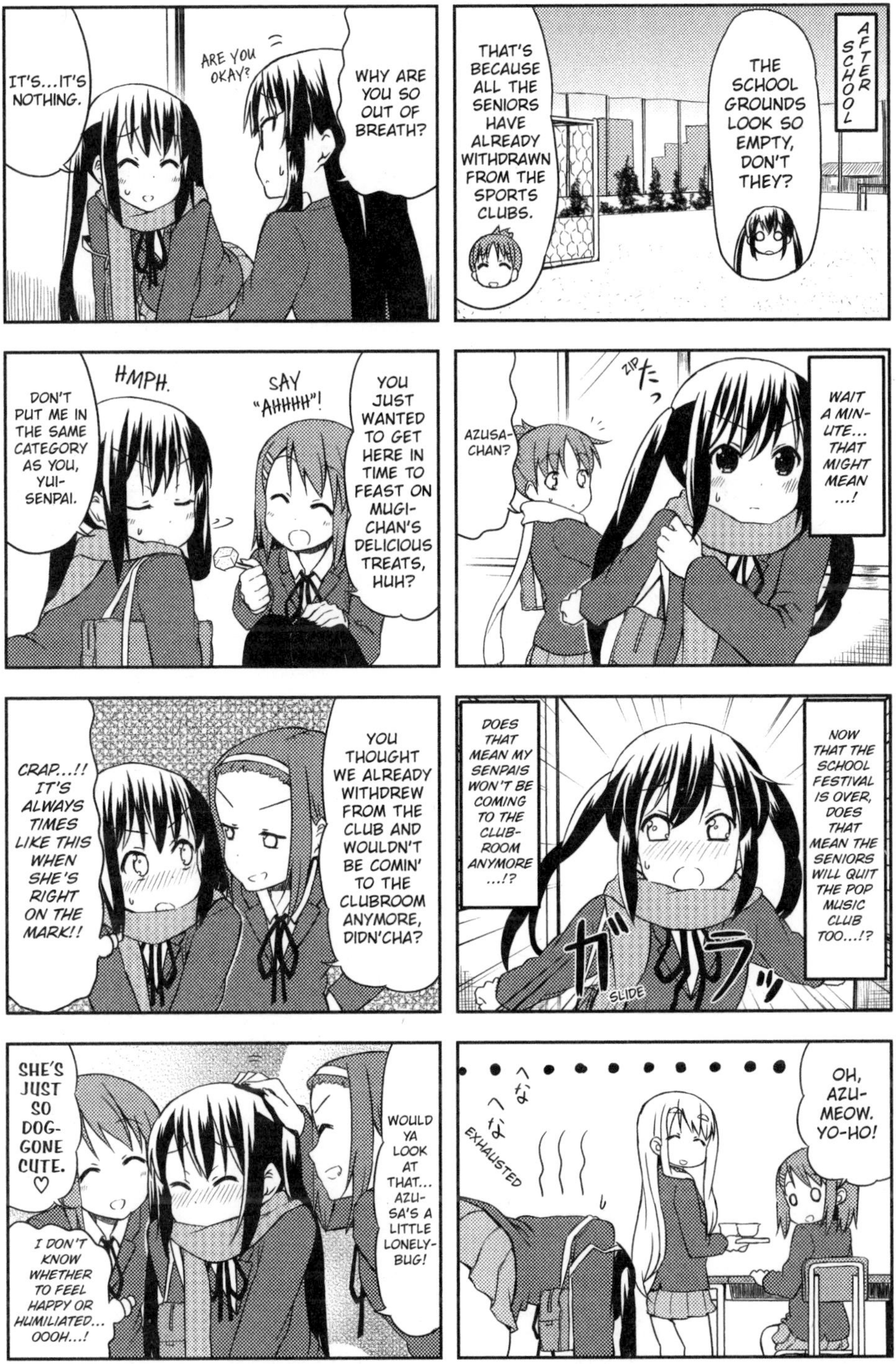
AFTER SCHOOL
THE SCHOOL GROUNDS LOOK SO EMPTY, DON'T THEY?
THAT'S BECAUSE ALL THE SENIORS HAVE ALREADY WITHDRAWN FROM THE SPORTS CLUBS.
WAIT A MIN-UTE... THAT MIGHT MEAN ...!
ZIP
AZUSA-CHAN?
NOW THAT THE SCHOOL FESTIVAL IS OVER, DOES THAT MEAN THE SENIORS WILL QUIT THE POP MUSIC CLUB TOO...!?
DOES THAT MEAN MY SENPAIS WON'T BE COMING TO THE CLUB-ROOM ANYMORE ...!?
SLIDE
OH, AZU-MEOW. YO-HO!
EXHAUSTED
WHY ARE YOU SO OUT OF BREATH?
ARE YOU OKAY?
IT'S...IT'S NOTHING.
YOU JUST WANTED TO GET HERE IN TIME TO FEAST ON MUGI-CHAN'S DELICIOUS TREATS, HUH?
SAY "AHHHH"!
HMPH.
DON'T PUT ME IN THE SAME CATEGORY AS YOU, YUI-SENPAI.
YOU THOUGHT WE ALREADY WITHDREW FROM THE CLUB AND WOULDN'T BE COMIN' TO THE CLUBROOM ANYMORE, DIDN'CHA?
CRAP...!! IT'S ALWAYS TIMES LIKE THIS WHEN SHE'S RIGHT ON THE MARK!!
WOULD YA LOOK AT THAT... AZUSA'S A LITTLE LONELY-BUG!
SHE'S JUST SO DOG-GONE CUTE. ♡
I DON'T KNOW WHETHER TO FEEL HAPPY OR HUMILIATED... OOOH...!

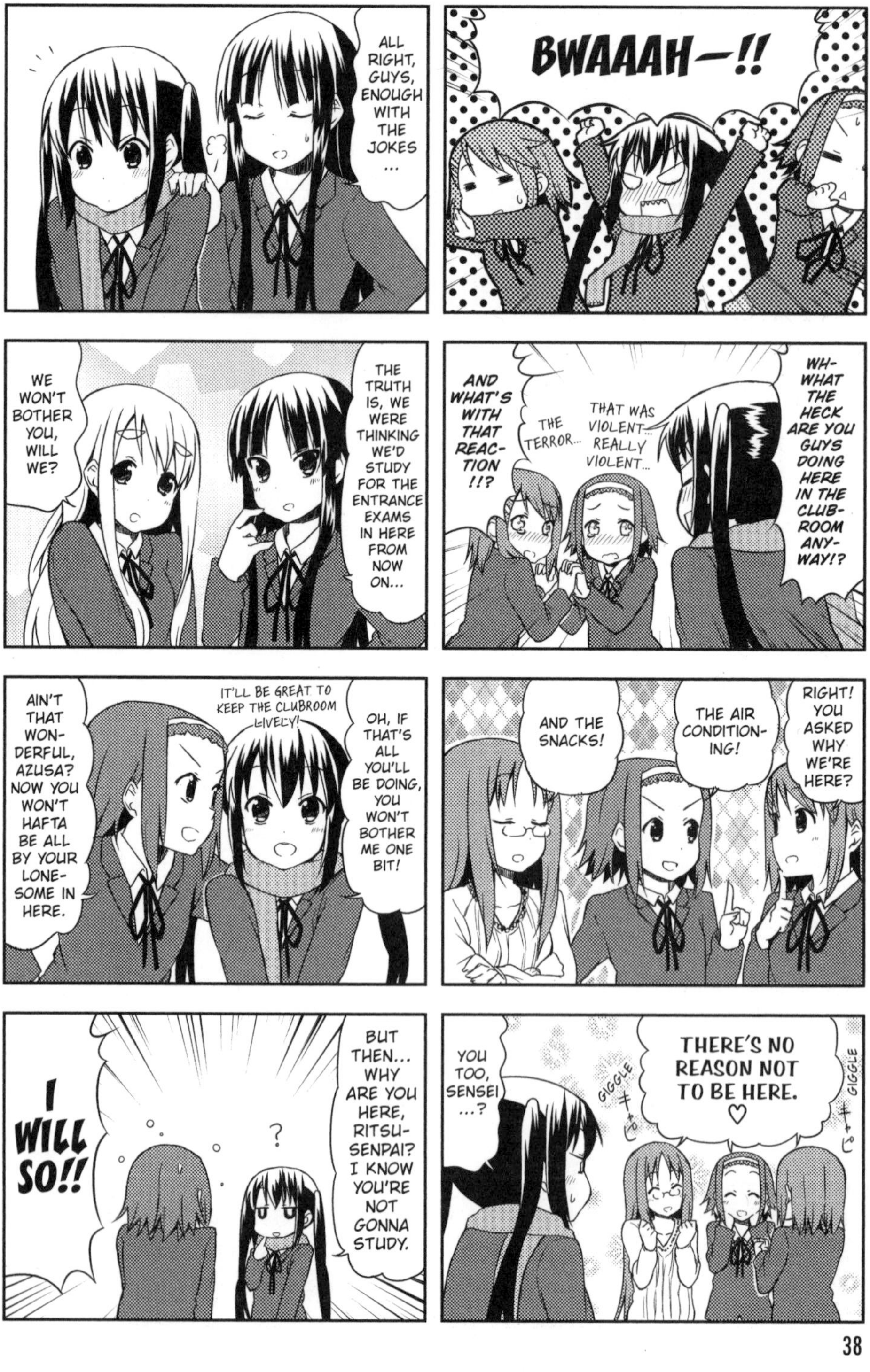
BWAAAH—!!
WH-WHAT THE HECK ARE YOU GUYS DOING HERE IN THE CLUBROOM ANYWAY!?
THAT WAS VIOLENT... REALLY VIOLENT...
THE TERROR...
AND WHAT'S WITH THAT REACTION!!?
RIGHT! YOU ASKED WHY WE'RE HERE?
THE AIR CONDITIONING!
AND THE SNACKS!
THERE'S NO REASON NOT TO BE HERE. ♡
GIGGLE
キャピ
GIGGLE
キャピ
YOU TOO, SENSEI ...?
ALL RIGHT, GUYS, ENOUGH WITH THE JOKES ...
THE TRUTH IS, WE WERE THINKING WE'D STUDY FOR THE ENTRANCE EXAMS IN HERE FROM NOW ON...
WE WON'T BOTHER YOU, WILL WE?
OH, IF THAT'S ALL YOU'LL BE DOING, YOU WON'T BOTHER ME ONE BIT!
IT'LL BE GREAT TO KEEP THE CLUBROOM LIVELY!
AIN'T THAT WONDERFUL, AZUSA? NOW YOU WON'T HAFTA BE ALL BY YOUR LONESOME IN HERE.
BUT THEN... WHY ARE YOU HERE, RITSU-SENPAI? I KNOW YOU'RE NOT GONNA STUDY.
?
I WILL SO!!

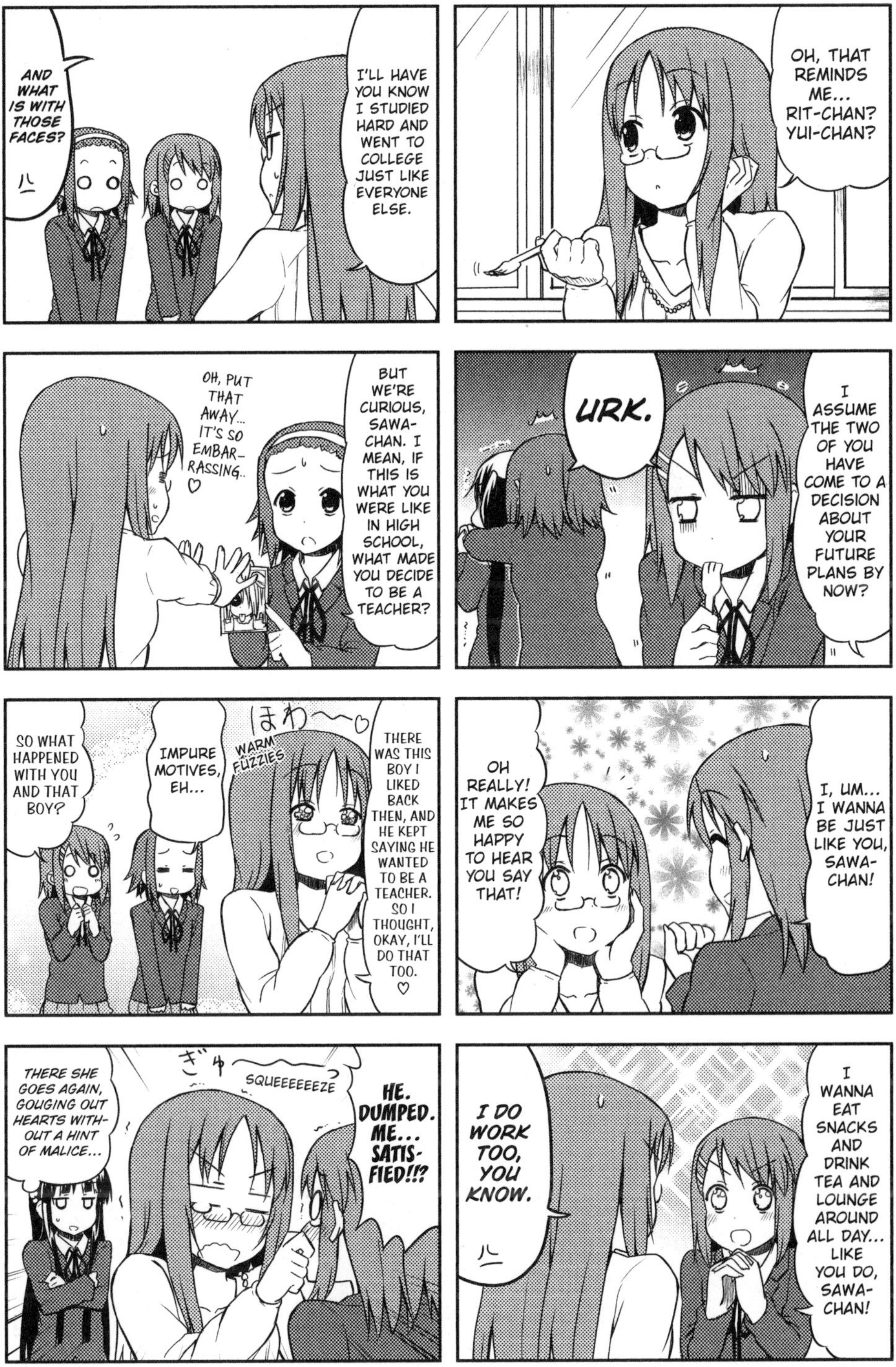
OH, THAT REMINDS ME... RIT-CHAN? YUI-CHAN?
I ASSUME THE TWO OF YOU HAVE COME TO A DECISION ABOUT YOUR FUTURE PLANS BY NOW?
URK.
I, UM... I WANNA BE JUST LIKE YOU, SAWA-CHAN!
OH REALLY! IT MAKES ME SO HAPPY TO HEAR YOU SAY THAT!
I WANNA EAT SNACKS AND DRINK TEA AND LOUNGE AROUND ALL DAY... LIKE YOU DO, SAWA-CHAN!
I DO WORK TOO, YOU KNOW.
I'LL HAVE YOU KNOW I STUDIED HARD AND WENT TO COLLEGE JUST LIKE EVERYONE ELSE.
AND WHAT IS WITH THOSE FACES?
BUT WE'RE CURIOUS, SAWA-CHAN. I MEAN, IF THIS IS WHAT YOU WERE LIKE IN HIGH SCHOOL, WHAT MADE YOU DECIDE TO BE A TEACHER?
OH, PUT THAT AWAY... IT'S SO EMBAR-RASSING.. ♡
THERE WAS THIS BOY I LIKED BACK THEN, AND HE KEPT SAYING HE WANTED TO BE A TEACHER. SO I THOUGHT, OKAY, I'LL DO THAT TOO. ♡
ほわ～～♡
WARM FUZZIES
IMPURE MOTIVES, EH...
SO WHAT HAPPENED WITH YOU AND THAT BOY?
HE. DUMPED. ME... SATIS-FIED!!?
ぎゅ～～っ
SQUEEEEEEEZE
THERE SHE GOES AGAIN, GOUGING OUT HEARTS WITH-OUT A HINT OF MALICE...

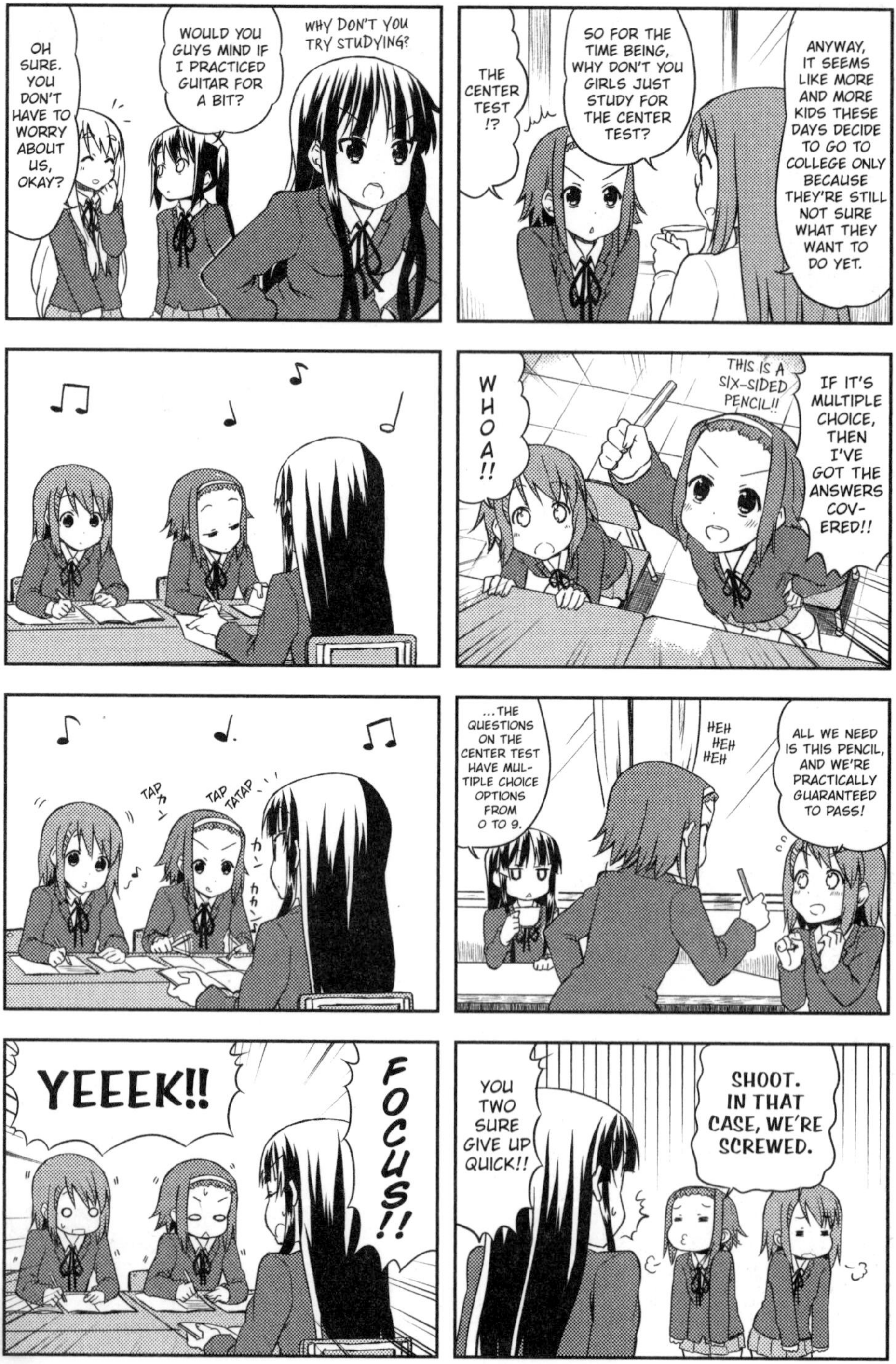
ANYWAY, IT SEEMS LIKE MORE AND MORE KIDS THESE DAYS DECIDE TO GO TO COLLEGE ONLY BECAUSE THEY'RE STILL NOT SURE WHAT THEY WANT TO DO YET.
SO FOR THE TIME BEING, WHY DON'T YOU GIRLS JUST STUDY FOR THE CENTER TEST?
THE CENTER TEST !?
IF IT'S MULTIPLE CHOICE, THEN I'VE GOT THE ANSWERS COVERED!!
THIS IS A SIX-SIDED PENCIL!!
WHOA!!
ALL WE NEED IS THIS PENCIL, AND WE'RE PRACTICALLY GUARANTEED TO PASS!
HEH HEH HEH
...THE QUESTIONS ON THE CENTER TEST HAVE MULTIPLE CHOICE OPTIONS FROM 0 TO 9.
SHOOT. IN THAT CASE, WE'RE SCREWED.
YOU TWO SURE GIVE UP QUICK!!
WHY DON'T YOU TRY STUDYING?
WOULD YOU GUYS MIND IF I PRACTICED GUITAR FOR A BIT?
OH SURE. YOU DON'T HAVE TO WORRY ABOUT US, OKAY?
TAP TATAP
TAP
FOCUS!!
YEEEK!!

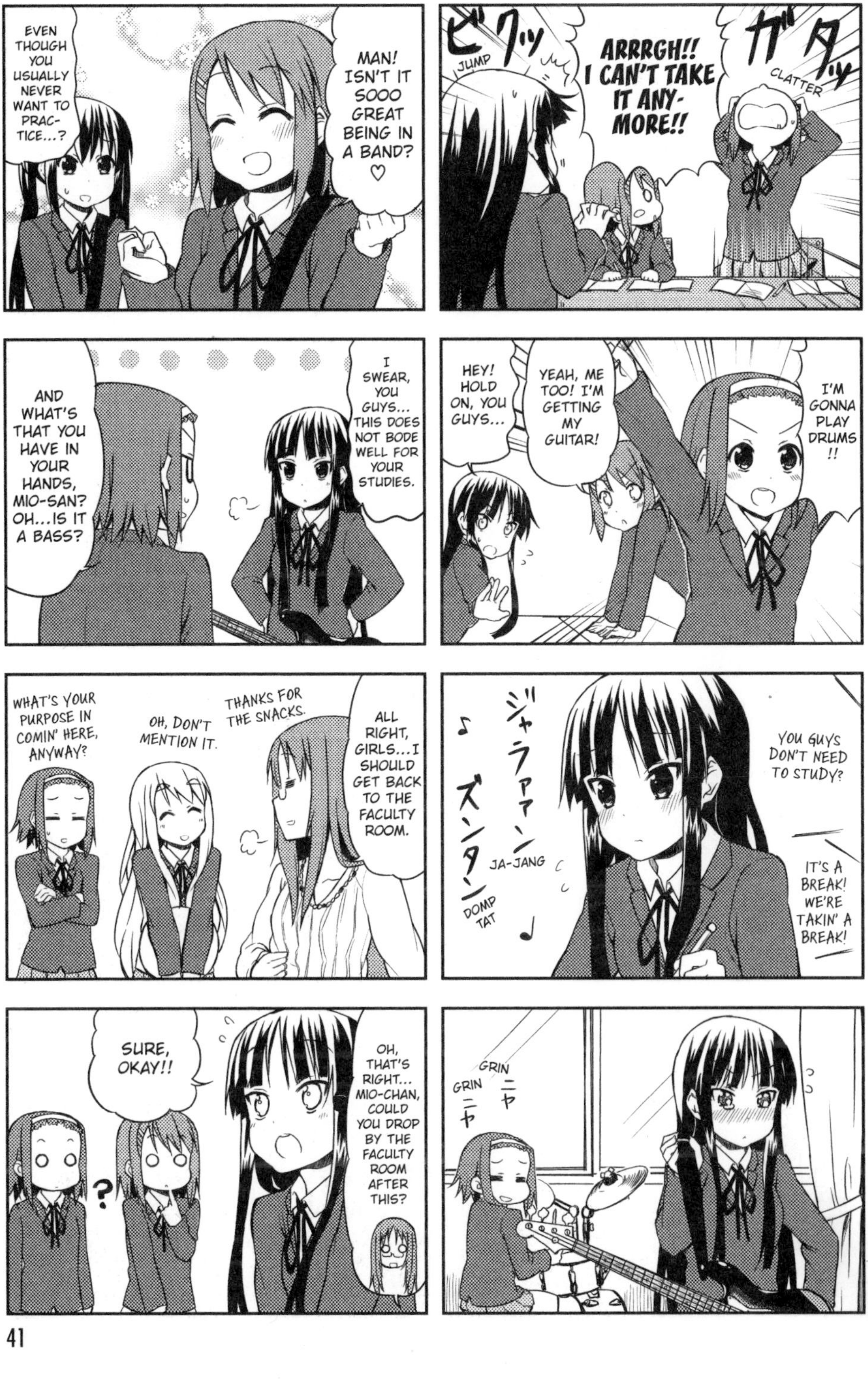
ガタッ
CLATTER
ARRRGH!! I CAN'T TAKE IT ANY-MORE!!
ビクッ
JUMP
I'M GONNA PLAY DRUMS!!
YEAH, ME TOO! I'M GETTING MY GUITAR!
HEY! HOLD ON, YOU GUYS...
YOU GUYS DON'T NEED TO STUDY?
IT'S A BREAK! WE'RE TAKIN' A BREAK!
ジャラァン
JA-JANG
ズンタン
DOMP TAT
GRIN
ニヤ
GRIN
ニヤ
MAN! ISN'T IT SOOO GREAT BEING IN A BAND? ♡
EVEN THOUGH YOU USUALLY NEVER WANT TO PRAC-TICE...?
I SWEAR, YOU GUYS... THIS DOES NOT BODE WELL FOR YOUR STUDIES.
AND WHAT'S THAT YOU HAVE IN YOUR HANDS, MIO-SAN? OH...IS IT A BASS?
ALL RIGHT, GIRLS...I SHOULD GET BACK TO THE FACULTY ROOM.
THANKS FOR THE SNACKS.
OH, DON'T MENTION IT.
WHAT'S YOUR PURPOSE IN COMIN' HERE, ANYWAY?
OH, THAT'S RIGHT... MIO-CHAN, COULD YOU DROP BY THE FACULTY ROOM AFTER THIS?
SURE, OKAY!!

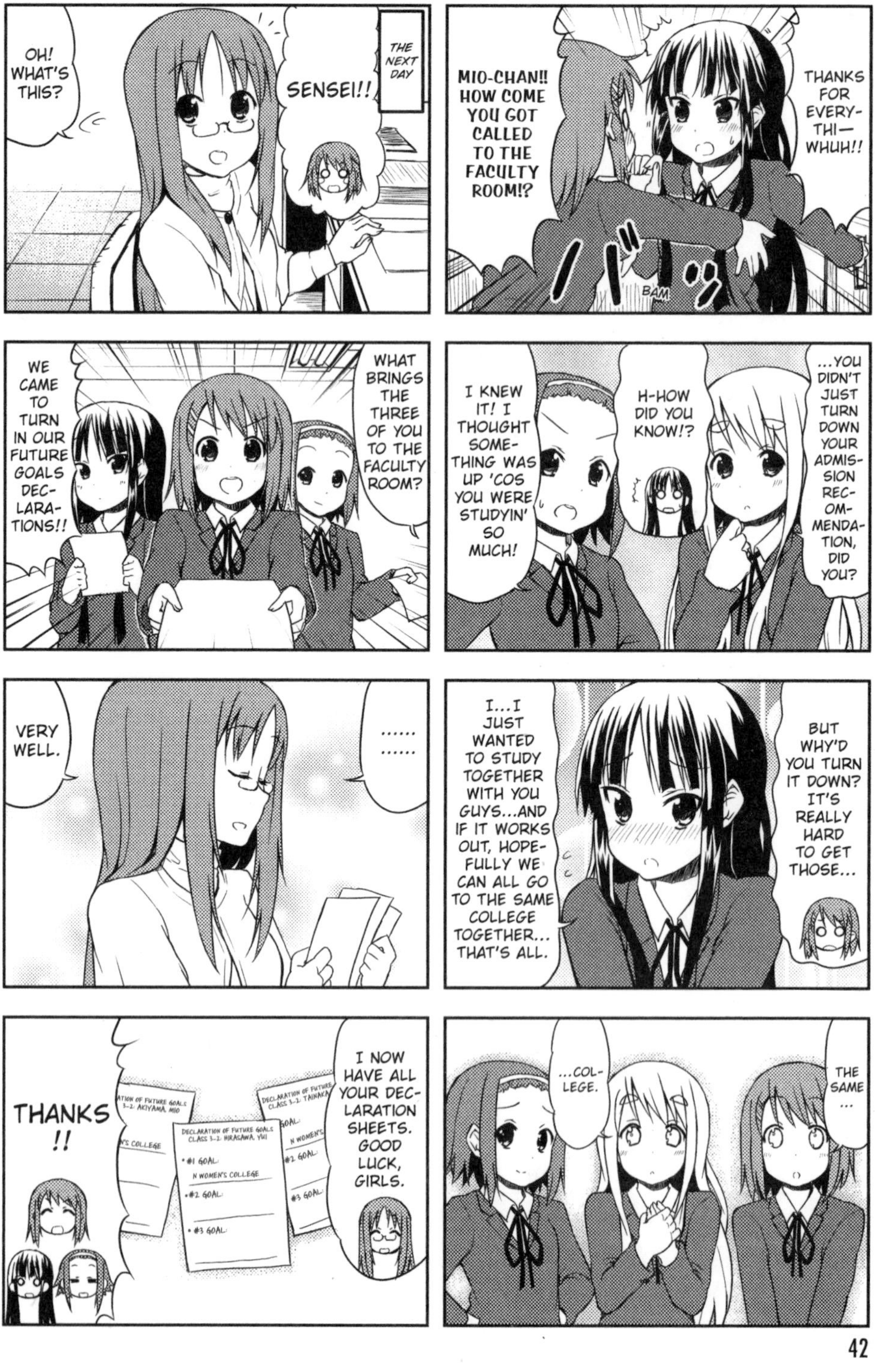
THANKS FOR EVERY-THI—WHUH!!
MIO-CHAN!! HOW COME YOU GOT CALLED TO THE FACULTY ROOM!?
BAM
...YOU DIDN'T JUST TURN DOWN YOUR ADMIS-SION REC-OM-MENDA-TION, DID YOU?
H-HOW DID YOU KNOW!?
I KNEW IT! I THOUGHT SOME-THING WAS UP 'COS YOU WERE STUDYIN' SO MUCH!
BUT WHY'D YOU TURN IT DOWN? IT'S REALLY HARD TO GET THOSE...
I...I JUST WANTED TO STUDY TOGETHER WITH YOU GUYS...AND IF IT WORKS OUT, HOPE-FULLY WE CAN ALL GO TO THE SAME COLLEGE TOGETHER... THAT'S ALL.
THE SAME...
...COL-LEGE.
THE NEXT DAY
SENSEI!!
OH! WHAT'S THIS?
WHAT BRINGS THE THREE OF YOU TO THE FACULTY ROOM?
WE CAME TO TURN IN OUR FUTURE GOALS DEC-LARA-TIONS!!
....
VERY WELL.
I NOW HAVE ALL YOUR DEC-LARATION SHEETS. GOOD LUCK, GIRLS.
DECLARATION OF FUTURE GOALS CLASS 3-2. HIRASAWA, YUI
#1 GOAL: N WOMEN'S COLLEGE
#2 GOAL:
#3 GOAL:
THANKS!!

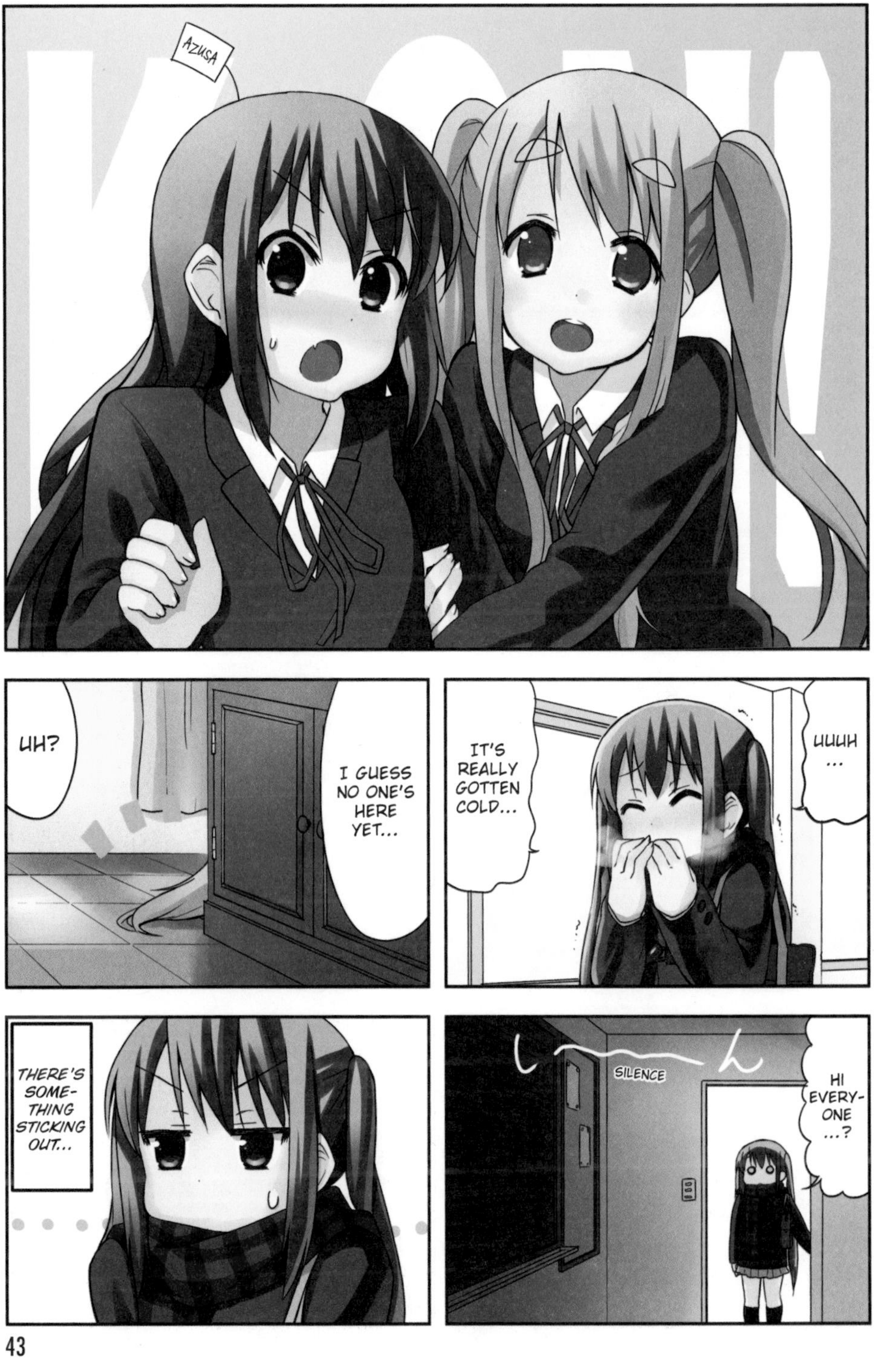
AZUSA
UUUH ...
IT'S REALLY GOTTEN COLD...
I GUESS NO ONE'S HERE YET...
UH?
HI EVERY-ONE ...?
しーん
SILENCE
THERE'S SOME-THING STICKING OUT...

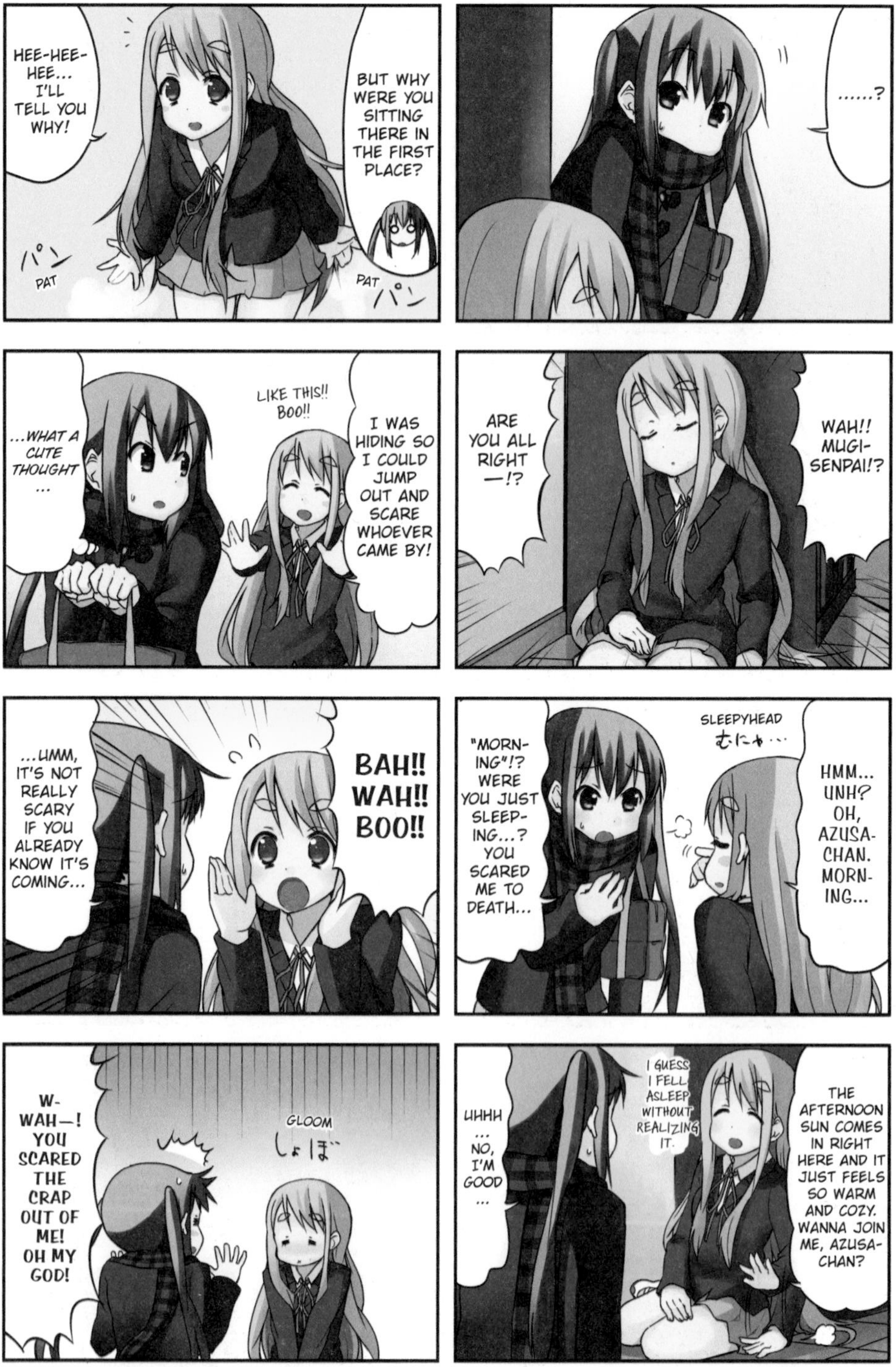
......?
WAH!! MUGI-SENPAI!?
ARE YOU ALL RIGHT—!?
HMM... UNH? OH, AZUSA-CHAN. MORNING...
SLEEPYHEAD
むにゃ…
"MORNING"!? WERE YOU JUST SLEEPING...? YOU SCARED ME TO DEATH...
THE AFTERNOON SUN COMES IN RIGHT HERE AND IT JUST FEELS SO WARM AND COZY. WANNA JOIN ME, AZUSA-CHAN?
I GUESS I FELL ASLEEP WITHOUT REALIZING IT.
UHHH... NO, I'M GOOD...
BUT WHY WERE YOU SITTING THERE IN THE FIRST PLACE?
HEE-HEE-HEE... I'LL TELL YOU WHY!
PAT
パン
PAT
パン
I WAS HIDING SO I COULD JUMP OUT AND SCARE WHOEVER CAME BY!
LIKE THIS!! BOO!!
...WHAT A CUTE THOUGHT...
BAH!! WAH!! BOO!!
...UMM, IT'S NOT REALLY SCARY IF YOU ALREADY KNOW IT'S COMING...
GLOOM
しょぼ
W-WAH—! YOU SCARED THE CRAP OUT OF ME! OH MY GOD!

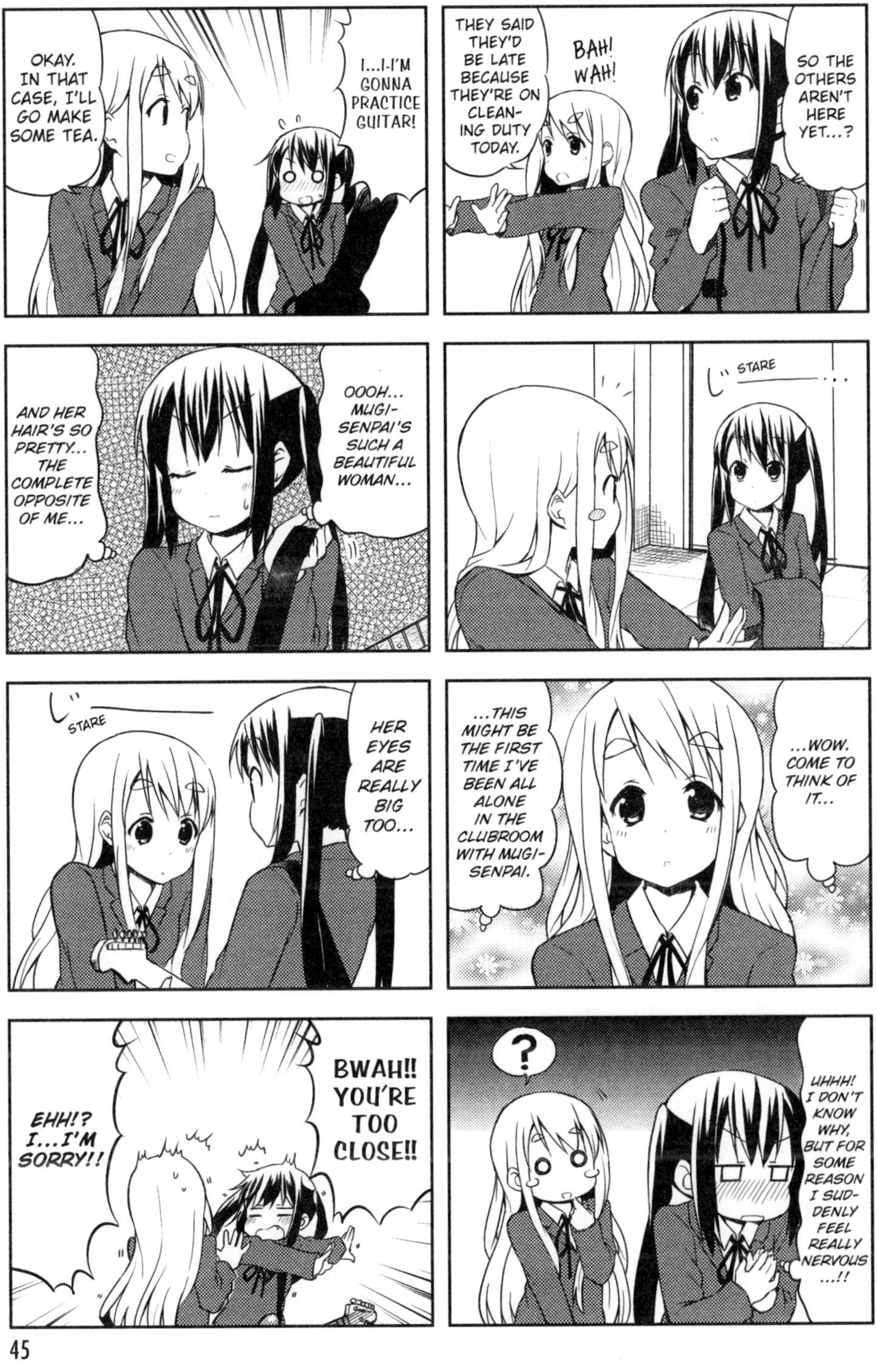
SO THE OTHERS AREN'T HERE YET...?
THEY SAID THEY'D BE LATE BECAUSE THEY'RE ON CLEANING DUTY TODAY.
BAH! WAH!
STARE
...WOW. COME TO THINK OF IT...
...THIS MIGHT BE THE FIRST TIME I'VE BEEN ALL ALONE IN THE CLUBROOM WITH MUGI-SENPAI.
UHHH! I DON'T KNOW WHY, BUT FOR SOME REASON I SUDDENLY FEEL REALLY NERVOUS ...!!
?
I...I-I'M GONNA PRACTICE GUITAR!
OKAY. IN THAT CASE, I'LL GO MAKE SOME TEA.
OOOH... MUGI-SENPAI'S SUCH A BEAUTIFUL WOMAN...
AND HER HAIR'S SO PRETTY... THE COMPLETE OPPOSITE OF ME...
HER EYES ARE REALLY BIG TOO...
STARE
BWAH!! YOU'RE TOO CLOSE!!
EHH!? I...I'M SORRY!!

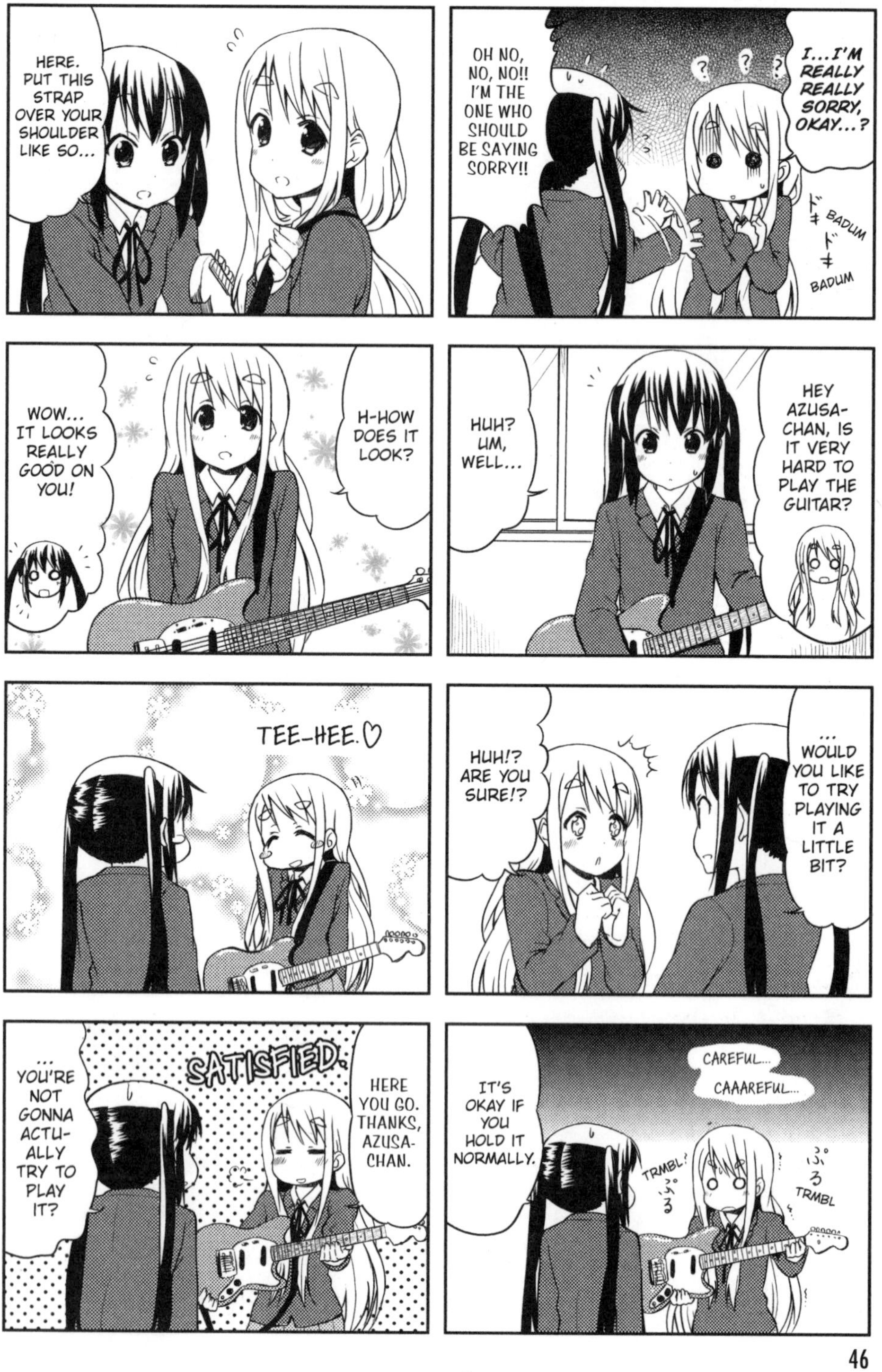

I...I'M REALLY REALLY SORRY, OKAY...?
OH NO, NO, NO!! I'M THE ONE WHO SHOULD BE SAYING SORRY!!
ドキ BADUM
ドキ BADUM
HEY AZUSA-CHAN, IS IT VERY HARD TO PLAY THE GUITAR?
HUH? UM, WELL...
...WOULD YOU LIKE TO TRY PLAYING IT A LITTLE BIT?
HUH!? ARE YOU SURE!?
CAREFUL...
CAAAREFUL...
IT'S OKAY IF YOU HOLD IT NORMALLY.
ぷる TRMBL
ぷる TRMBL
HERE. PUT THIS STRAP OVER YOUR SHOULDER LIKE SO...
H-HOW DOES IT LOOK?
WOW... IT LOOKS REALLY GOOD ON YOU!
TEE-HEE.♡
HERE YOU GO. THANKS, AZUSA-CHAN.
SATISFIED.
...YOU'RE NOT GONNA ACTU-ALLY TRY TO PLAY IT?

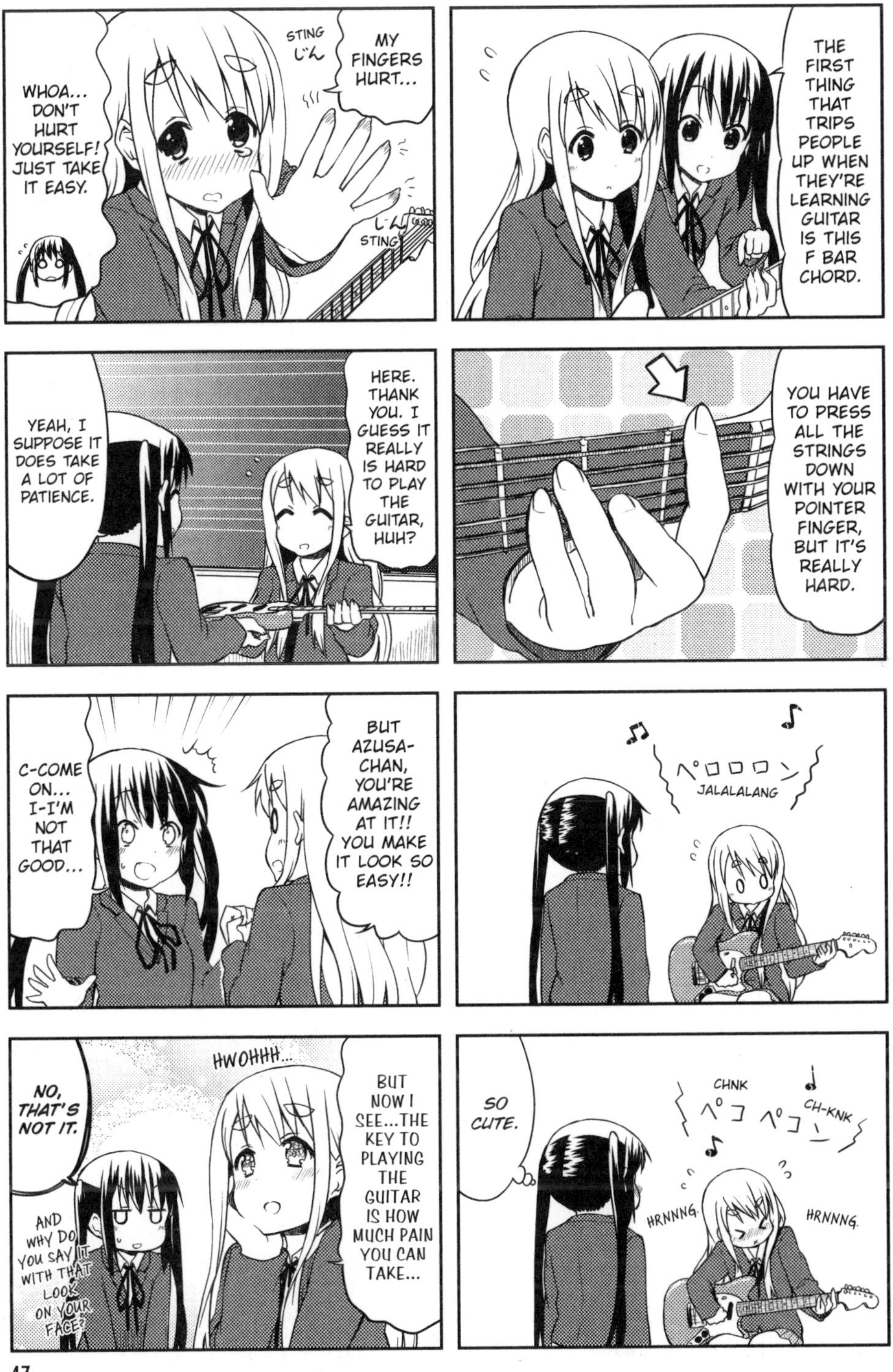
THE FIRST THING THAT TRIPS PEOPLE UP WHEN THEY'RE LEARNING GUITAR IS THIS F BAR CHORD.
YOU HAVE TO PRESS ALL THE STRINGS DOWN WITH YOUR POINTER FINGER, BUT IT'S REALLY HARD.
ペロロロン
JALALALANG
ペコ ペコン
CHNK CH-KNK
HRNNNG.
HRNNNG.
SO CUTE.
STING
じん
MY FINGERS HURT...
じん
STING
WHOA... DON'T HURT YOURSELF! JUST TAKE IT EASY.
HERE. THANK YOU. I GUESS IT REALLY IS HARD TO PLAY THE GUITAR, HUH?
YEAH, I SUPPOSE IT DOES TAKE A LOT OF PATIENCE.
BUT AZUSA-CHAN, YOU'RE AMAZING AT IT!! YOU MAKE IT LOOK SO EASY!!
C-COME ON... I-I'M NOT THAT GOOD...
HWOHHH...
BUT NOW I SEE...THE KEY TO PLAYING THE GUITAR IS HOW MUCH PAIN YOU CAN TAKE...
NO, THAT'S NOT IT.
AND WHY DO YOU SAY IT WITH THAT LOOK ON YOUR FACE?

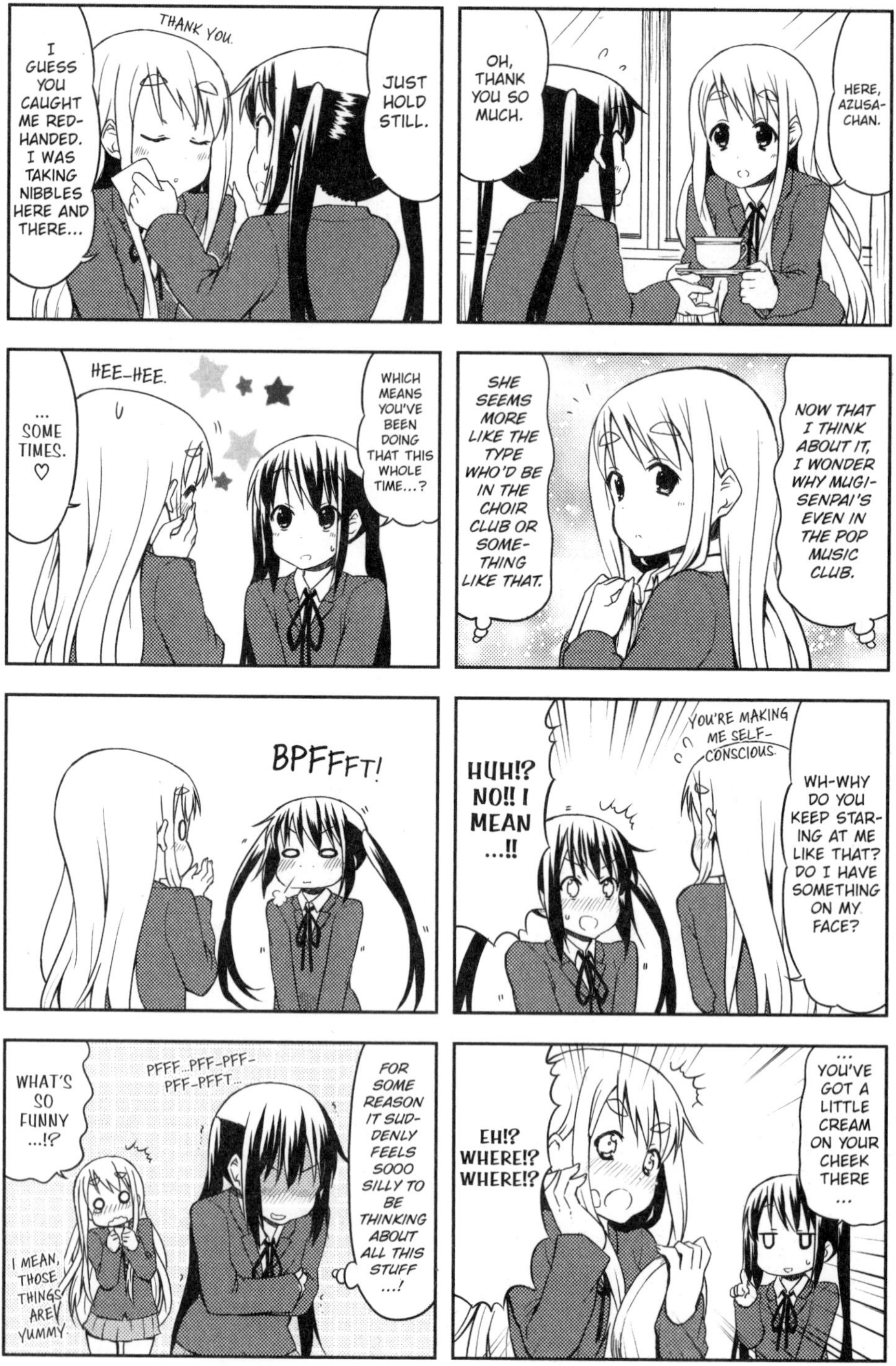
HERE, AZUSA-CHAN.
OH, THANK YOU SO MUCH.
NOW THAT I THINK ABOUT IT, I WONDER WHY MUGI-SENPAI'S EVEN IN THE POP MUSIC CLUB.
SHE SEEMS MORE LIKE THE TYPE WHO'D BE IN THE CHOIR CLUB OR SOMETHING LIKE THAT.
WH-WHY DO YOU KEEP STARING AT ME LIKE THAT? DO I HAVE SOMETHING ON MY FACE?
YOU'RE MAKING ME SELF-CONSCIOUS.
HUH!? NO!! I MEAN ...!!
... YOU'VE GOT A LITTLE CREAM ON YOUR CHEEK THERE ...
EH!? WHERE!? WHERE!?
JUST HOLD STILL.
THANK YOU.
I GUESS YOU CAUGHT ME RED-HANDED. I WAS TAKING NIBBLES HERE AND THERE...
WHICH MEANS YOU'VE BEEN DOING THAT THIS WHOLE TIME...?
HEE-HEE.
... SOMETIMES. ♡
BPFFFFT!
FOR SOME REASON IT SUDDENLY FEELS SOOO SILLY TO BE THINKING ABOUT ALL THIS STUFF ...!
PFFF...PFF-PFF-PFF-PFFT...
WHAT'S SO FUNNY ...!?
I MEAN, THOSE THINGS ARE YUMMY.

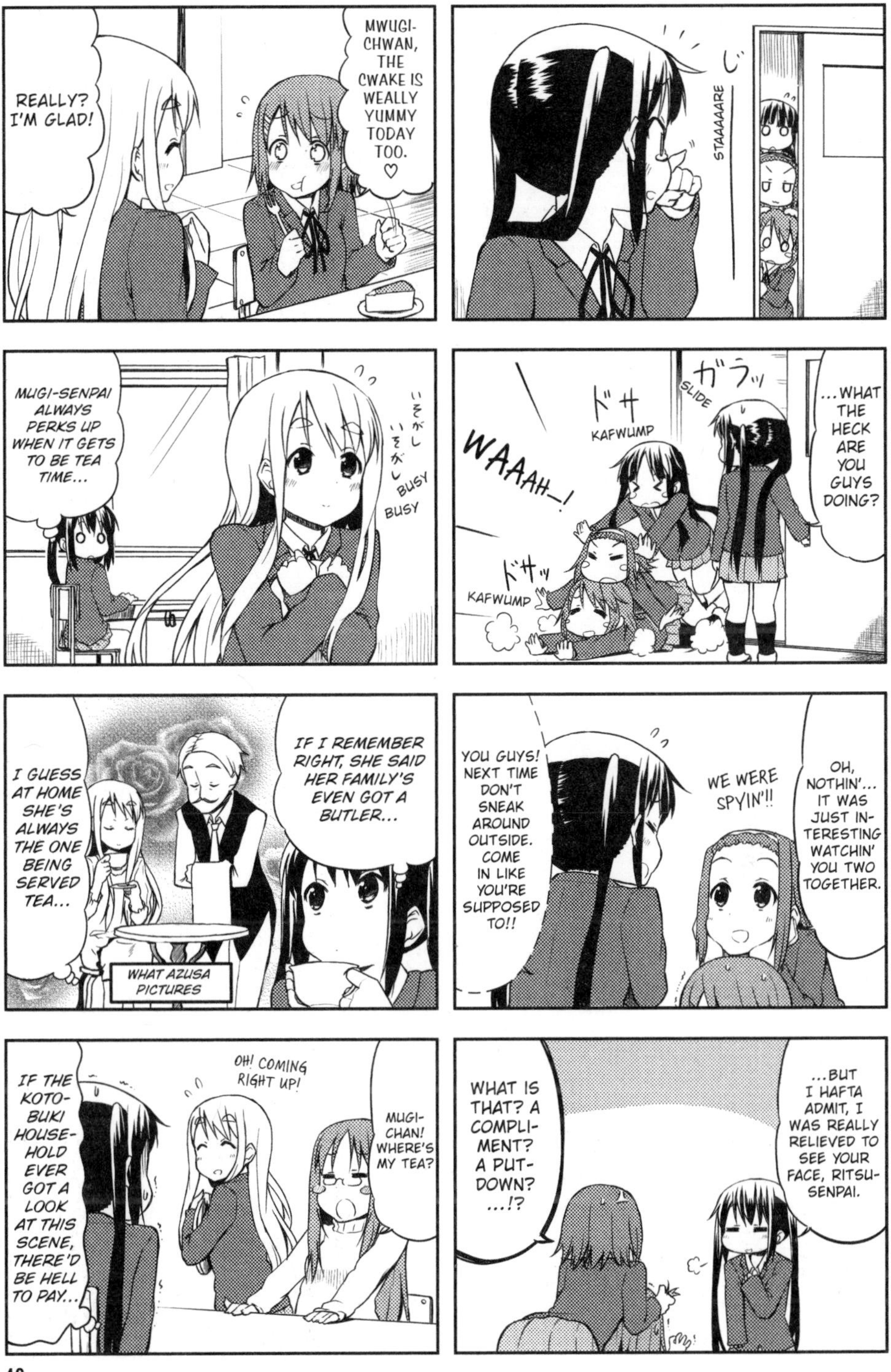
じ
STAAAAARE
ガラッ
SLIDE
...WHAT THE HECK ARE YOU GUYS DOING?
ドサ
KAFWUMP
WAAAH—!
ドサッ
KAFWUMP
OH, NOTHIN'... IT WAS JUST IN-TERESTING WATCHIN' YOU TWO TOGETHER.
WE WERE SPYIN'!!
YOU GUYS! NEXT TIME DON'T SNEAK AROUND OUTSIDE. COME IN LIKE YOU'RE SUPPOSED TO!!
...BUT I HAFTA ADMIT, I WAS REALLY RELIEVED TO SEE YOUR FACE, RITSU-SENPAI.
WHAT IS THAT? A COMPLI-MENT? A PUT-DOWN? ...!?
MWUGI-CHWAN, THE CWAKE IS WEALLY YUMMY TODAY TOO. ♡
REALLY? I'M GLAD!
いそがしいそがし
BUSY BUSY
MUGI-SENPAI ALWAYS PERKS UP WHEN IT GETS TO BE TEA TIME...
IF I REMEMBER RIGHT, SHE SAID HER FAMILY'S EVEN GOT A BUTLER...
I GUESS AT HOME SHE'S ALWAYS THE ONE BEING SERVED TEA...
WHAT AZUSA PICTURES
MUGI-CHAN! WHERE'S MY TEA?
OH! COMING RIGHT UP!
IF THE KOTO-BUKI HOUSE-HOLD EVER GOT A LOOK AT THIS SCENE, THERE'D BE HELL TO PAY...

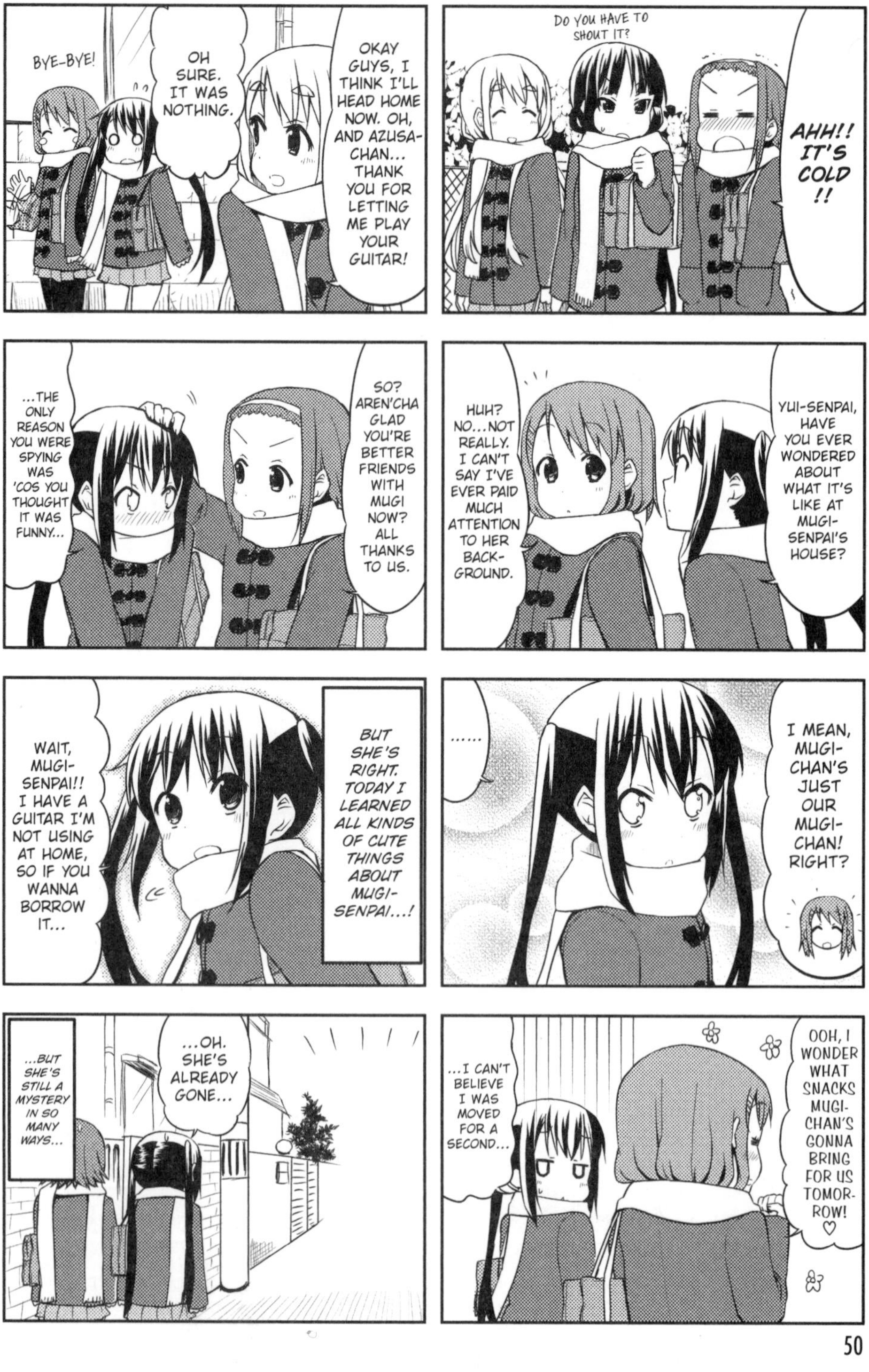
AHH!! IT'S COLD!!
DO YOU HAVE TO SHOUT IT?
YUI-SENPAI, HAVE YOU EVER WONDERED ABOUT WHAT IT'S LIKE AT MUGI-SENPAI'S HOUSE?
HUH? NO...NOT REALLY. I CAN'T SAY I'VE EVER PAID MUCH ATTENTION TO HER BACK-GROUND.
I MEAN, MUGI-CHAN'S JUST OUR MUGI-CHAN! RIGHT?
......
OOH, I WONDER WHAT SNACKS MUGI-CHAN'S GONNA BRING FOR US TOMOR-ROW! ♡
...I CAN'T BELIEVE I WAS MOVED FOR A SECOND...
OKAY GUYS, I THINK I'LL HEAD HOME NOW. OH, AND AZUSA-CHAN... THANK YOU FOR LETTING ME PLAY YOUR GUITAR!
OH SURE. IT WAS NOTHING.
BYE-BYE!
SO? AREN'CHA GLAD YOU'RE BETTER FRIENDS WITH MUGI NOW? ALL THANKS TO US.
...THE ONLY REASON YOU WERE SPYING WAS 'COS YOU THOUGHT IT WAS FUNNY...
BUT SHE'S RIGHT. TODAY I LEARNED ALL KINDS OF CUTE THINGS ABOUT MUGI-SENPAI...!
WAIT, MUGI-SENPAI!! I HAVE A GUITAR I'M NOT USING AT HOME, SO IF YOU WANNA BORROW IT...
...OH. SHE'S ALREADY GONE...
...BUT SHE'S STILL A MYSTERY IN SO MANY WAYS...

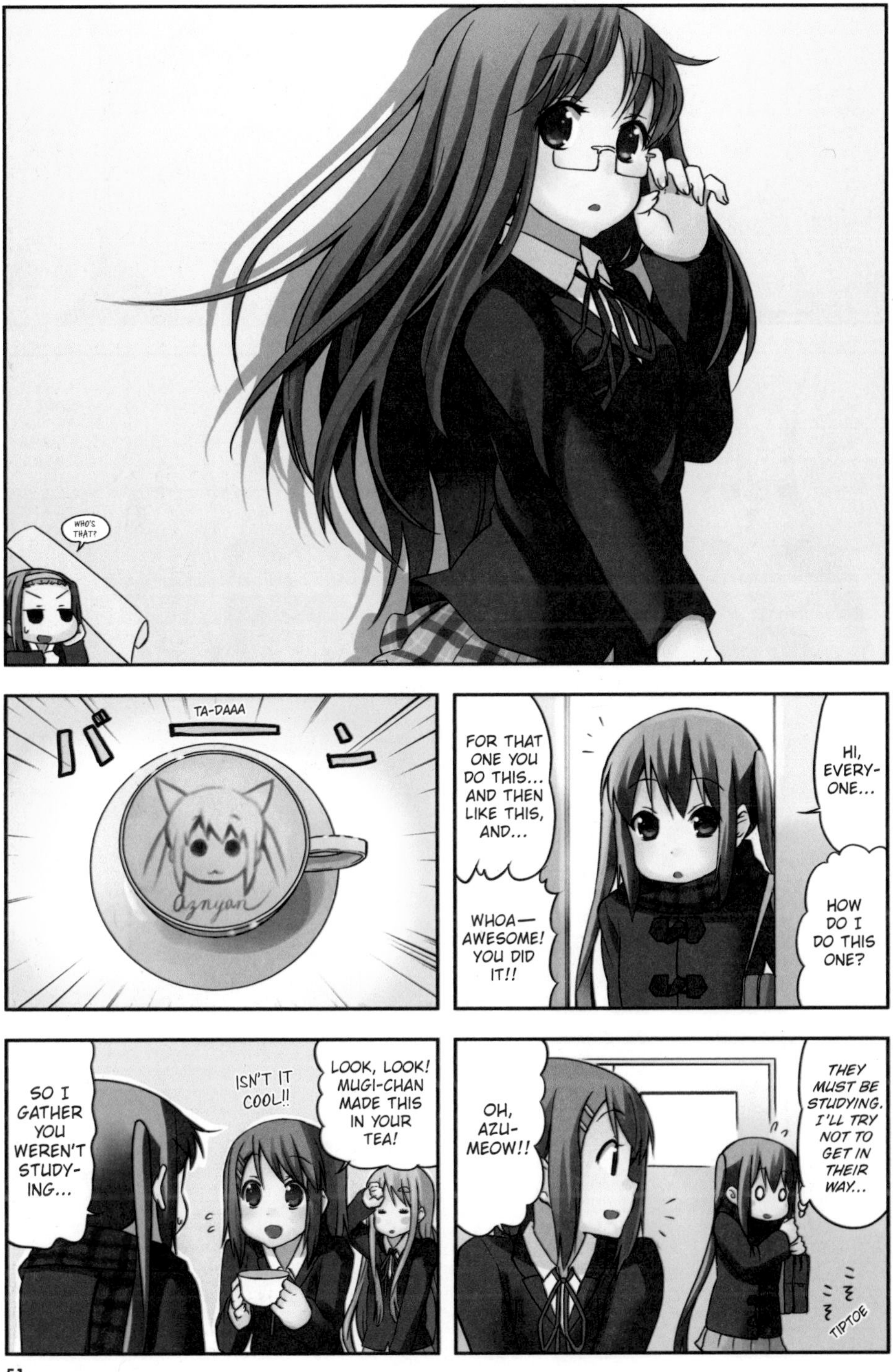
WHO'S THAT?
HI, EVERY-ONE...
HOW DO I DO THIS ONE?
FOR THAT ONE YOU DO THIS... AND THEN LIKE THIS, AND...
WHOA— AWESOME! YOU DID IT!!
TA-DAAA
Aznyan
THEY MUST BE STUDYING. I'LL TRY NOT TO GET IN THEIR WAY...
OH, AZU-MEOW!!
TIPTOE
LOOK, LOOK! MUGI-CHAN MADE THIS IN YOUR TEA!
ISN'T IT COOL!!
SO I GATHER YOU WEREN'T STUDY-ING...

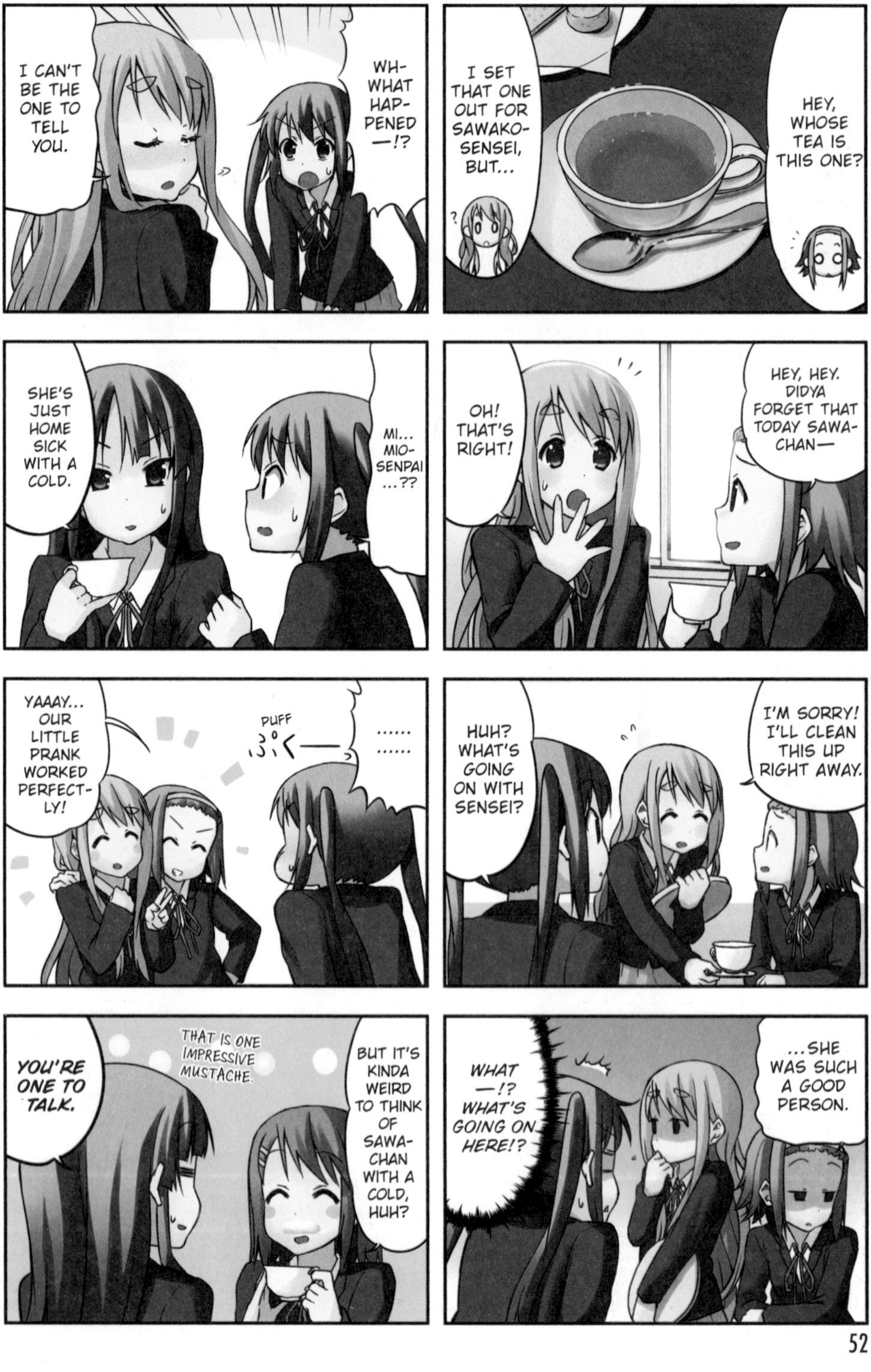
HEY, WHOSE TEA IS THIS ONE?
I SET THAT ONE OUT FOR SAWAKO-SENSEI, BUT...
HEY, HEY. DIDYA FORGET THAT TODAY SAWA-CHAN—
OH! THAT'S RIGHT!
I'M SORRY! I'LL CLEAN THIS UP RIGHT AWAY.
HUH? WHAT'S GOING ON WITH SENSEI?
...SHE WAS SUCH A GOOD PERSON.
WHAT—!? WHAT'S GOING ON HERE!?
WH-WHAT HAPPENED—!?
I CAN'T BE THE ONE TO TELL YOU.
MI... MIO-SENPAI...??
SHE'S JUST HOME SICK WITH A COLD.
......
......
PUFF
ぷくー
YAAAY... OUR LITTLE PRANK WORKED PERFECTLY!
BUT IT'S KINDA WEIRD TO THINK OF SAWA-CHAN WITH A COLD, HUH?
THAT IS ONE IMPRESSIVE MUSTACHE.
YOU'RE ONE TO TALK.

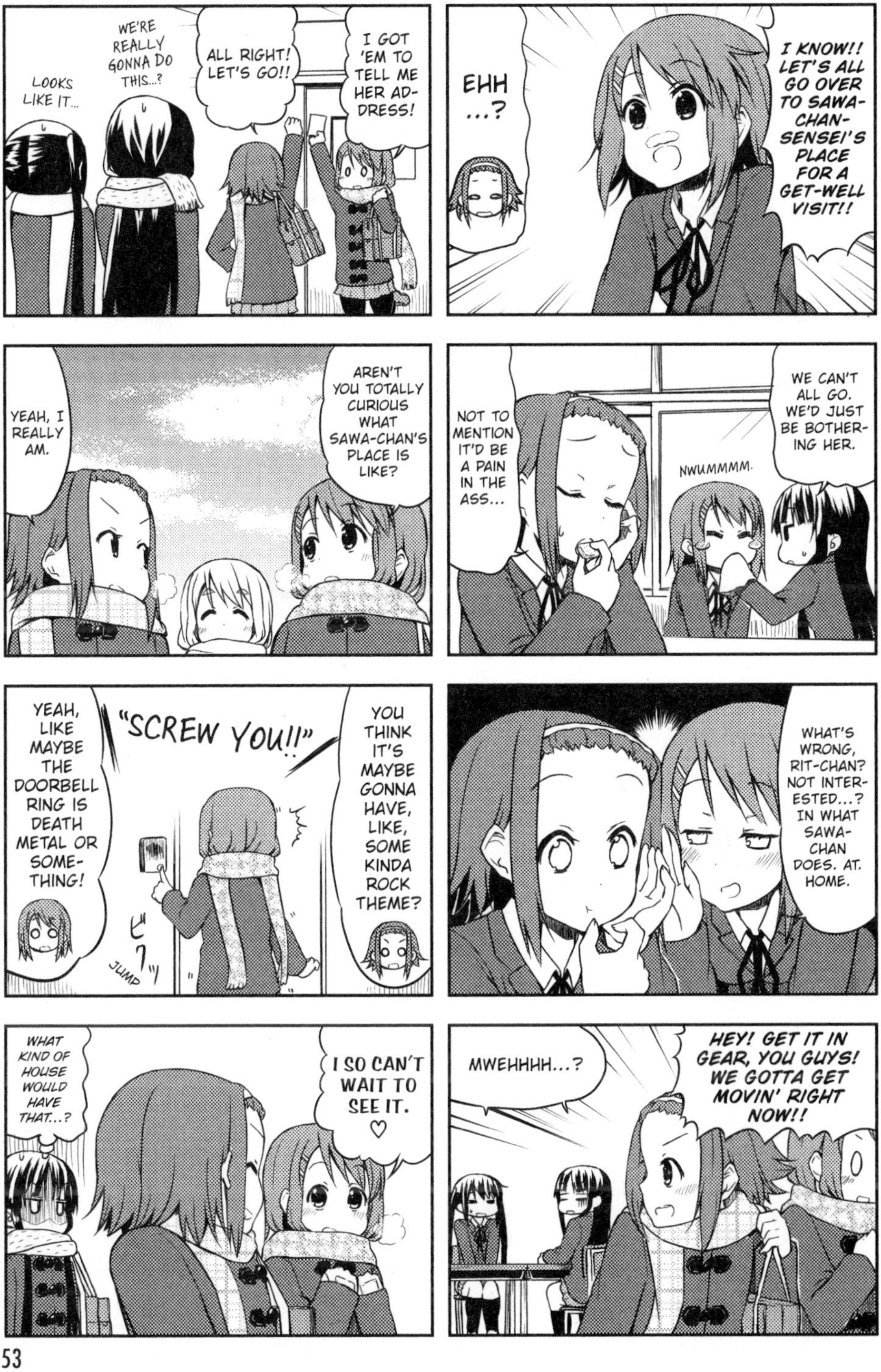

I KNOW!! LET'S ALL GO OVER TO SAWA-CHAN-SENSEI'S PLACE FOR A GET-WELL VISIT!!
EHH ...?
WE CAN'T ALL GO. WE'D JUST BE BOTHERING HER.
NWUMMMM.
NOT TO MENTION IT'D BE A PAIN IN THE ASS...
WHAT'S WRONG, RIT-CHAN? NOT INTERESTED...? IN WHAT SAWA-CHAN DOES. AT HOME.
HEY! GET IT IN GEAR, YOU GUYS! WE GOTTA GET MOVIN' RIGHT NOW!!
MWEHHHH...?
I GOT 'EM TO TELL ME HER ADDRESS!
ALL RIGHT! LET'S GO!!
WE'RE REALLY GONNA DO THIS...?
LOOKS LIKE IT...
AREN'T YOU TOTALLY CURIOUS WHAT SAWA-CHAN'S PLACE IS LIKE?
YEAH, I REALLY AM.
YOU THINK IT'S MAYBE GONNA HAVE, LIKE, SOME KINDA ROCK THEME?
"SCREW YOU!!"
YEAH, LIKE MAYBE THE DOORBELL RING IS DEATH METAL OR SOMETHING!
ビクッ
JUMP
I SO CAN'T WAIT TO SEE IT. ♡
WHAT KIND OF HOUSE WOULD HAVE THAT...?

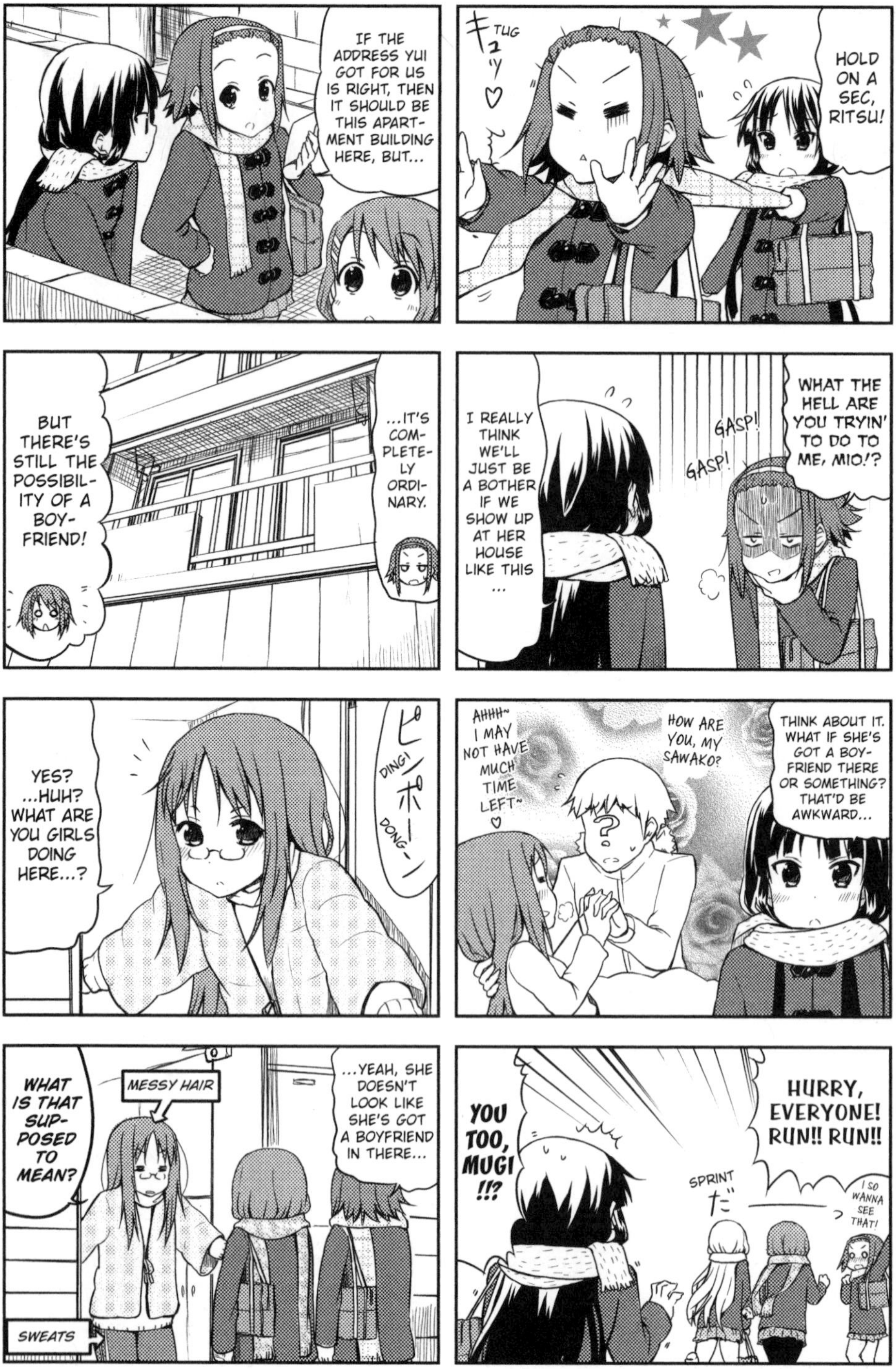
HOLD ON A SEC, RITSU!
TUG キュッ ♡
WHAT THE HELL ARE YOU TRYIN' TO DO TO ME, MIO!?
GASP!
GASP!
I REALLY THINK WE'LL JUST BE A BOTHER IF WE SHOW UP AT HER HOUSE LIKE THIS ...
THINK ABOUT IT. WHAT IF SHE'S GOT A BOY-FRIEND THERE OR SOMETHING? THAT'D BE AWKWARD...
HOW ARE YOU, MY SAWAKO?
AHHH~ I MAY NOT HAVE MUCH TIME LEFT~ ♡
HURRY, EVERYONE! RUN!! RUN!!
I SO WANNA SEE THAT!
SPRINT だ
YOU TOO, MUGI!!?
IF THE ADDRESS YUI GOT FOR US IS RIGHT, THEN IT SHOULD BE THIS APARTMENT BUILDING HERE, BUT...
...IT'S COMPLETELY ORDINARY.
BUT THERE'S STILL THE POSSIBILITY OF A BOYFRIEND!
ピンポーン DING! DONG~
YES? ...HUH? WHAT ARE YOU GIRLS DOING HERE...?
...YEAH, SHE DOESN'T LOOK LIKE SHE'S GOT A BOYFRIEND IN THERE...
MESSY HAIR
WHAT IS THAT SUPPOSED TO MEAN?
SWEATS

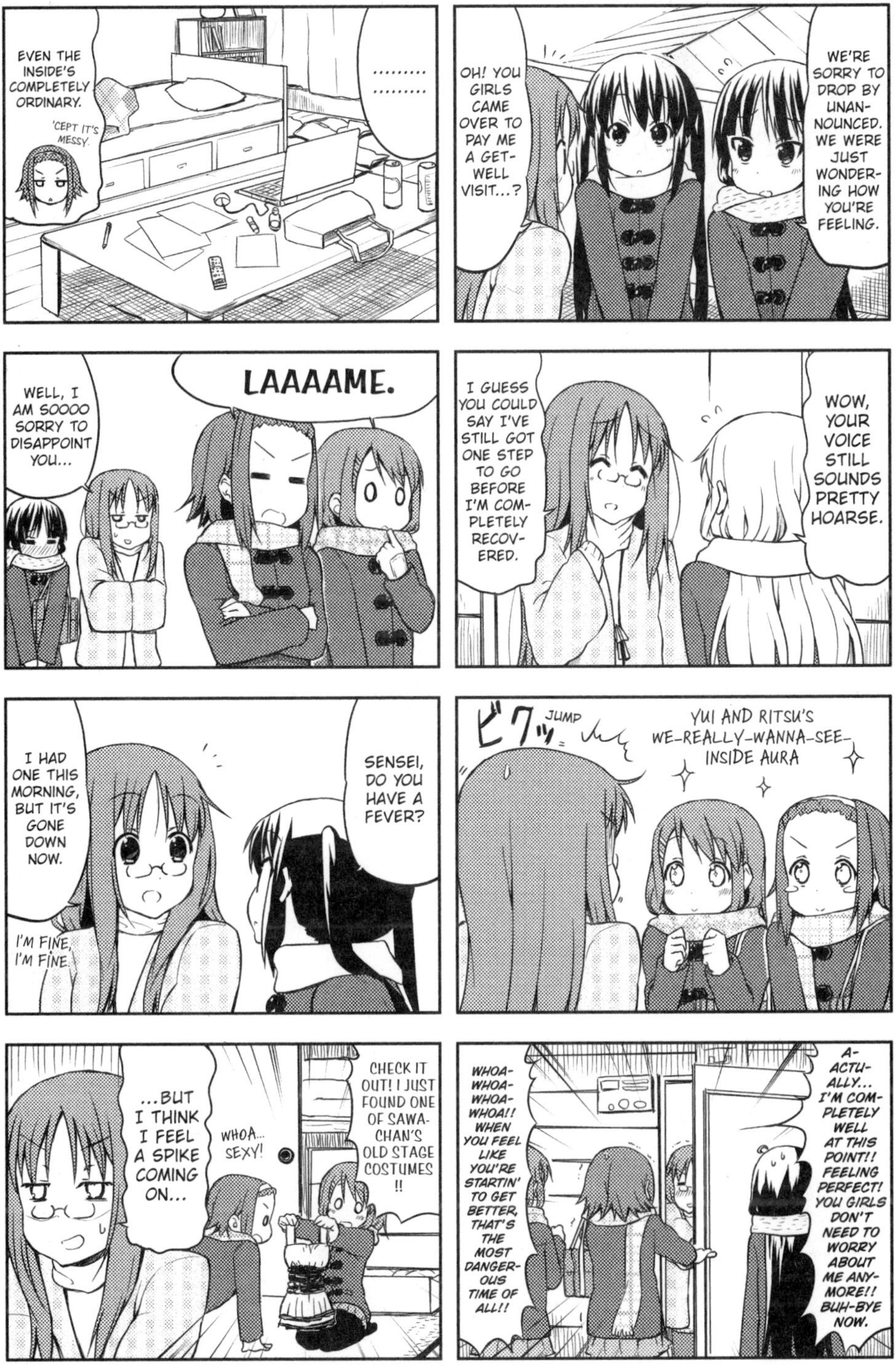
WE'RE SORRY TO DROP BY UNANNOUNCED. WE WERE JUST WONDERING HOW YOU'RE FEELING.
OH! YOU GIRLS CAME OVER TO PAY ME A GET-WELL VISIT...?
WOW, YOUR VOICE STILL SOUNDS PRETTY HOARSE.
I GUESS YOU COULD SAY I'VE STILL GOT ONE STEP TO GO BEFORE I'M COMPLETELY RECOVERED.
YUI AND RITSU'S WE-REALLY-WANNA-SEE-INSIDE AURA
ビクッ
JUMP
A-ACTUALLY... I'M COMPLETELY WELL AT THIS POINT!! FEELING PERFECT! YOU GIRLS DON'T NEED TO WORRY ABOUT ME ANYMORE!! BUH-BYE NOW.
WHOA-WHOA-WHOA!! WHEN YOU FEEL LIKE YOU'RE STARTIN' TO GET BETTER, THAT'S THE MOST DANGEROUS TIME OF ALL!!
....
....
EVEN THE INSIDE'S COMPLETELY ORDINARY.
'CEPT IT'S MESSY.
LAAAAME.
WELL, I AM SOOOO SORRY TO DISAPPOINT YOU...
SENSEI, DO YOU HAVE A FEVER?
I HAD ONE THIS MORNING, BUT IT'S GONE DOWN NOW.
I'M FINE, I'M FINE.
CHECK IT OUT! I JUST FOUND ONE OF SAWA-CHAN'S OLD STAGE COSTUMES!!
WHOA... SEXY!
...BUT I THINK I FEEL A SPIKE COMING ON...

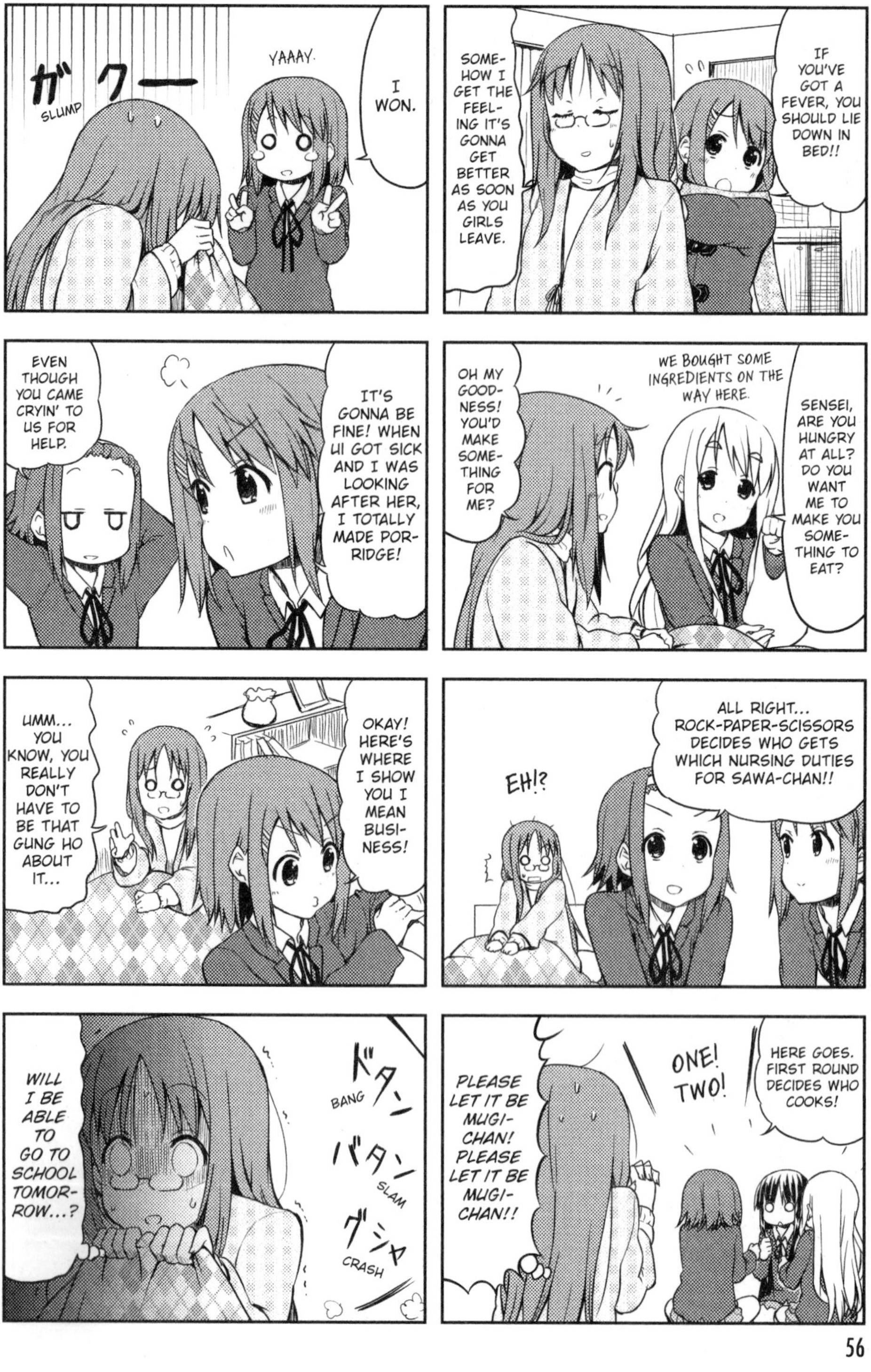
IF YOU'VE GOT A FEVER, YOU SHOULD LIE DOWN IN BED!!
SOMEHOW I GET THE FEELING IT'S GONNA GET BETTER AS SOON AS YOU GIRLS LEAVE.
SENSEI, ARE YOU HUNGRY AT ALL? DO YOU WANT ME TO MAKE YOU SOMETHING TO EAT?
WE BOUGHT SOME INGREDIENTS ON THE WAY HERE.
OH MY GOODNESS! YOU'D MAKE SOMETHING FOR ME?
ALL RIGHT... ROCK-PAPER-SCISSORS DECIDES WHO GETS WHICH NURSING DUTIES FOR SAWA-CHAN!!
EH!?
HERE GOES. FIRST ROUND DECIDES WHO COOKS!
ONE! TWO!
PLEASE LET IT BE MUGI-CHAN! PLEASE LET IT BE MUGI-CHAN!!
I WON.
YAAAY.
ガクー
SLUMP
IT'S GONNA BE FINE! WHEN UI GOT SICK AND I WAS LOOKING AFTER HER, I TOTALLY MADE PORRIDGE!
EVEN THOUGH YOU CAME CRYIN' TO US FOR HELP.
OKAY! HERE'S WHERE I SHOW YOU I MEAN BUSINESS!
UMM... YOU KNOW, YOU REALLY DON'T HAVE TO BE THAT GUNG HO ABOUT IT...
ドタン
BANG
バタン
SLAM
グシャ
CRASH
WILL I BE ABLE TO GO TO SCHOOL TOMORROW...?

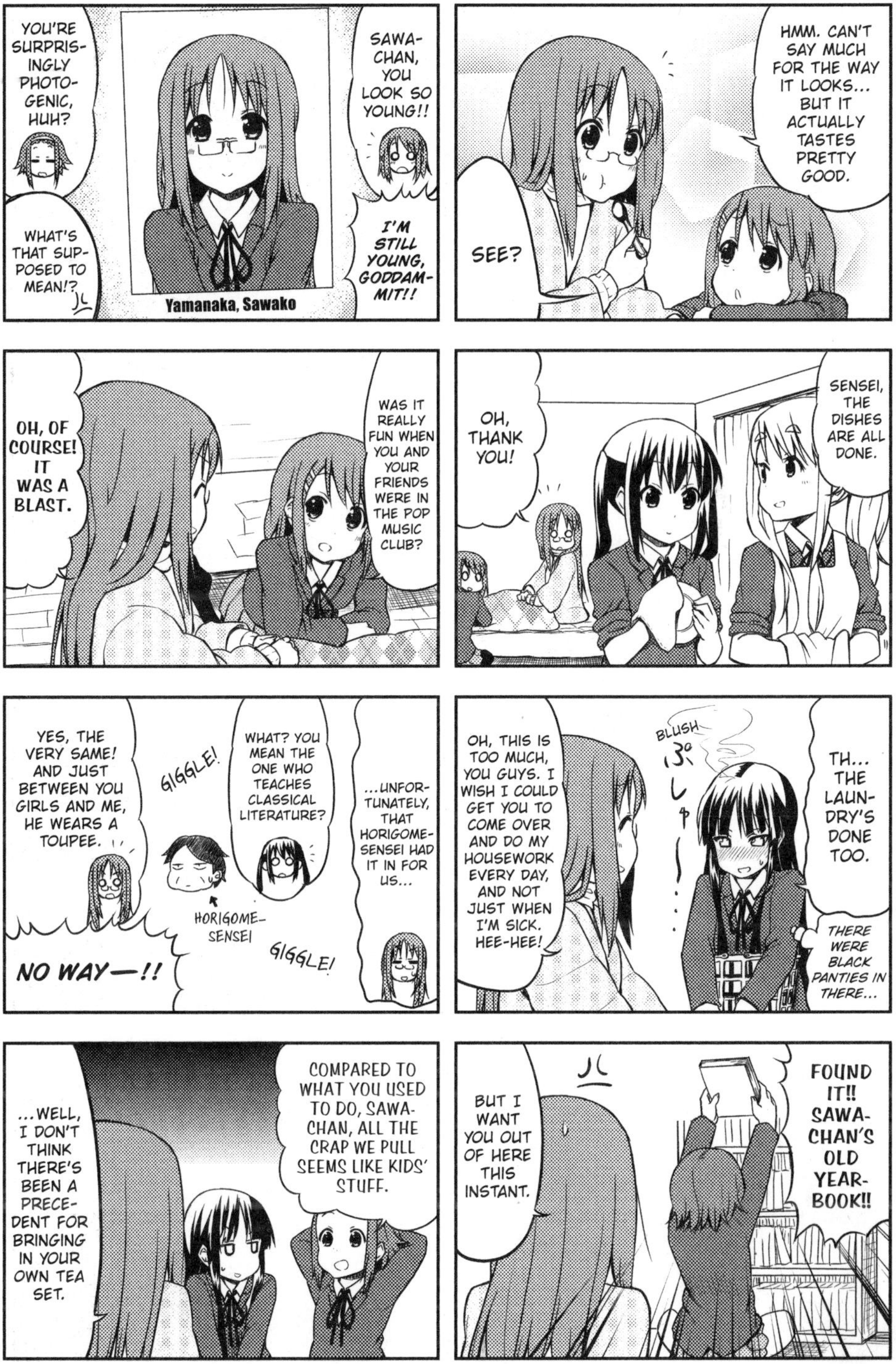
HMM. CAN'T SAY MUCH FOR THE WAY IT LOOKS... BUT IT ACTUALLY TASTES PRETTY GOOD.
SEE?
SENSEI, THE DISHES ARE ALL DONE.
OH, THANK YOU!
TH... THE LAUNDRY'S DONE TOO.
BLUSH
ぷしゅ〜…
THERE WERE BLACK PANTIES IN THERE...
OH, THIS IS TOO MUCH, YOU GUYS. I WISH I COULD GET YOU TO COME OVER AND DO MY HOUSEWORK EVERY DAY, AND NOT JUST WHEN I'M SICK. HEE-HEE!
FOUND IT!! SAWA-CHAN'S OLD YEARBOOK!!
BUT I WANT YOU OUT OF HERE THIS INSTANT.
SAWA-CHAN, YOU LOOK SO YOUNG!!
I'M STILL YOUNG, GODDAMMIT!!
Yamanaka, Sawako
YOU'RE SURPRISINGLY PHOTOGENIC, HUH?
WHAT'S THAT SUPPOSED TO MEAN!?
WAS IT REALLY FUN WHEN YOU AND YOUR FRIENDS WERE IN THE POP MUSIC CLUB?
OH, OF COURSE! IT WAS A BLAST.
...UNFORTUNATELY, THAT HORIGOME-SENSEI HAD IT IN FOR US...
WHAT? YOU MEAN THE ONE WHO TEACHES CLASSICAL LITERATURE?
YES, THE VERY SAME! AND JUST BETWEEN YOU GIRLS AND ME, HE WEARS A TOUPEE.
GIGGLE!
HORIGOME-SENSEI
GIGGLE!
NO WAY—!!
COMPARED TO WHAT YOU USED TO DO, SAWA-CHAN, ALL THE CRAP WE PULL SEEMS LIKE KIDS' STUFF.
...WELL, I DON'T THINK THERE'S BEEN A PRECEDENT FOR BRINGING IN YOUR OWN TEA SET.

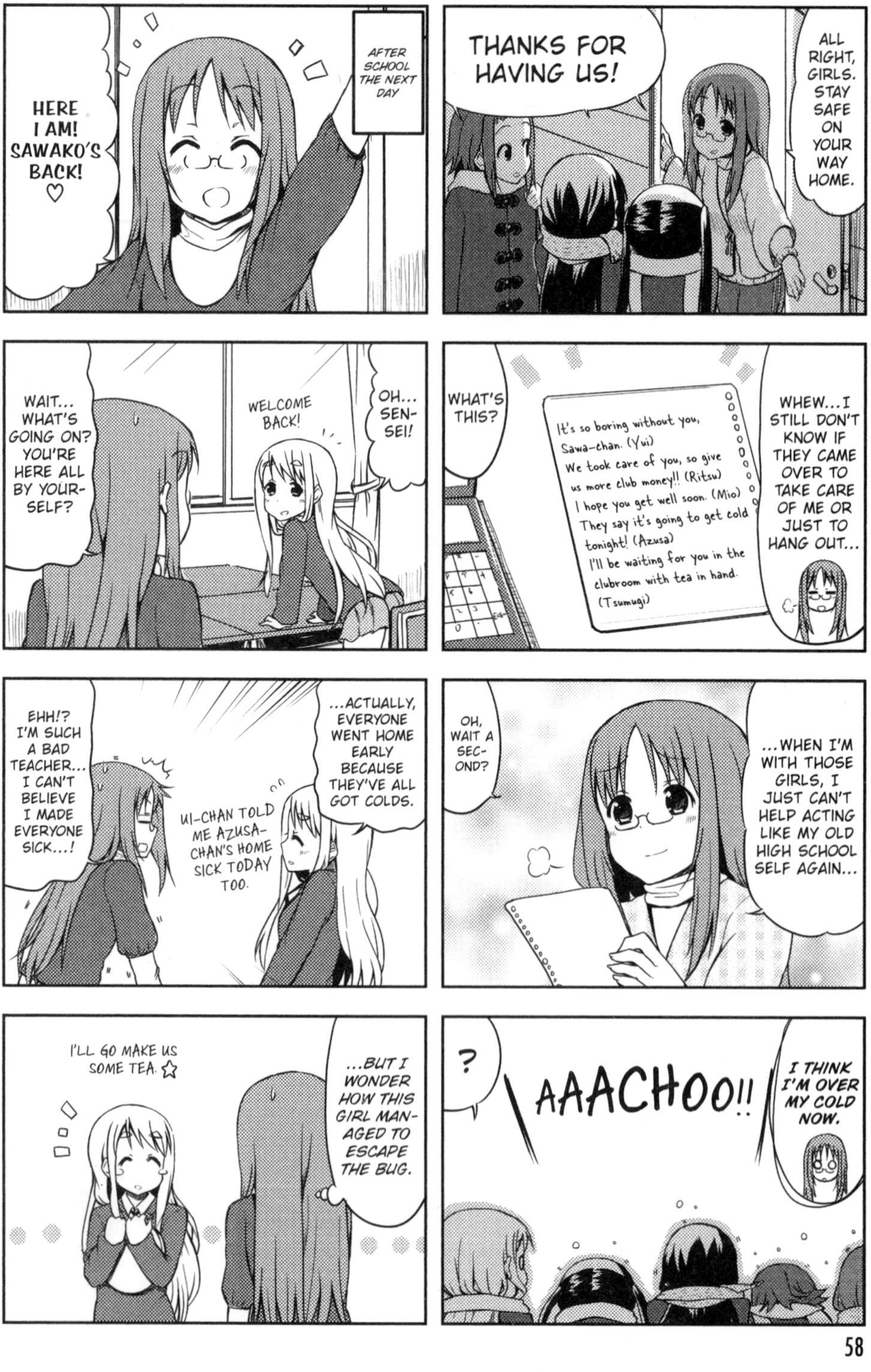
ALL RIGHT, GIRLS. STAY SAFE ON YOUR WAY HOME.
THANKS FOR HAVING US!
WHEW... I STILL DON'T KNOW IF THEY CAME OVER TO TAKE CARE OF ME OR JUST TO HANG OUT...
It's so boring without you, Sawa-chan. (Yui)
We took care of you, so give us more club money!! (Ritsu)
I hope you get well soon. (Mio)
They say it's going to get cold tonight! (Azusa)
I'll be waiting for you in the clubroom with tea in hand. (Tsumugi)
WHAT'S THIS?
...WHEN I'M WITH THOSE GIRLS, I JUST CAN'T HELP ACTING LIKE MY OLD HIGH SCHOOL SELF AGAIN...
OH, WAIT A SEC-OND?
I THINK I'M OVER MY COLD NOW.
AAACHOO!!
?
AFTER SCHOOL THE NEXT DAY
HERE I AM! SAWAKO'S BACK! ♡
OH... SEN-SEI!
WELCOME BACK!
WAIT... WHAT'S GOING ON? YOU'RE HERE ALL BY YOUR-SELF?
...ACTUALLY, EVERYONE WENT HOME EARLY BECAUSE THEY'VE ALL GOT COLDS.
UI-CHAN TOLD ME AZUSA-CHAN'S HOME SICK TODAY TOO.
EHH!? I'M SUCH A BAD TEACHER... I CAN'T BELIEVE I MADE EVERYONE SICK...!
...BUT I WONDER HOW THIS GIRL MAN-AGED TO ESCAPE THE BUG.
I'LL GO MAKE US SOME TEA. ☆

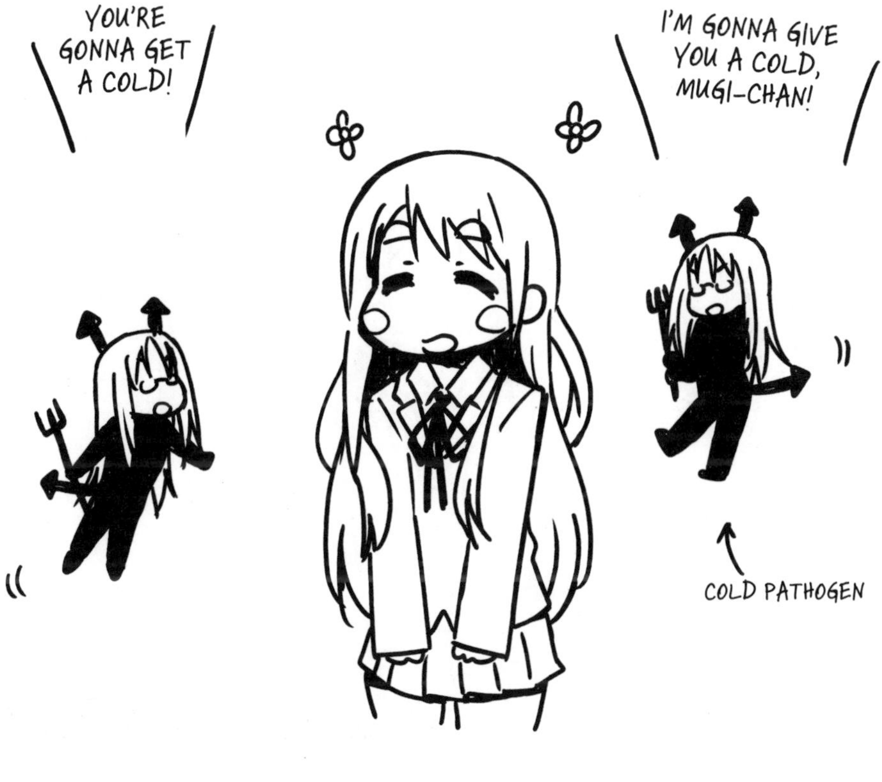
I'M GONNA GIVE YOU A COLD, MUGI-CHAN!
YOU'RE GONNA GET A COLD!
COLD PATHOGEN

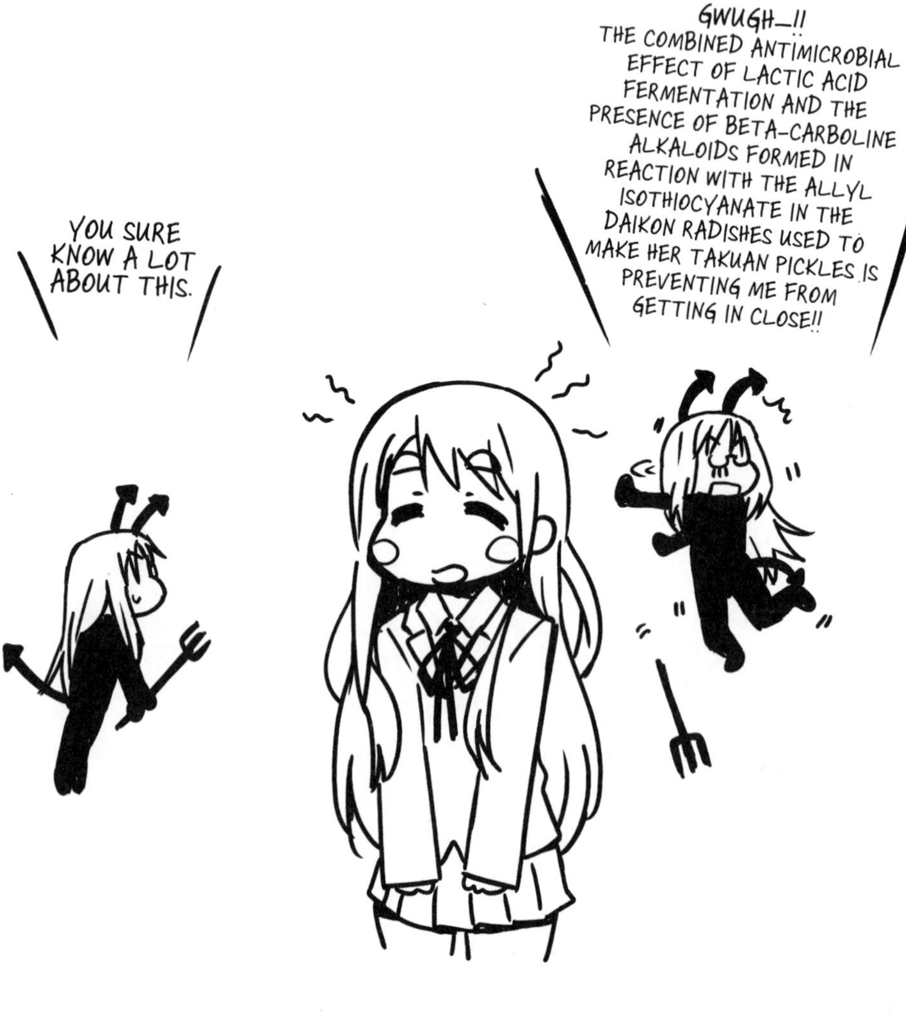
GWUGH...!! THE COMBINED ANTIMICROBIAL EFFECT OF LACTIC ACID FERMENTATION AND THE PRESENCE OF BETA-CARBOLINE ALKALOIDS FORMED IN REACTION WITH THE ALLYL ISOTHIOCYANATE IN THE DAIKON RADISHES USED TO MAKE HER TAKUAN PICKLES IS PREVENTING ME FROM GETTING IN CLOSE!!
YOU SURE KNOW A LOT ABOUT THIS.

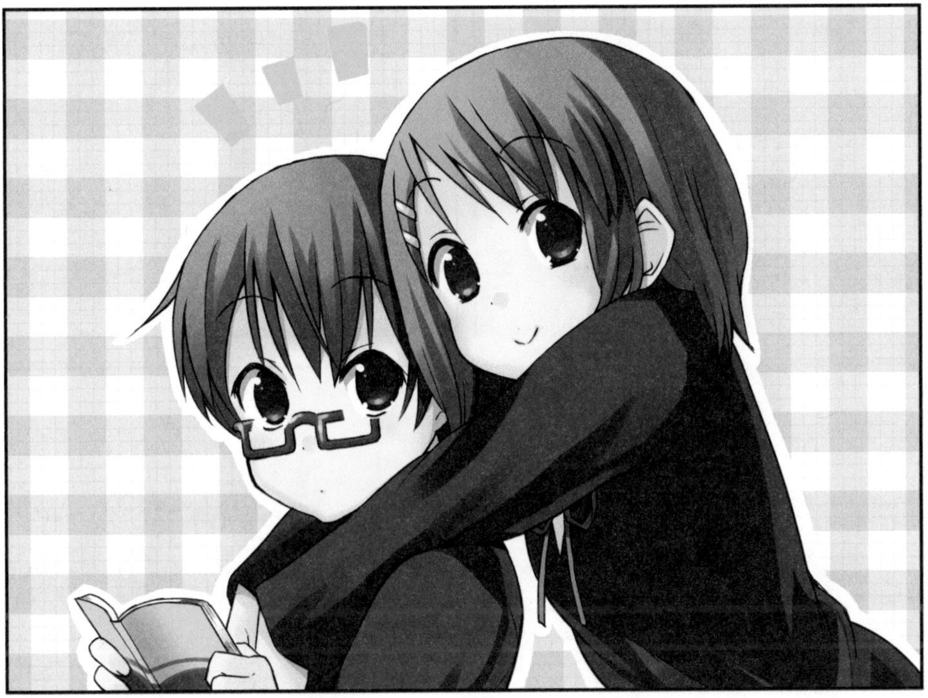

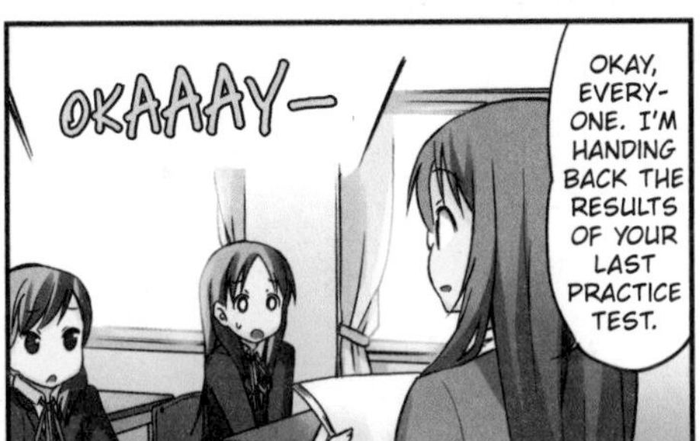
OKAY, EVERYONE. I'M HANDING BACK THE RESULTS OF YOUR LAST PRACTICE TEST.
OKAAAY—

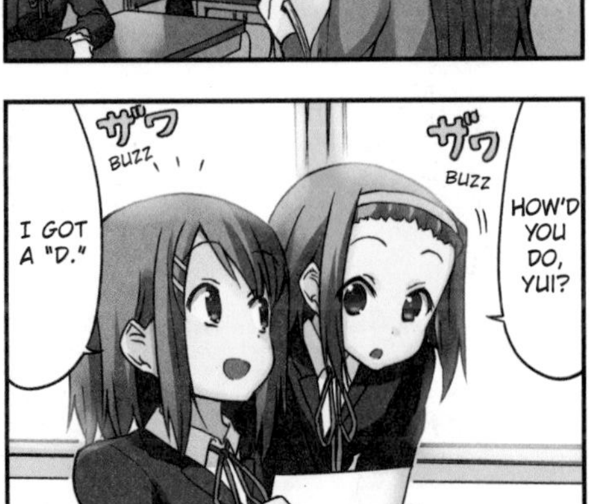
ザワ
BUZZ
HOW'D YOU DO, YUI?
ザワ
BUZZ
I GOT A "D."

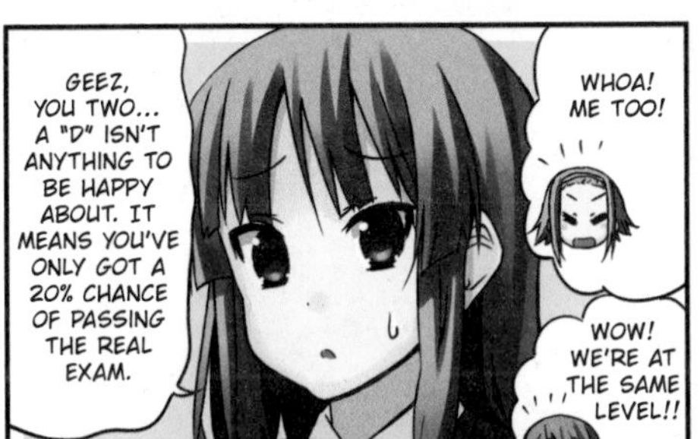
WHOA! ME TOO!
WOW! WE'RE AT THE SAME LEVEL!!
GEEZ, YOU TWO... A "D" ISN'T ANYTHING TO BE HAPPY ABOUT. IT MEANS YOU'VE ONLY GOT A 20% CHANCE OF PASSING THE REAL EXAM.

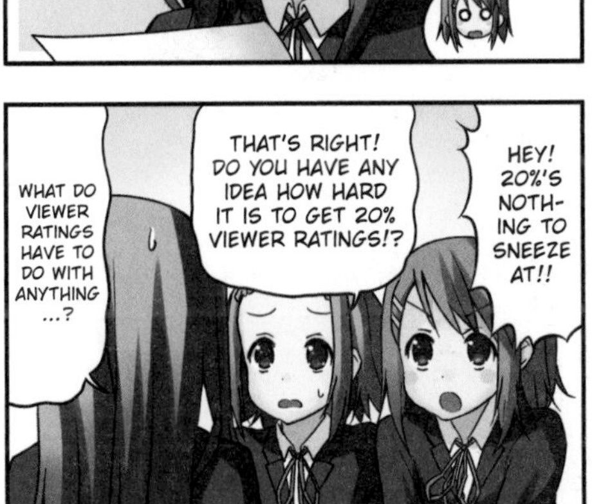
HEY! 20%'S NOTHING TO SNEEZE AT!!
THAT'S RIGHT! DO YOU HAVE ANY IDEA HOW HARD IT IS TO GET 20% VIEWER RATINGS!?
WHAT DO VIEWER RATINGS HAVE TO DO WITH ANYTHING ...?

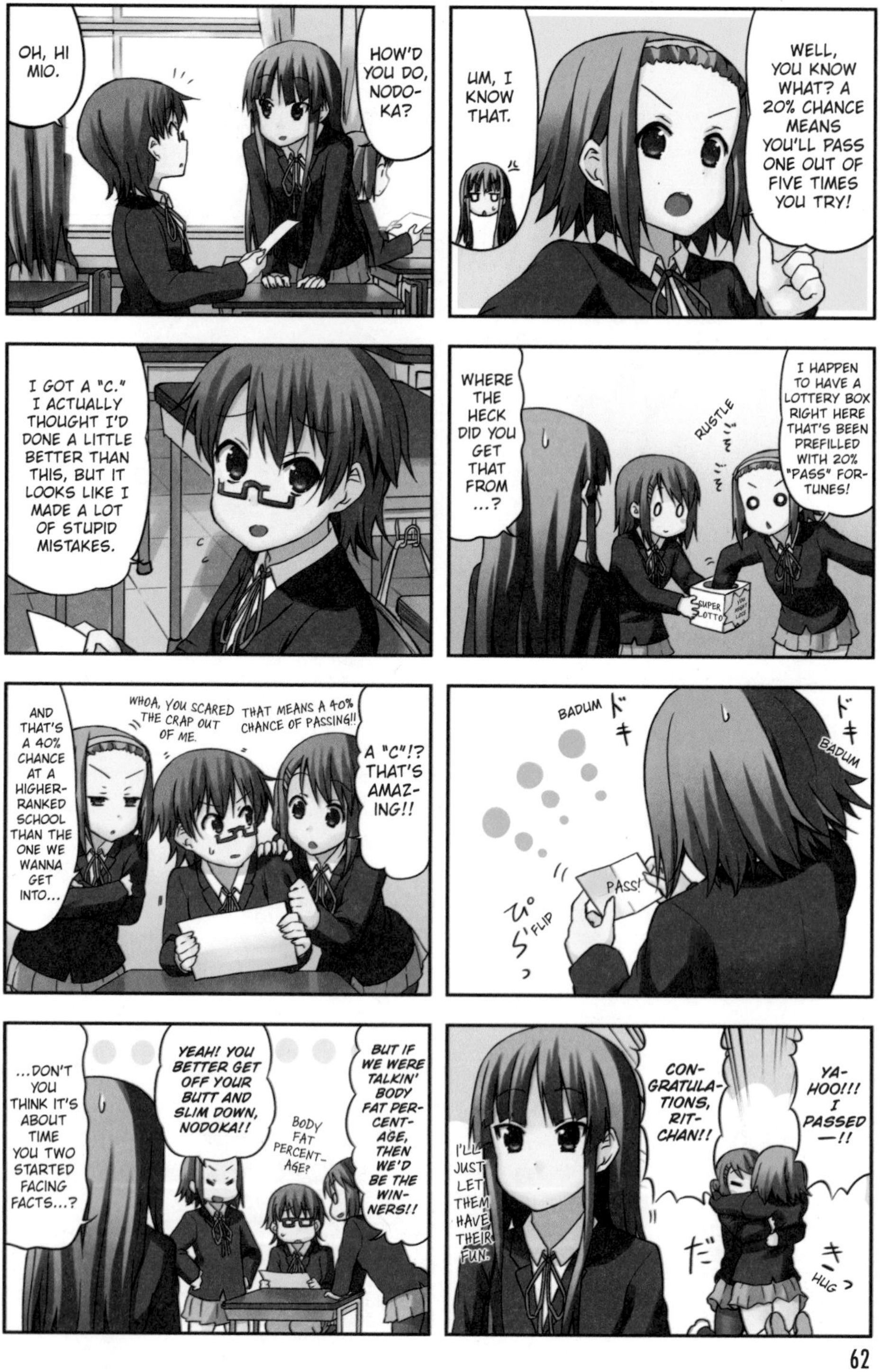
WELL, YOU KNOW WHAT? A 20% CHANCE MEANS YOU'LL PASS ONE OUT OF FIVE TIMES YOU TRY!
UM, I KNOW THAT.
I HAPPEN TO HAVE A LOTTERY BOX RIGHT HERE THAT'S BEEN PREFILLED WITH 20% "PASS" FORTUNES!
RUSTLE
WHERE THE HECK DID YOU GET THAT FROM ...?
SUPER LOTTO
BADUM
BADUM
PASS!
FLIP
YA-HOO!!! I PASSED—!!
CONGRATULATIONS, RITCHAN!!
HUG
I'LL JUST LET THEM HAVE THEIR FUN.
HOW'D YOU DO, NODOKA?
OH, HI MIO.
I GOT A "C." I ACTUALLY THOUGHT I'D DONE A LITTLE BETTER THAN THIS, BUT IT LOOKS LIKE I MADE A LOT OF STUPID MISTAKES.
A "C"!? THAT'S AMAZING!!
THAT MEANS A 40% CHANCE OF PASSING!!
WHOA, YOU SCARED THE CRAP OUT OF ME.
AND THAT'S A 40% CHANCE AT A HIGHER-RANKED SCHOOL THAN THE ONE WE WANNA GET INTO...
BUT IF WE WERE TALKIN' BODY FAT PERCENTAGE, THEN WE'D BE THE WINNERS!!
BODY FAT PERCENTAGE?
YEAH! YOU BETTER GET OFF YOUR BUTT AND SLIM DOWN, NODOKA!!
...DON'T YOU THINK IT'S ABOUT TIME YOU TWO STARTED FACING FACTS...?

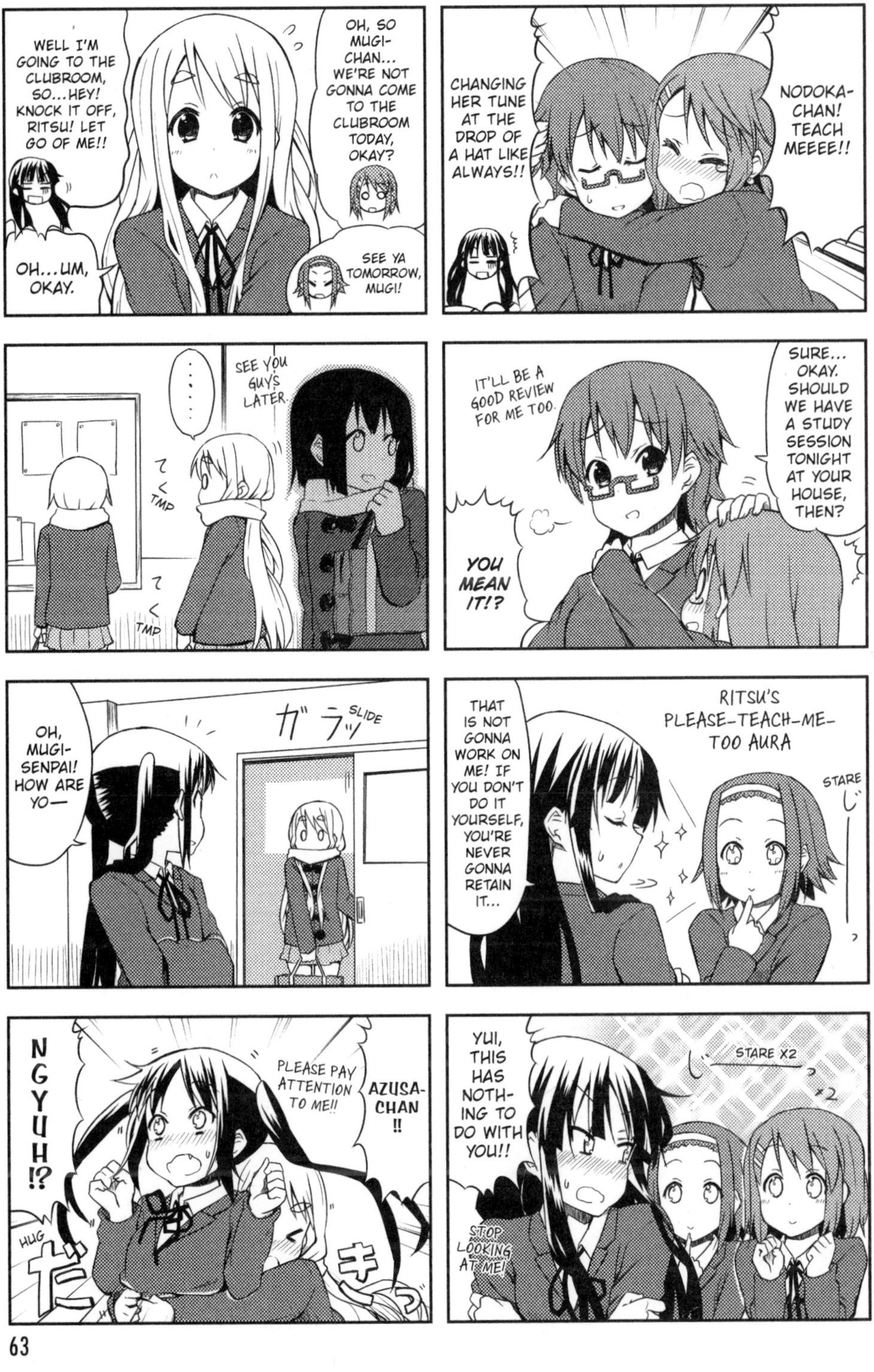
NODOKA-CHAN! TEACH MEEEE!!
CHANGING HER TUNE AT THE DROP OF A HAT LIKE ALWAYS!!
SURE... OKAY. SHOULD WE HAVE A STUDY SESSION TONIGHT AT YOUR HOUSE, THEN?
IT'LL BE A GOOD REVIEW FOR ME TOO.
YOU MEAN IT!?
STARE
RITSU'S PLEASE-TEACH-ME-TOO AURA
THAT IS NOT GONNA WORK ON ME! IF YOU DON'T DO IT YOURSELF, YOU'RE NEVER GONNA RETAIN IT...
STARE X2
YUI, THIS HAS NOTHING TO DO WITH YOU!!
STOP LOOKING AT ME!
OH, SO MUGI-CHAN... WE'RE NOT GONNA COME TO THE CLUBROOM TODAY, OKAY?
SEE YA TOMORROW, MUGI!
WELL I'M GOING TO THE CLUBROOM, SO...HEY! KNOCK IT OFF, RITSU! LET GO OF ME!!
OH...UM, OKAY.
SEE YOU GUYS LATER.
......
TMP
TMP
SLIDE
OH, MUGI-SENPAI! HOW ARE YO—
AZUSA-CHAN!!
PLEASE PAY ATTENTION TO ME!!
NGYUH!?
HUG

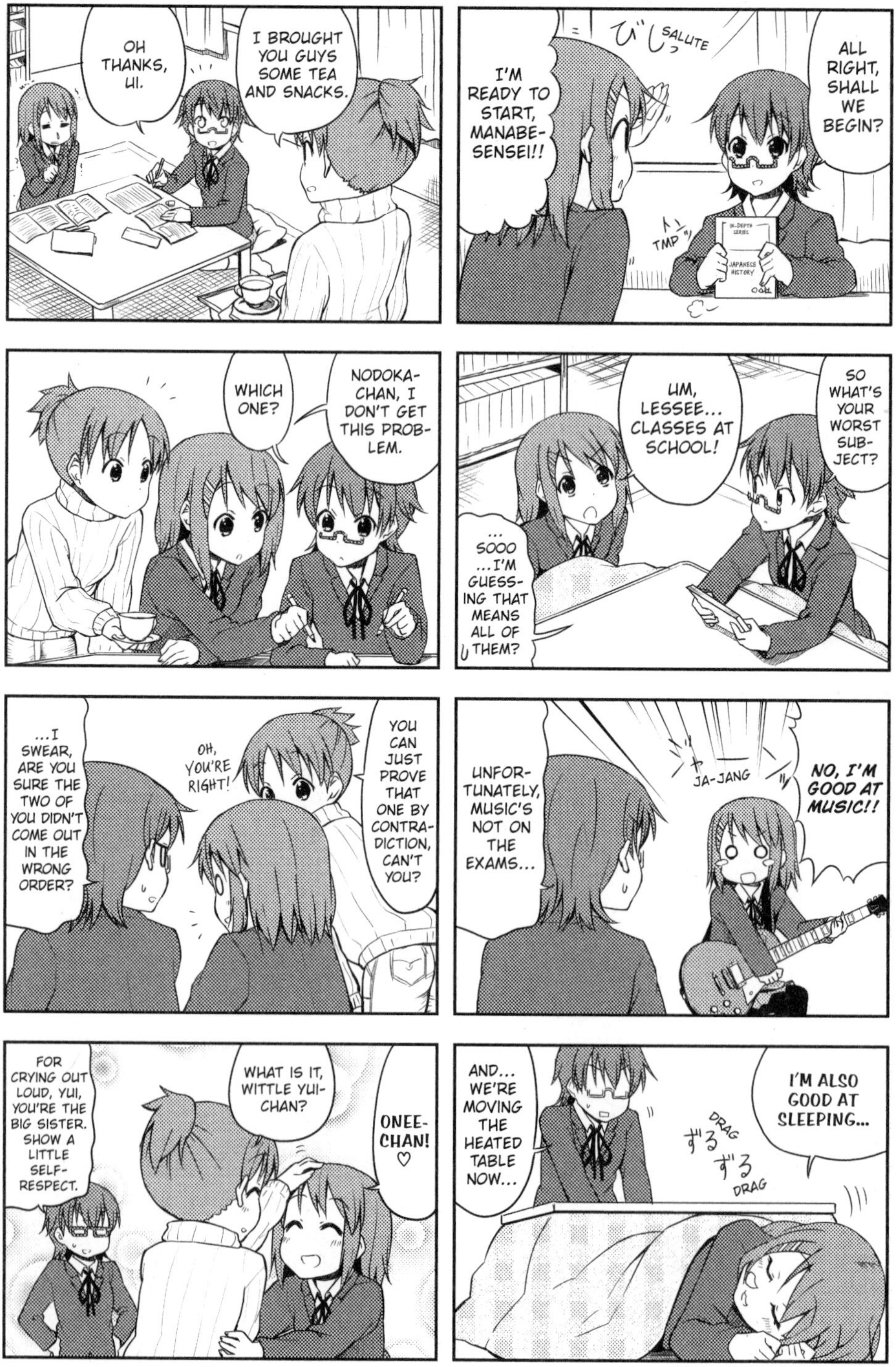
ALL RIGHT, SHALL WE BEGIN?
びしっ SALUTE
I'M READY TO START, MANABE-SENSEI!!
TMP
SO WHAT'S YOUR WORST SUBJECT?
UM, LESSEE... CLASSES AT SCHOOL!
...SOOO ...I'M GUESSING THAT MEANS ALL OF THEM?
NO, I'M GOOD AT MUSIC!!
JA-JANG
UNFORTUNATELY, MUSIC'S NOT ON THE EXAMS...
I'M ALSO GOOD AT SLEEPING...
ずる DRAG ずる DRAG
AND... WE'RE MOVING THE HEATED TABLE NOW...
I BROUGHT YOU GUYS SOME TEA AND SNACKS.
OH THANKS, UI.
NODOKA-CHAN, I DON'T GET THIS PROBLEM.
WHICH ONE?
YOU CAN JUST PROVE THAT ONE BY CONTRADICTION, CAN'T YOU?
OH, YOU'RE RIGHT!
...I SWEAR, ARE YOU SURE THE TWO OF YOU DIDN'T COME OUT IN THE WRONG ORDER?
ONEE-CHAN! ♡
WHAT IS IT, WITTLE YUI-CHAN?
FOR CRYING OUT LOUD, YUI, YOU'RE THE BIG SISTER. SHOW A LITTLE SELF-RESPECT.

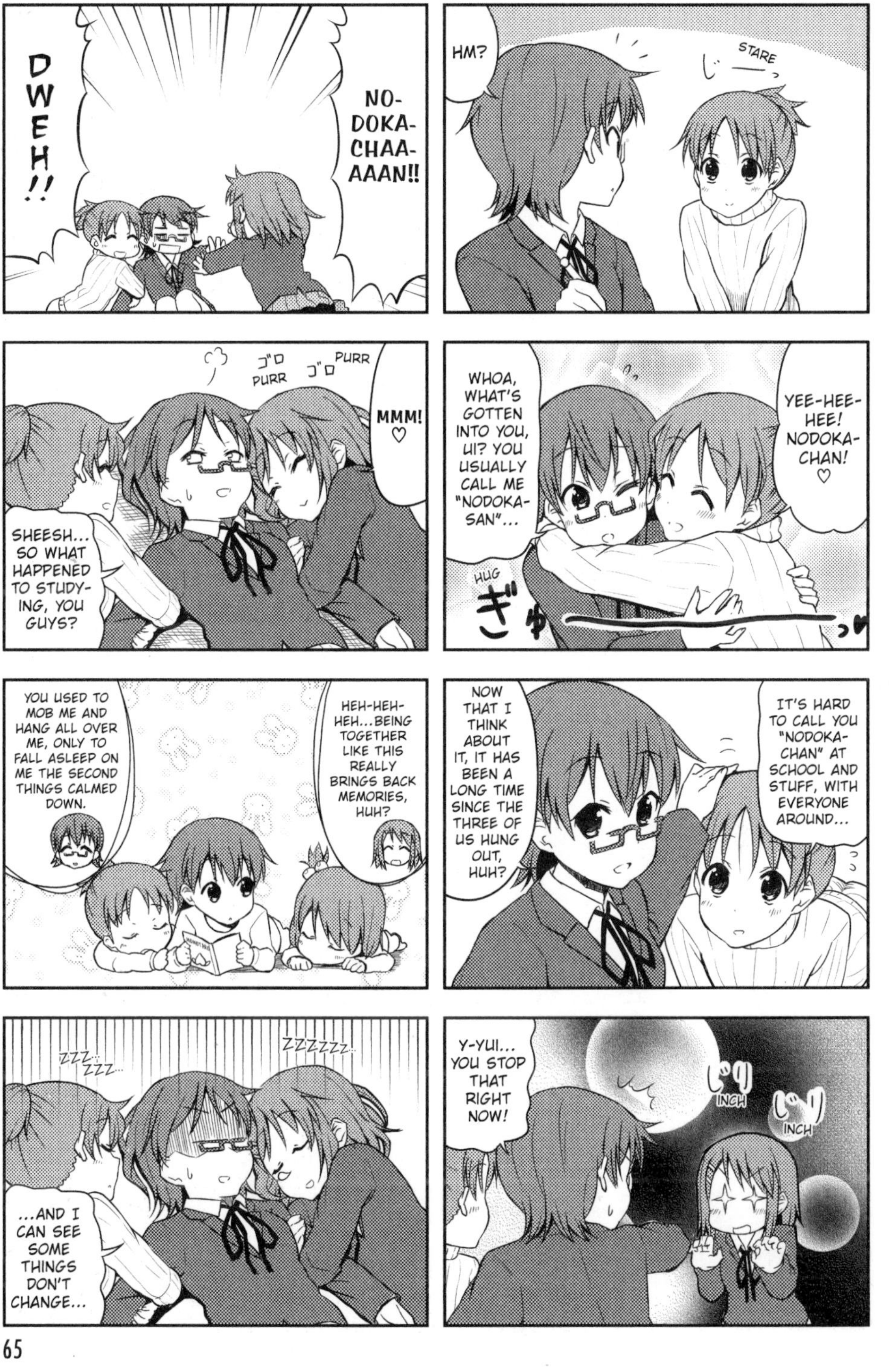
HM?
STARE
じーっ
YEE-HEE-HEE! NODOKA-CHAN! ♡
WHOA, WHAT'S GOTTEN INTO YOU, UI? YOU USUALLY CALL ME "NODOKA-SAN"...
HUG
ぎゅ
IT'S HARD TO CALL YOU "NODOKA-CHAN" AT SCHOOL AND STUFF, WITH EVERYONE AROUND...
NOW THAT I THINK ABOUT IT, IT HAS BEEN A LONG TIME SINCE THE THREE OF US HUNG OUT, HUH?
Y-YUI... YOU STOP THAT RIGHT NOW!
じり
INCH
じり
INCH
NO-DOKA-CHAAA-AAAN!!
DWEH!!
MMM! ♡
ゴロ
PURR
ゴロ
PURR
SHEESH... SO WHAT HAPPENED TO STUDY-ING, YOU GUYS?
HEH-HEH-HEH...BEING TOGETHER LIKE THIS REALLY BRINGS BACK MEMORIES, HUH?
YOU USED TO MOB ME AND HANG ALL OVER ME, ONLY TO FALL ASLEEP ON ME THE SECOND THINGS CALMED DOWN.
ZZZZZZ...
ZZZ... ZZZ...
...AND I CAN SEE SOME THINGS DON'T CHANGE...

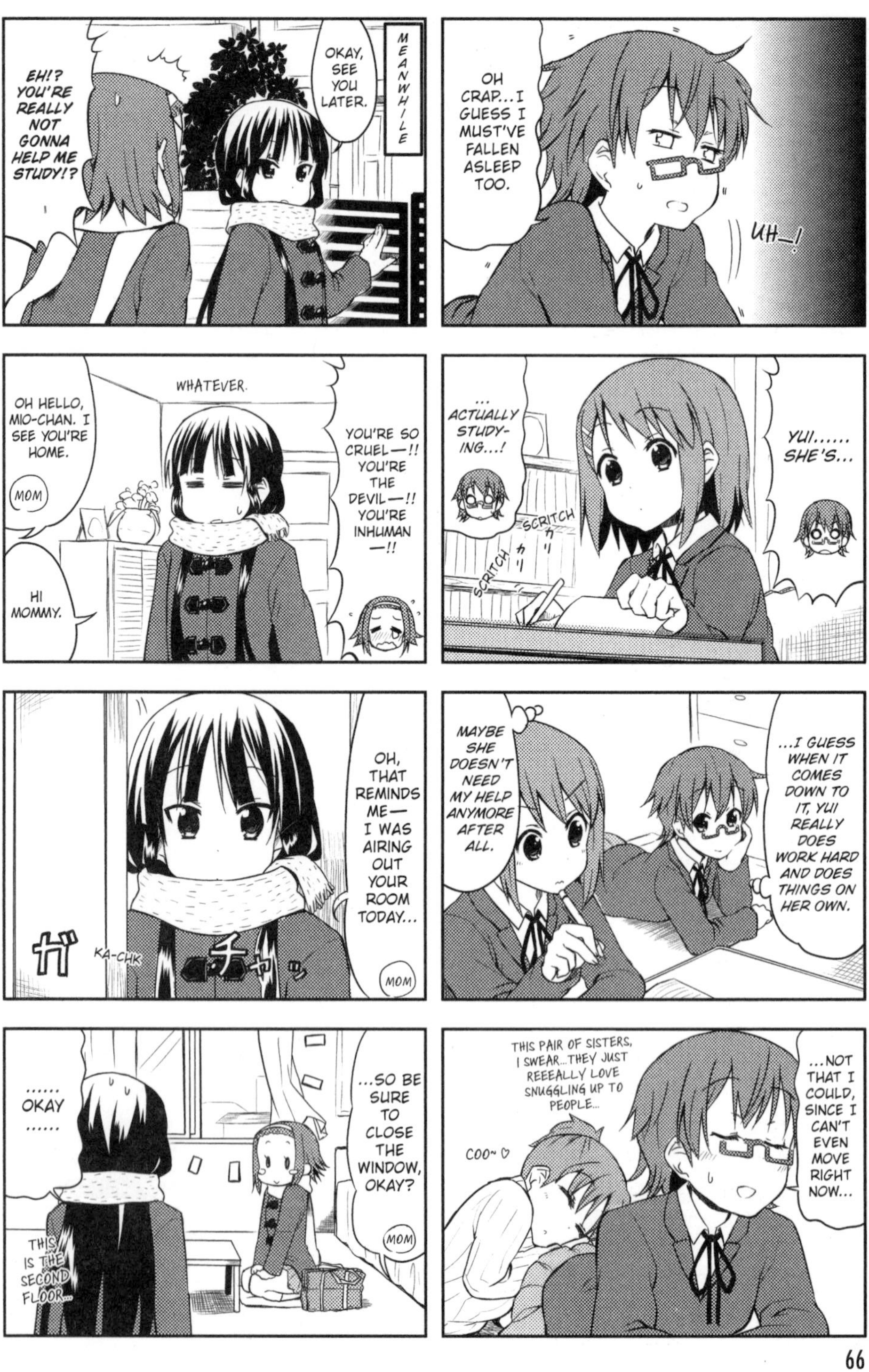
OH CRAP... I GUESS I MUST'VE FALLEN ASLEEP TOO.
UH—!
YUI...... SHE'S...
...ACTUALLY STUDYING...!
SCRITCH カリ
SCRITCH カリ
...I GUESS WHEN IT COMES DOWN TO IT, YUI REALLY DOES WORK HARD AND DOES THINGS ON HER OWN.
MAYBE SHE DOESN'T NEED MY HELP ANYMORE AFTER ALL.
...NOT THAT I COULD, SINCE I CAN'T EVEN MOVE RIGHT NOW...
THIS PAIR OF SISTERS, I SWEAR... THEY JUST REEEALLY LOVE SNUGGLING UP TO PEOPLE...
COO~ ♡
MEANWHILE
OKAY, SEE YOU LATER.
EH!? YOU'RE REALLY NOT GONNA HELP ME STUDY!?
YOU'RE SO CRUEL—!! YOU'RE THE DEVIL—!! YOU'RE INHUMAN—!!
WHATEVER.
OH HELLO, MIO-CHAN. I SEE YOU'RE HOME.
MOM
HI MOMMY.
OH, THAT REMINDS ME— I WAS AIRING OUT YOUR ROOM TODAY...
MOM
ガチャッ
KA-CHK
...SO BE SURE TO CLOSE THE WINDOW, OKAY?
MOM
......OKAY......
THIS IS THE SECOND FLOOR...

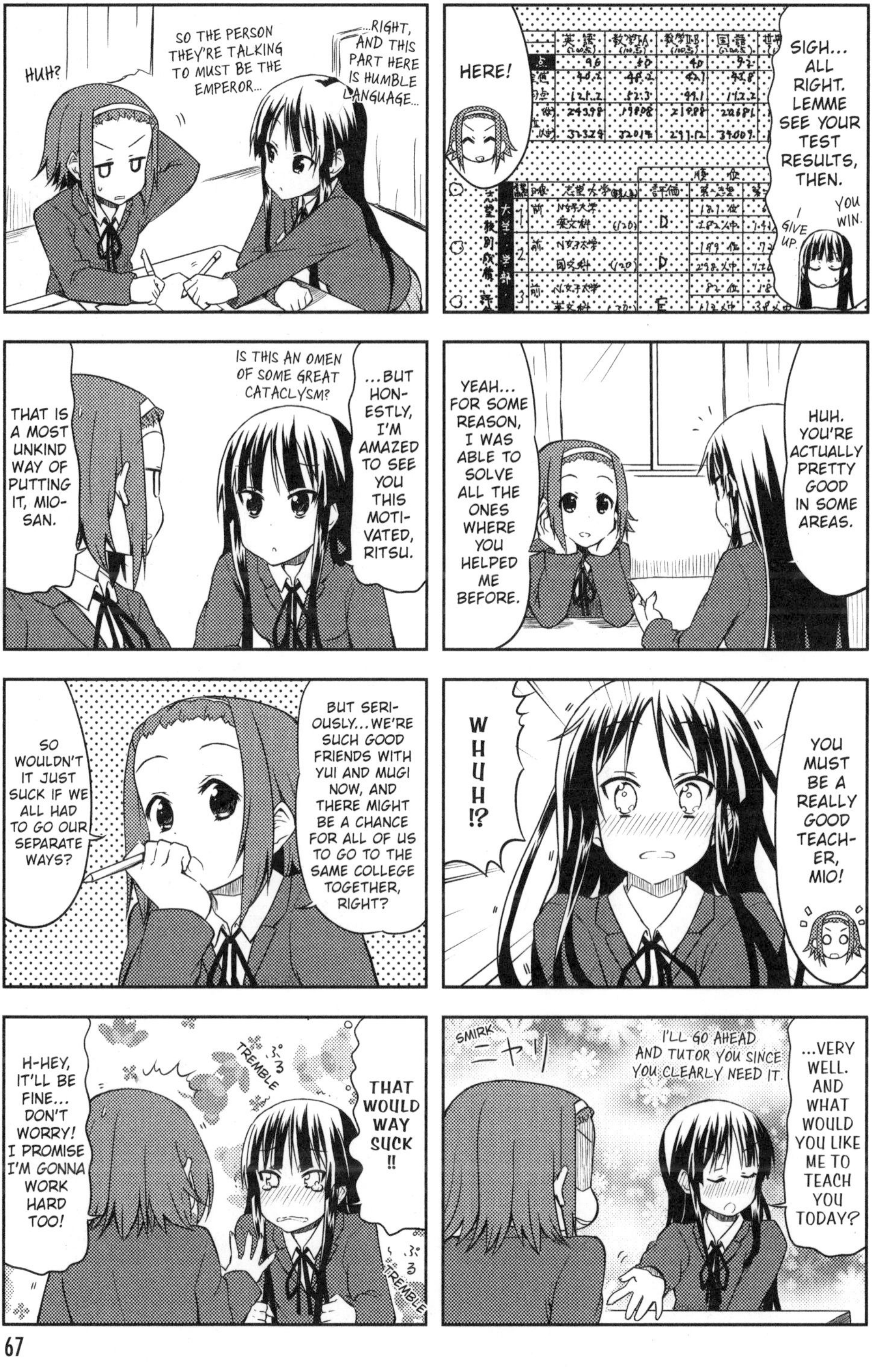

SIGH... ALL RIGHT. LEMME SEE YOUR TEST RESULTS, THEN.
HERE!
YOU WIN.
I GIVE UP.
HUH. YOU'RE ACTUALLY PRETTY GOOD IN SOME AREAS.
YEAH... FOR SOME REASON, I WAS ABLE TO SOLVE ALL THE ONES WHERE YOU HELPED ME BEFORE.
YOU MUST BE A REALLY GOOD TEACHER, MIO!
WHUH!?
...VERY WELL. AND WHAT WOULD YOU LIKE ME TO TEACH YOU TODAY?
I'LL GO AHEAD AND TUTOR YOU SINCE YOU CLEARLY NEED IT.
SMIRK
ニヤリ
...RIGHT, AND THIS PART HERE IS HUMBLE LANGUAGE...
SO THE PERSON THEY'RE TALKING TO MUST BE THE EMPEROR...
HUH?
...BUT HON-ESTLY, I'M AMAZED TO SEE YOU THIS MOTI-VATED, RITSU.
IS THIS AN OMEN OF SOME GREAT CATACLYSM?
THAT IS A MOST UNKIND WAY OF PUTTING IT, MIO-SAN.
BUT SERI-OUSLY...WE'RE SUCH GOOD FRIENDS WITH YUI AND MUGI NOW, AND THERE MIGHT BE A CHANCE FOR ALL OF US TO GO TO THE SAME COLLEGE TOGETHER, RIGHT?
SO WOULDN'T IT JUST SUCK IF WE ALL HAD TO GO OUR SEPARATE WAYS?
THAT WOULD WAY SUCK!!
ぷる
TREMBLE
ぷる
TREMBLE
H-HEY, IT'LL BE FINE... DON'T WORRY! I PROMISE I'M GONNA WORK HARD TOO!

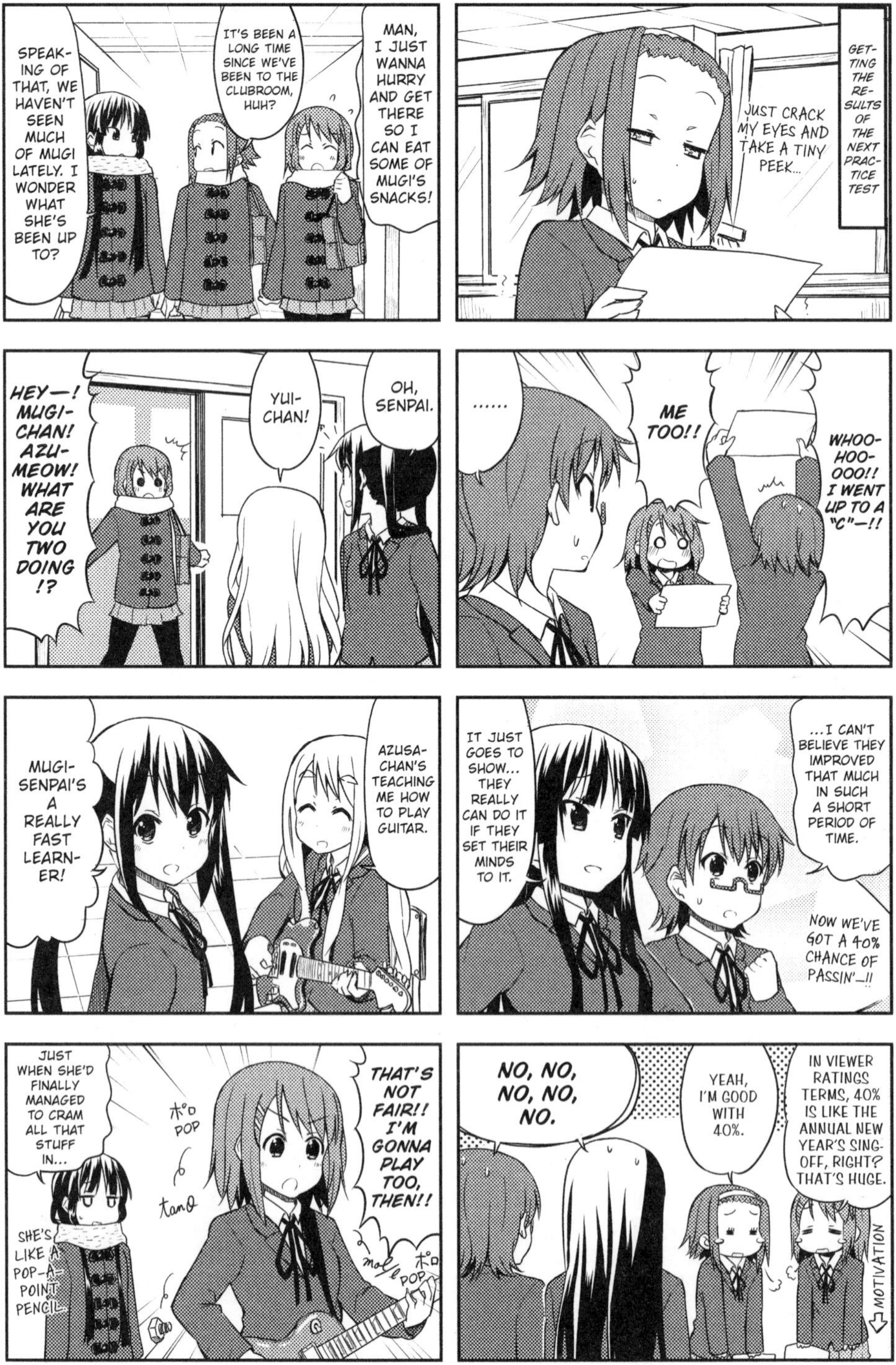
GETTING THE RESULTS OF THE NEXT PRACTICE TEST
JUST CRACK MY EYES AND TAKE A TINY PEEK...
WHOO-HOO-OOO!! I WENT UP TO A "C"—!!
ME TOO!!
......
...I CAN'T BELIEVE THEY IMPROVED THAT MUCH IN SUCH A SHORT PERIOD OF TIME.
IT JUST GOES TO SHOW... THEY REALLY CAN DO IT IF THEY SET THEIR MINDS TO IT.
NOW WE'VE GOT A 40% CHANCE OF PASSIN'—!!
IN VIEWER RATINGS TERMS, 40% IS LIKE THE ANNUAL NEW YEAR'S SING-OFF, RIGHT? THAT'S HUGE.
YEAH, I'M GOOD WITH 40%.
NO, NO, NO, NO, NO.
MOTIVATION
MAN, I JUST WANNA HURRY AND GET THERE SO I CAN EAT SOME OF MUGI'S SNACKS!
IT'S BEEN A LONG TIME SINCE WE'VE BEEN TO THE CLUBROOM, HUH?
SPEAKING OF THAT, WE HAVEN'T SEEN MUCH OF MUGI LATELY. I WONDER WHAT SHE'S BEEN UP TO?
OH, SENPAI.
YUI-CHAN!
HEY—! MUGI-CHAN! AZU-MEOW! WHAT ARE YOU TWO DOING!?
AZUSA-CHAN'S TEACHING ME HOW TO PLAY GUITAR.
MUGI-SENPAI'S A REALLY FAST LEARNER!
THAT'S NOT FAIR!! I'M GONNA PLAY TOO, THEN!!
ポロ POP
ポロ POP
JUST WHEN SHE'D FINALLY MANAGED TO CRAM ALL THAT STUFF IN...
SHE'S LIKE A POP-A-POINT PENCIL.

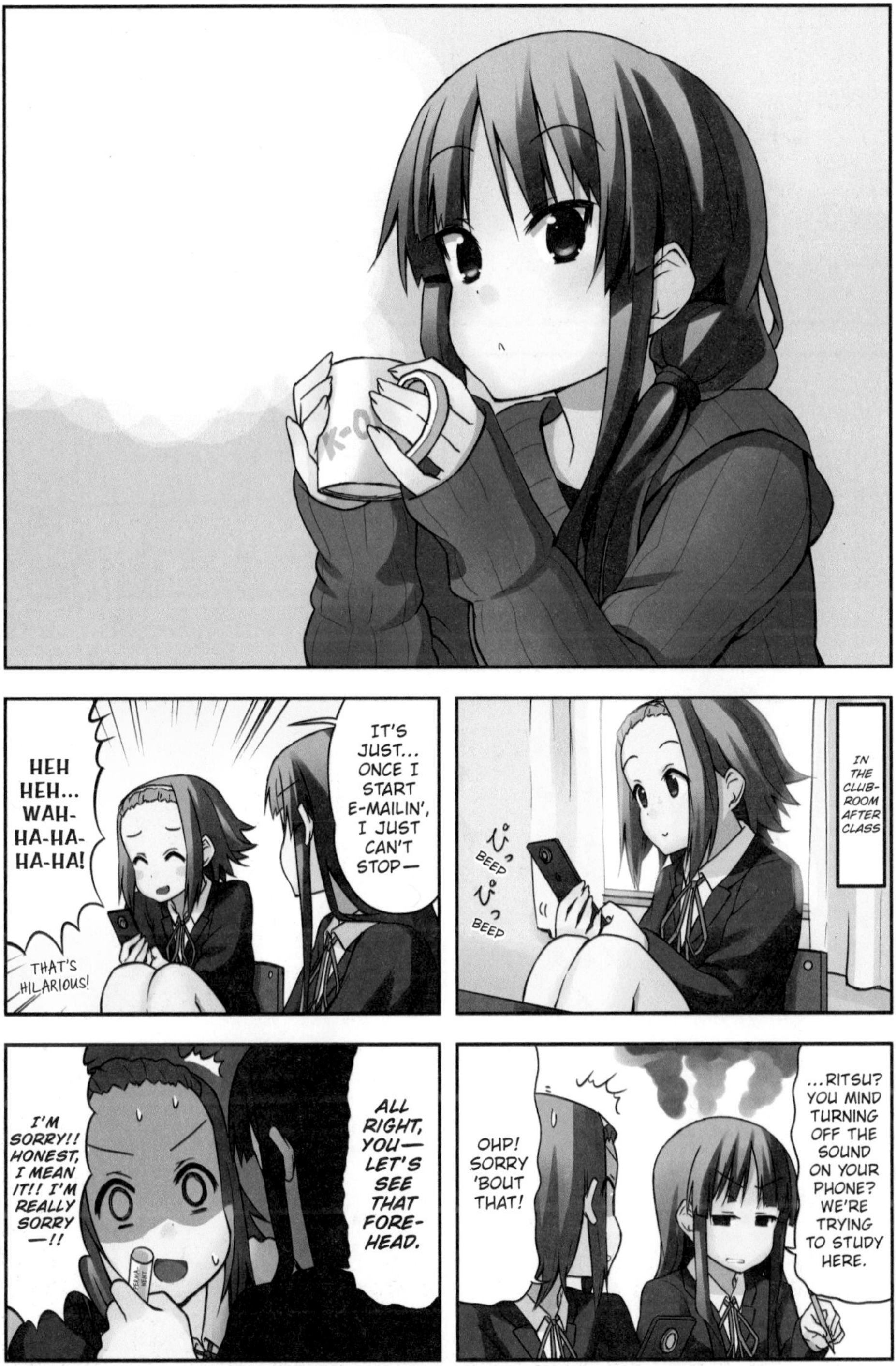
IN THE CLUBROOM AFTER CLASS
ぴっ BEEP
ぴっ BEEP
IT'S JUST... ONCE I START E-MAILIN', I JUST CAN'T STOP—
HEH HEH... WAH-HA-HA-HA-HA!
THAT'S HILARIOUS!
...RITSU? YOU MIND TURNING OFF THE SOUND ON YOUR PHONE? WE'RE TRYING TO STUDY HERE.
ムッ
OHP! SORRY 'BOUT THAT!
ALL RIGHT, YOU— LET'S SEE THAT FORE-HEAD.
I'M SORRY!! HONEST, I MEAN IT!! I'M REALLY SORRY—!!

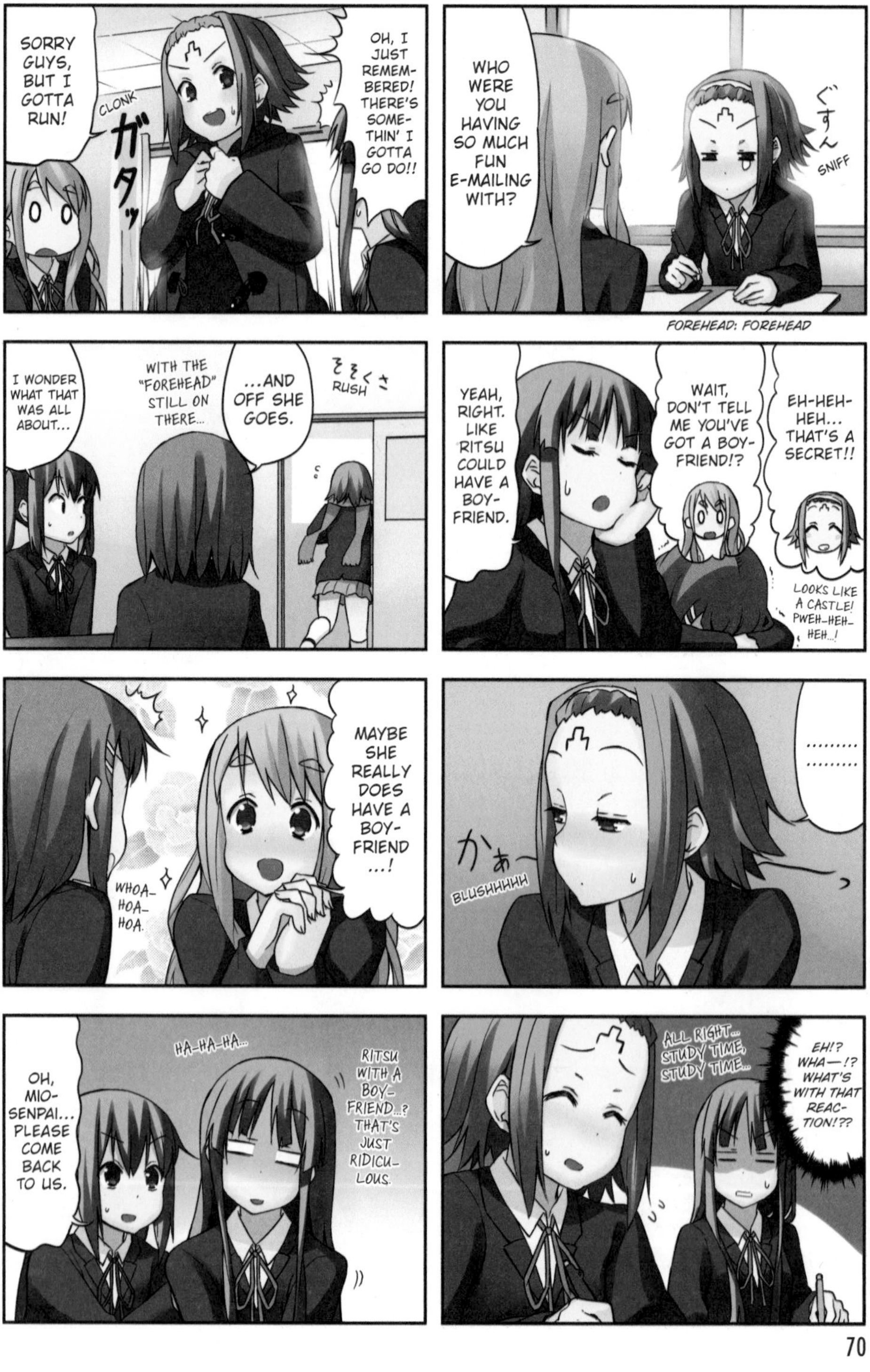
ぐすん
SNIFF
WHO WERE YOU HAVING SO MUCH FUN E-MAILING WITH?
FOREHEAD: FOREHEAD
EH-HEH-HEH... THAT'S A SECRET!!
LOOKS LIKE A CASTLE! PWEH-HEH-HEH...!
WAIT, DON'T TELL ME YOU'VE GOT A BOY-FRIEND!?
YEAH, RIGHT. LIKE RITSU COULD HAVE A BOY-FRIEND.
....
かぁ～
BLUSHHHHH
EH!? WHA—!? WHAT'S WITH THAT REAC-TION!??
ALL RIGHT... STUDY TIME, STUDY TIME...
OH, I JUST REMEM-BERED! THERE'S SOME-THIN' I GOTTA GO DO!!
CLONK
ガタッ
SORRY GUYS, BUT I GOTTA RUN!
そそくさ
RUSH
...AND OFF SHE GOES.
WITH THE "FOREHEAD" STILL ON THERE...
I WONDER WHAT THAT WAS ALL ABOUT...
MAYBE SHE REALLY DOES HAVE A BOY-FRIEND...!
WHOA-HOA-HOA.
RITSU WITH A BOY-FRIEND...? THAT'S JUST RIDICU-LOUS.
HA-HA-HA...
OH, MIO-SENPAI... PLEASE COME BACK TO US.

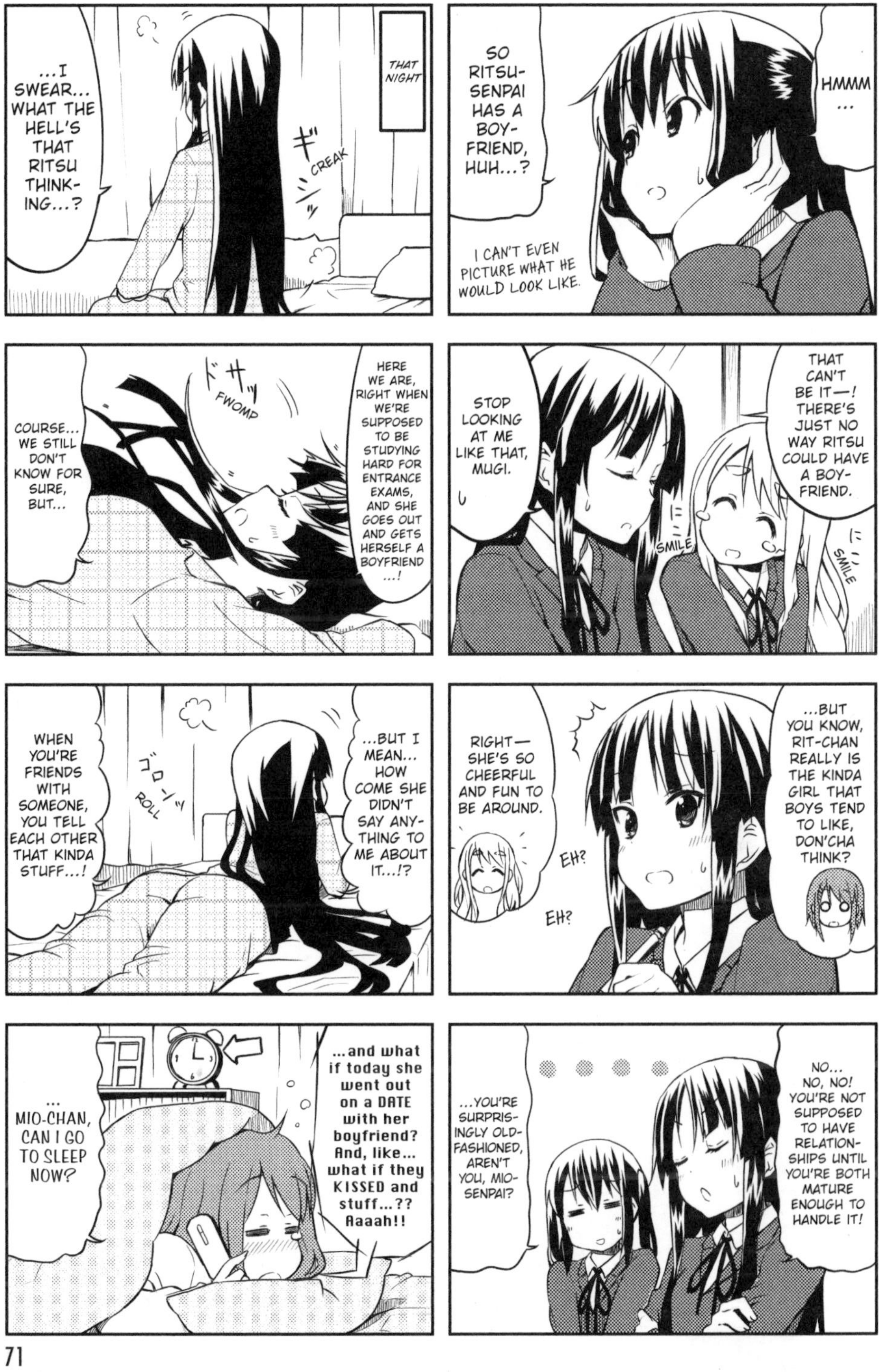

HMMM...
SO RITSU-SENPAI HAS A BOY-FRIEND, HUH...?
I CAN'T EVEN PICTURE WHAT HE WOULD LOOK LIKE.
THAT CAN'T BE IT—! THERE'S JUST NO WAY RITSU COULD HAVE A BOY-FRIEND.
SMILE
SMILE
STOP LOOKING AT ME LIKE THAT, MUGI.
...BUT YOU KNOW, RIT-CHAN REALLY IS THE KINDA GIRL THAT BOYS TEND TO LIKE, DON'CHA THINK?
RIGHT— SHE'S SO CHEERFUL AND FUN TO BE AROUND.
EH?
EH?
NO... NO, NO! YOU'RE NOT SUPPOSED TO HAVE RELATION-SHIPS UNTIL YOU'RE BOTH MATURE ENOUGH TO HANDLE IT!
...YOU'RE SURPRIS-INGLY OLD-FASHIONED, AREN'T YOU, MIO-SENPAI?
THAT NIGHT
CREAK
...I SWEAR... WHAT THE HELL'S THAT RITSU THINKING...?
HERE WE ARE, RIGHT WHEN WE'RE SUPPOSED TO BE STUDYING HARD FOR ENTRANCE EXAMS, AND SHE GOES OUT AND GETS HERSELF A BOYFRIEND...!
FWOMP
COURSE... WE STILL DON'T KNOW FOR SURE, BUT...
...BUT I MEAN... HOW COME SHE DIDN'T SAY ANY-THING TO ME ABOUT IT...!?
ROLL
WHEN YOU'RE FRIENDS WITH SOMEONE, YOU TELL EACH OTHER THAT KINDA STUFF...!
...and what if today she went out on a DATE with her boyfriend? And, like... what if they KISSED and stuff...?? Aaaah!!
...MIO-CHAN, CAN I GO TO SLEEP NOW?

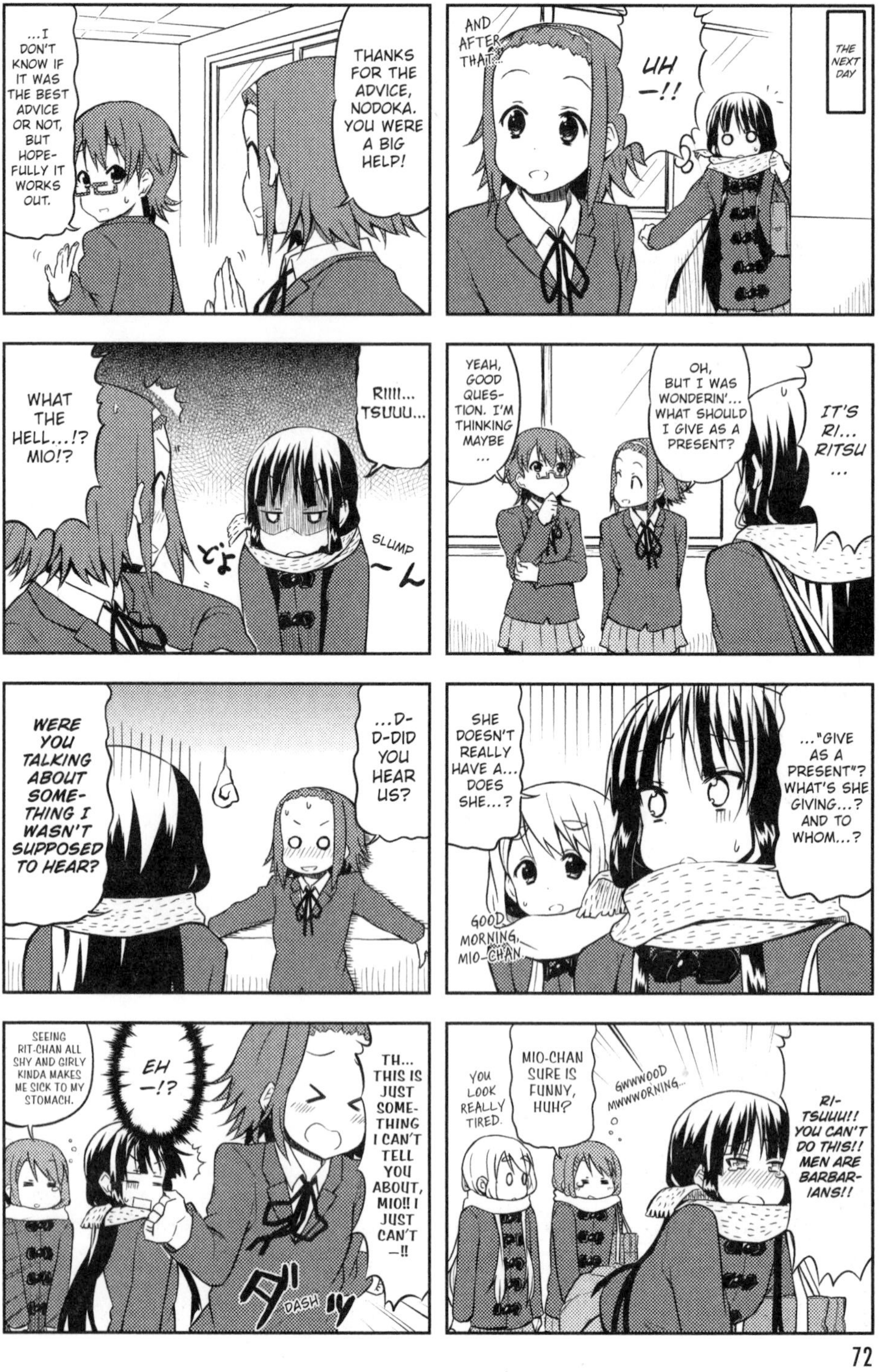
THE NEXT DAY
UH —!!
AND AFTER THAT...
IT'S RI... RITSU ...
OH, BUT I WAS WONDERIN'... WHAT SHOULD I GIVE AS A PRESENT?
YEAH, GOOD QUES-TION. I'M THINKING MAYBE ...
..."GIVE AS A PRESENT"? WHAT'S SHE GIVING...? AND TO WHOM...?
SHE DOESN'T REALLY HAVE A... DOES SHE...?
GOOD MORNING, MIO-CHAN.
RI-TSUUU!! YOU CAN'T DO THIS!! MEN ARE BARBAR-IANS!!
GWWWOOD MWWWORNING...
MIO-CHAN SURE IS FUNNY, HUH?
YOU LOOK REALLY TIRED.
THANKS FOR THE ADVICE, NODOKA. YOU WERE A BIG HELP!
...I DON'T KNOW IF IT WAS THE BEST ADVICE OR NOT, BUT HOPE-FULLY IT WORKS OUT.
RIIII... TSUUU...
SLUMP
WHAT THE HELL...!? MIO!?
...D-D-DID YOU HEAR US?
WERE YOU TALKING ABOUT SOME-THING I WASN'T SUPPOSED TO HEAR?
TH... THIS IS JUST SOME-THING I CAN'T TELL YOU ABOUT, MIO!! I JUST CAN'T —!!
DASH
EH —!?
SEEING RIT-CHAN ALL SHY AND GIRLY KINDA MAKES ME SICK TO MY STOMACH.

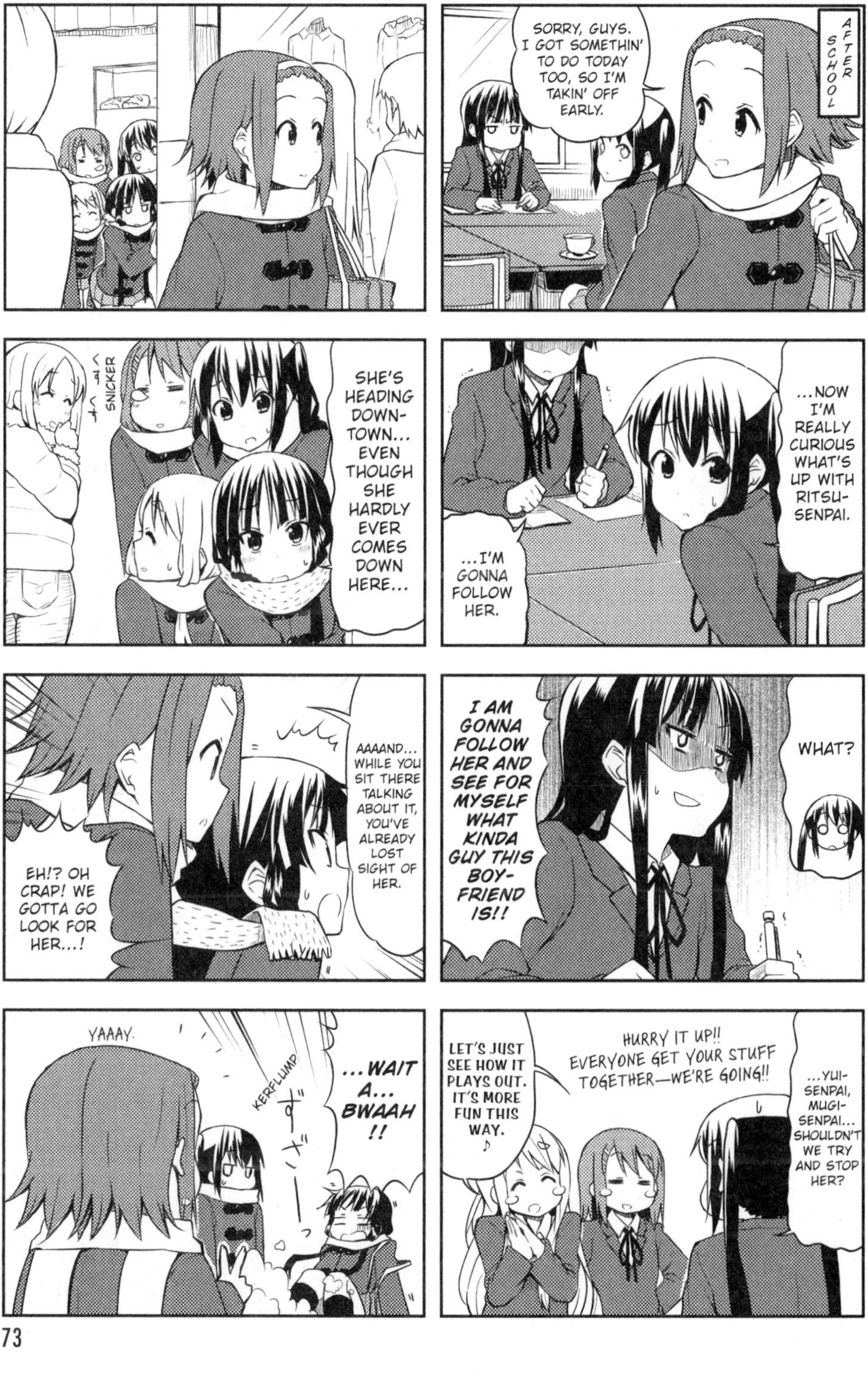
AFTER SCHOOL
SORRY, GUYS. I GOT SOMETHIN' TO DO TODAY TOO, SO I'M TAKIN' OFF EARLY.
...NOW I'M REALLY CURIOUS WHAT'S UP WITH RITSU-SENPAI.
...I'M GONNA FOLLOW HER.
WHAT?
I AM GONNA FOLLOW HER AND SEE FOR MYSELF WHAT KINDA GUY THIS BOYFRIEND IS!!
...YUI-SENPAI, MUGI-SENPAI... SHOULDN'T WE TRY AND STOP HER?
HURRY IT UP!! EVERYONE GET YOUR STUFF TOGETHER—WE'RE GOING!!
LET'S JUST SEE HOW IT PLAYS OUT. IT'S MORE FUN THIS WAY. ♪
SHE'S HEADING DOWNTOWN... EVEN THOUGH SHE HARDLY EVER COMES DOWN HERE...
くすくす
SNICKER
AAAAND... WHILE YOU SIT THERE TALKING ABOUT IT, YOU'VE ALREADY LOST SIGHT OF HER.
EH!? OH CRAP! WE GOTTA GO LOOK FOR HER...!
...WAIT A... BWAAH!!
ずざー
KERFLUMP
YAAAY.

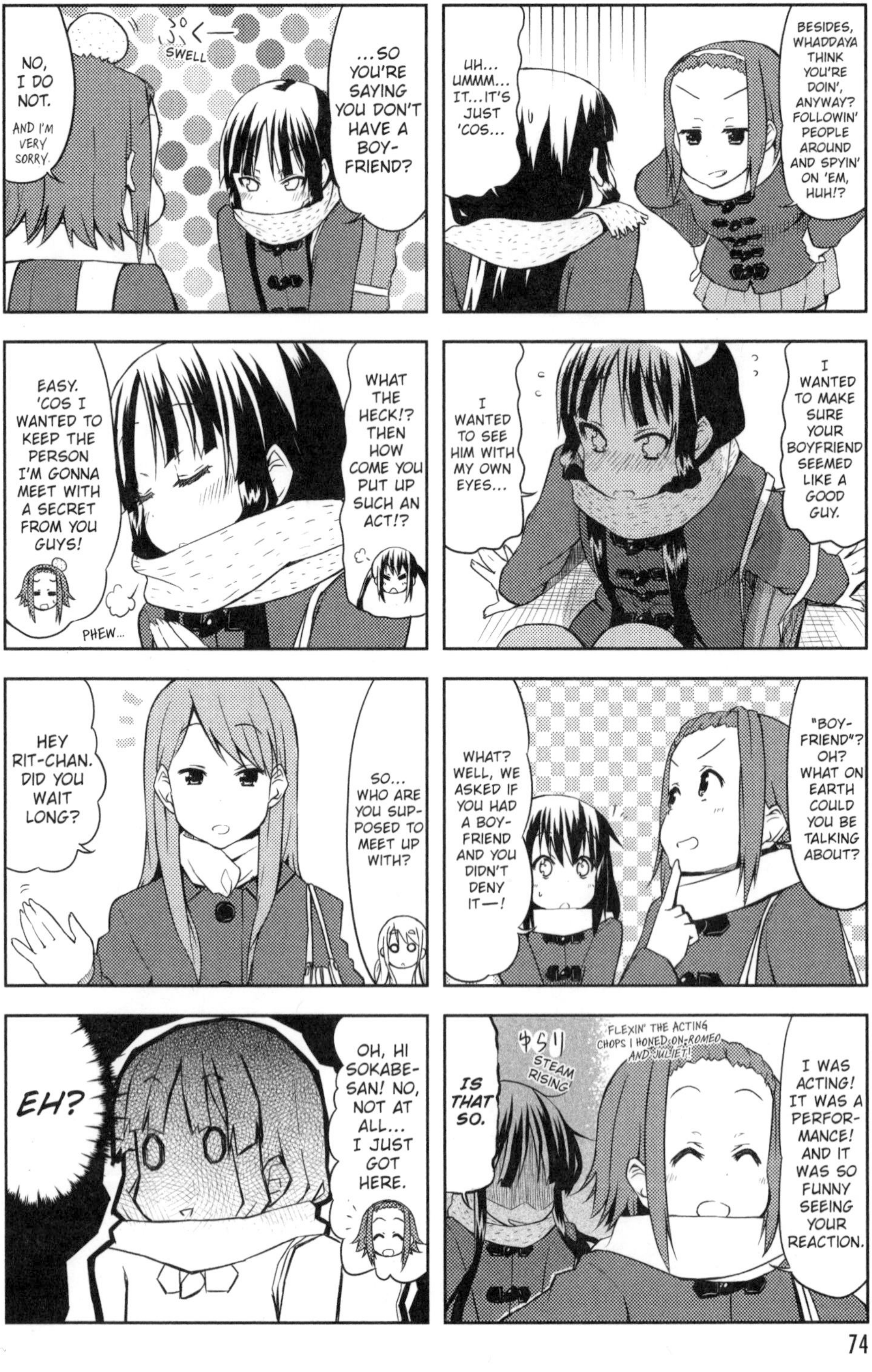
BESIDES, WHADDAYA THINK YOU'RE DOIN', ANYWAY? FOLLOWIN' PEOPLE AROUND AND SPYIN' ON 'EM, HUH!?
UH... UMMM... IT...IT'S JUST 'COS...
I WANTED TO MAKE SURE YOUR BOYFRIEND SEEMED LIKE A GOOD GUY.
I WANTED TO SEE HIM WITH MY OWN EYES...
"BOY-FRIEND"? OH? WHAT ON EARTH COULD YOU BE TALKING ABOUT?
WHAT? WELL, WE ASKED IF YOU HAD A BOY-FRIEND AND YOU DIDN'T DENY IT—!
I WAS ACTING! IT WAS A PERFOR-MANCE! AND IT WAS SO FUNNY SEEING YOUR REACTION.
FLEXIN' THE ACTING CHOPS I HONED ON ROMEO AND JULIET!
ゆらり
STEAM RISING
IS THAT SO.
...SO YOU'RE SAYING YOU DON'T HAVE A BOY-FRIEND?
ぷくー
SWELL
NO, I DO NOT.
AND I'M VERY SORRY.
WHAT THE HECK!? THEN HOW COME YOU PUT UP SUCH AN ACT!?
EASY. 'COS I WANTED TO KEEP THE PERSON I'M GONNA MEET WITH A SECRET FROM YOU GUYS!
PHEW...
SO... WHO ARE YOU SUP-POSED TO MEET UP WITH?
HEY RIT-CHAN. DID YOU WAIT LONG?
OH, HI SOKABE-SAN! NO, NOT AT ALL... I JUST GOT HERE.
EH?

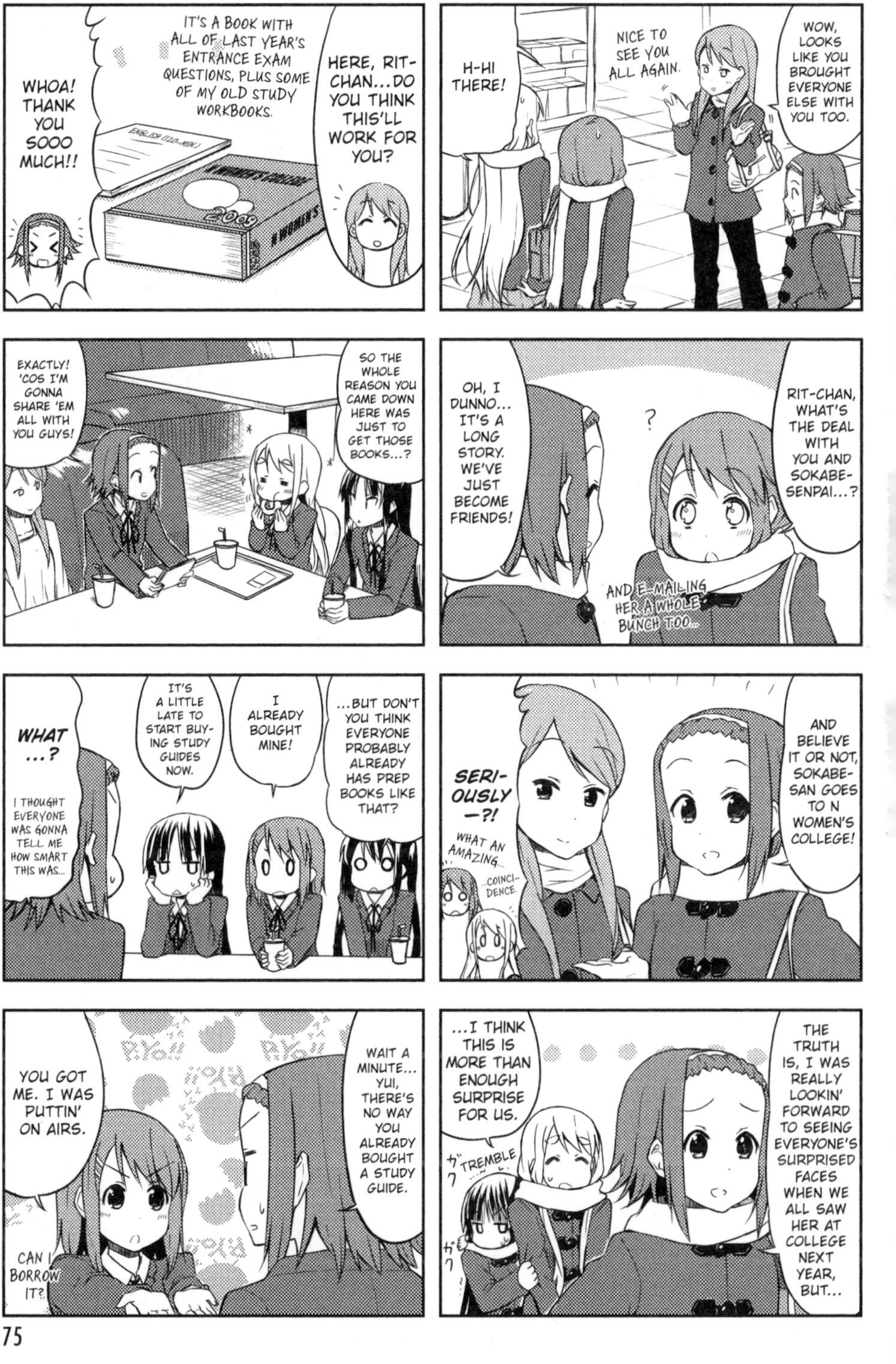
WOW, LOOKS LIKE YOU BROUGHT EVERYONE ELSE WITH YOU TOO.
NICE TO SEE YOU ALL AGAIN.
H-HI THERE!
RIT-CHAN, WHAT'S THE DEAL WITH YOU AND SOKABE-SENPAI...?
?
OH, I DUNNO... IT'S A LONG STORY. WE'VE JUST BECOME FRIENDS!
AND E-MAILING HER A WHOLE BUNCH TOO...
AND BELIEVE IT OR NOT, SOKABE-SAN GOES TO N WOMEN'S COLLEGE!
SERI-OUSLY—?!
WHAT AN AMAZING...
...COINCI-DENCE.
THE TRUTH IS, I WAS REALLY LOOKIN' FORWARD TO SEEING EVERYONE'S SURPRISED FACES WHEN WE ALL SAW HER AT COLLEGE NEXT YEAR, BUT...
...I THINK THIS IS MORE THAN ENOUGH SURPRISE FOR US.
TREMBLE
HERE, RIT-CHAN...DO YOU THINK THIS'LL WORK FOR YOU?
IT'S A BOOK WITH ALL OF LAST YEAR'S ENTRANCE EXAM QUESTIONS, PLUS SOME OF MY OLD STUDY WORKBOOKS.
WHOA! THANK YOU SOOO MUCH!!
SO THE WHOLE REASON YOU CAME DOWN HERE WAS JUST TO GET THOSE BOOKS...?
EXACTLY! 'COS I'M GONNA SHARE 'EM ALL WITH YOU GUYS!
...BUT DON'T YOU THINK EVERYONE PROBABLY ALREADY HAS PREP BOOKS LIKE THAT?
I ALREADY BOUGHT MINE!
IT'S A LITTLE LATE TO START BUYING STUDY GUIDES NOW.
WHAT...?
I THOUGHT EVERYONE WAS GONNA TELL ME HOW SMART THIS WAS...
WAIT A MINUTE... YUI, THERE'S NO WAY YOU ALREADY BOUGHT A STUDY GUIDE.
YOU GOT ME. I WAS PUTTIN' ON AIRS.
CAN I BORROW IT?

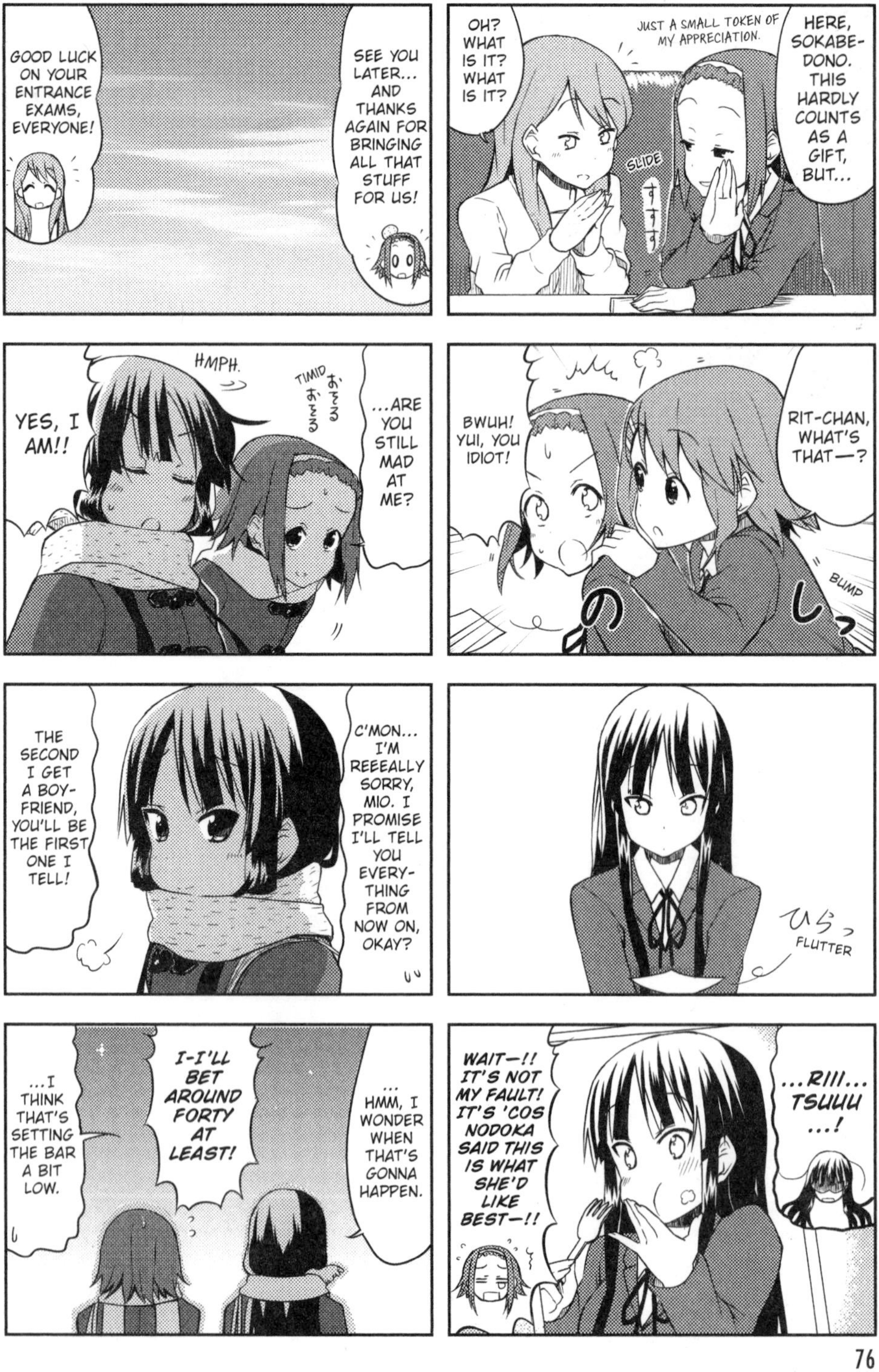
HERE, SOKABE-DONO. THIS HARDLY COUNTS AS A GIFT, BUT...
JUST A SMALL TOKEN OF MY APPRECIATION.
OH? WHAT IS IT? WHAT IS IT?
すすす
SLIDE
RIT-CHAN, WHAT'S THAT—?
BUMP
しっ
BWUH! YUI, YOU IDIOT!
の
ひらっ
FLUTTER
...RIII... TSUUU...!
WAIT—!! IT'S NOT MY FAULT! IT'S 'COS NODOKA SAID THIS IS WHAT SHE'D LIKE BEST—!!
SEE YOU LATER... AND THANKS AGAIN FOR BRINGING ALL THAT STUFF FOR US!
GOOD LUCK ON YOUR ENTRANCE EXAMS, EVERYONE!
...ARE YOU STILL MAD AT ME?
おそるおそる
TIMID
HMPH.
YES, I AM!!
C'MON... I'M REEEALLY SORRY, MIO. I PROMISE I'LL TELL YOU EVERYTHING FROM NOW ON, OKAY?
THE SECOND I GET A BOY-FRIEND, YOU'LL BE THE FIRST ONE I TELL!
...HMM, I WONDER WHEN THAT'S GONNA HAPPEN.
I-I'LL BET AROUND FORTY AT LEAST!
...I THINK THAT'S SETTING THE BAR A BIT LOW.

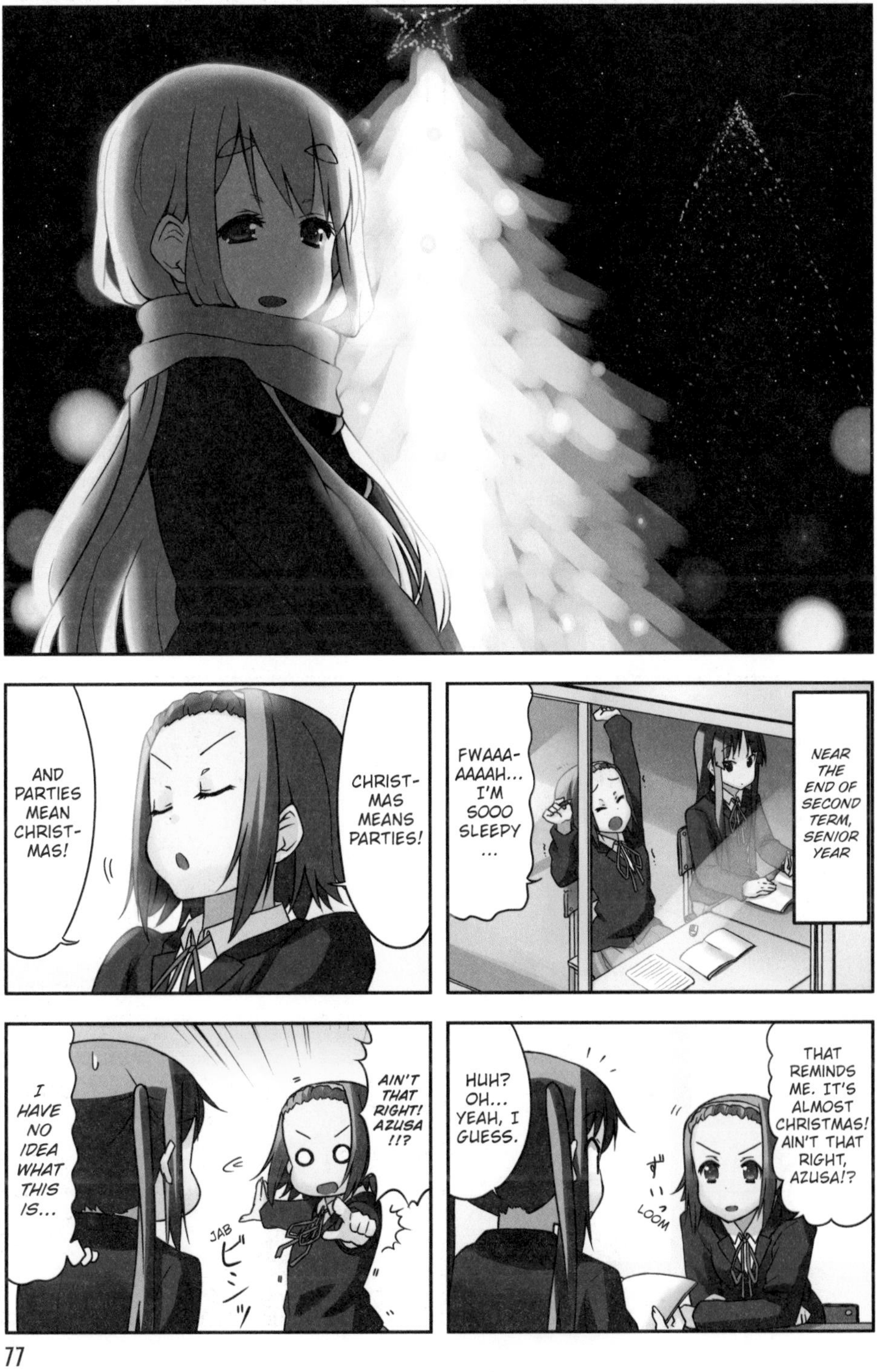
NEAR THE END OF SECOND TERM, SENIOR YEAR
FWAAA-AAAAH... I'M SOOO SLEEPY ...
CHRIST-MAS MEANS PARTIES!
AND PARTIES MEAN CHRIST-MAS!
THAT REMINDS ME. IT'S ALMOST CHRISTMAS! AIN'T THAT RIGHT, AZUSA!?
LOOM
HUH? OH... YEAH, I GUESS.
AIN'T THAT RIGHT! AZUSA!!?
JAB
I HAVE NO IDEA WHAT THIS IS...

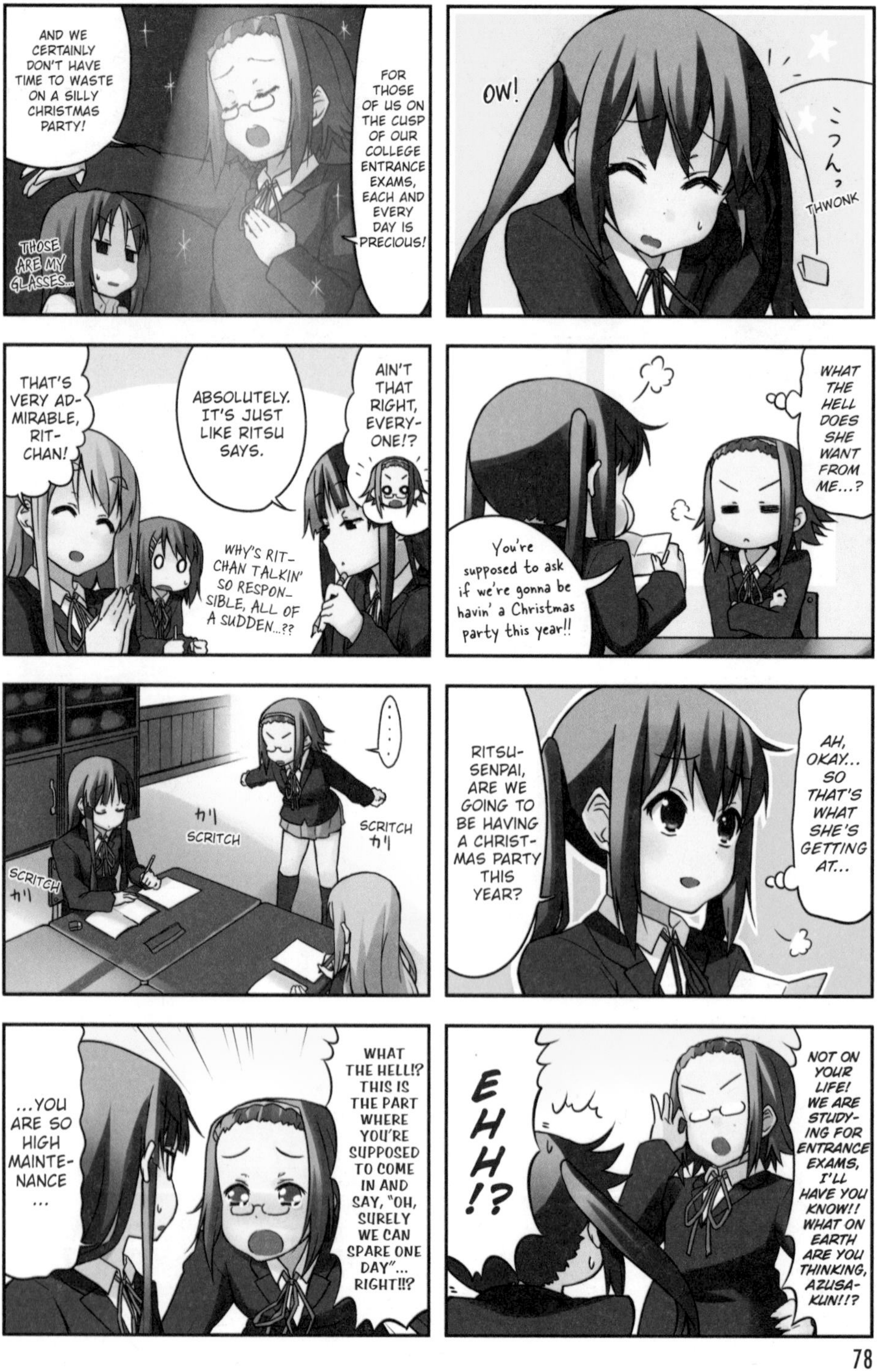

こつん
THWONK
OW!
WHAT THE HELL DOES SHE WANT FROM ME...?
You're supposed to ask if we're gonna be havin' a Christmas party this year!!
AH, OKAY... SO THAT'S WHAT SHE'S GETTING AT...
RITSU-SENPAI, ARE WE GOING TO BE HAVING A CHRISTMAS PARTY THIS YEAR?
NOT ON YOUR LIFE! WE ARE STUDYING FOR ENTRANCE EXAMS, I'LL HAVE YOU KNOW!! WHAT ON EARTH ARE YOU THINKING, AZUSA-KUN!!?
EHH!?
FOR THOSE OF US ON THE CUSP OF OUR COLLEGE ENTRANCE EXAMS, EACH AND EVERY DAY IS PRECIOUS!
AND WE CERTAINLY DON'T HAVE TIME TO WASTE ON A SILLY CHRISTMAS PARTY!
THOSE ARE MY GLASSES...
AIN'T THAT RIGHT, EVERYONE!?
ABSOLUTELY. IT'S JUST LIKE RITSU SAYS.
THAT'S VERY ADMIRABLE, RIT-CHAN!
WHY'S RIT-CHAN TALKIN' SO RESPONSIBLE, ALL OF A SUDDEN...??
. . . .
SCRITCH カリ
カリ SCRITCH
SCRITCH カリ
WHAT THE HELL!? THIS IS THE PART WHERE YOU'RE SUPPOSED TO COME IN AND SAY, "OH, SURELY WE CAN SPARE ONE DAY"... RIGHT!!?
...YOU ARE SO HIGH MAINTENANCE...

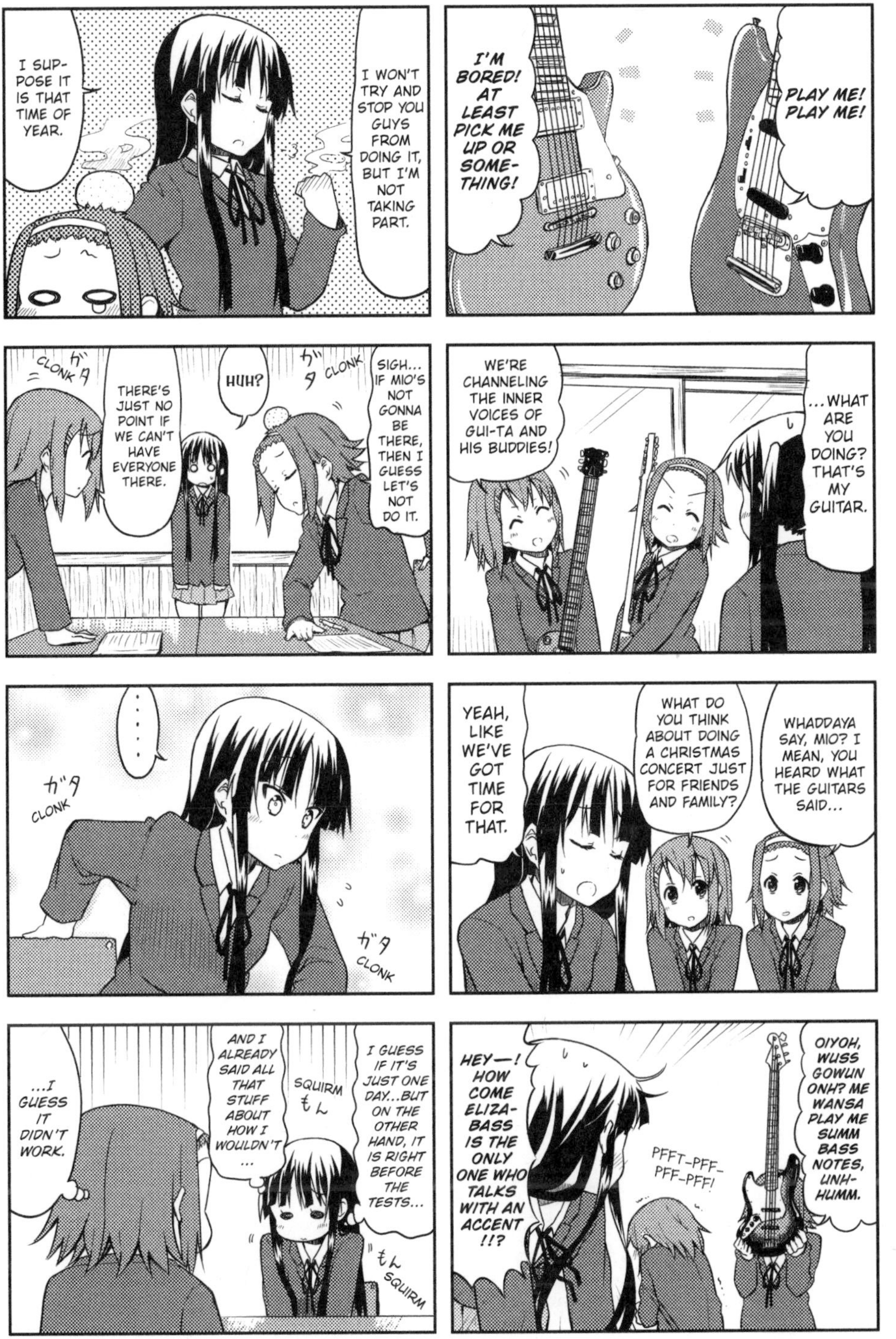
PLAY ME! PLAY ME!
I'M BORED! AT LEAST PICK ME UP OR SOMETHING!
...WHAT ARE YOU DOING? THAT'S MY GUITAR.
WE'RE CHANNELING THE INNER VOICES OF GUI-TA AND HIS BUDDIES!
WHADDAYA SAY, MIO? I MEAN, YOU HEARD WHAT THE GUITARS SAID...
WHAT DO YOU THINK ABOUT DOING A CHRISTMAS CONCERT JUST FOR FRIENDS AND FAMILY?
YEAH, LIKE WE'VE GOT TIME FOR THAT.
OIYOH, WUSS GOWUN ONH? ME WANSA PLAY ME SUMM BASS NOTES, UNH-HUMM.
PFFT-PFF-PFF-PFF!
HEY—! HOW COME ELIZA-BASS IS THE ONLY ONE WHO TALKS WITH AN ACCENT!!?
I WON'T TRY AND STOP YOU GUYS FROM DOING IT, BUT I'M NOT TAKING PART.
I SUPPOSE IT IS THAT TIME OF YEAR.
ガタ CLONK
SIGH... IF MIO'S NOT GONNA BE THERE, THEN I GUESS LET'S NOT DO IT.
HUH?
THERE'S JUST NO POINT IF WE CAN'T HAVE EVERYONE THERE.
ガタ CLONK
......
ガタ CLONK
ガタ CLONK
I GUESS IF IT'S JUST ONE DAY...BUT ON THE OTHER HAND, IT IS RIGHT BEFORE THE TESTS...
SQUIRM もん
AND I ALREADY SAID ALL THAT STUFF ABOUT HOW I WOULDN'T...
もん SQUIRM
...I GUESS IT DIDN'T WORK.

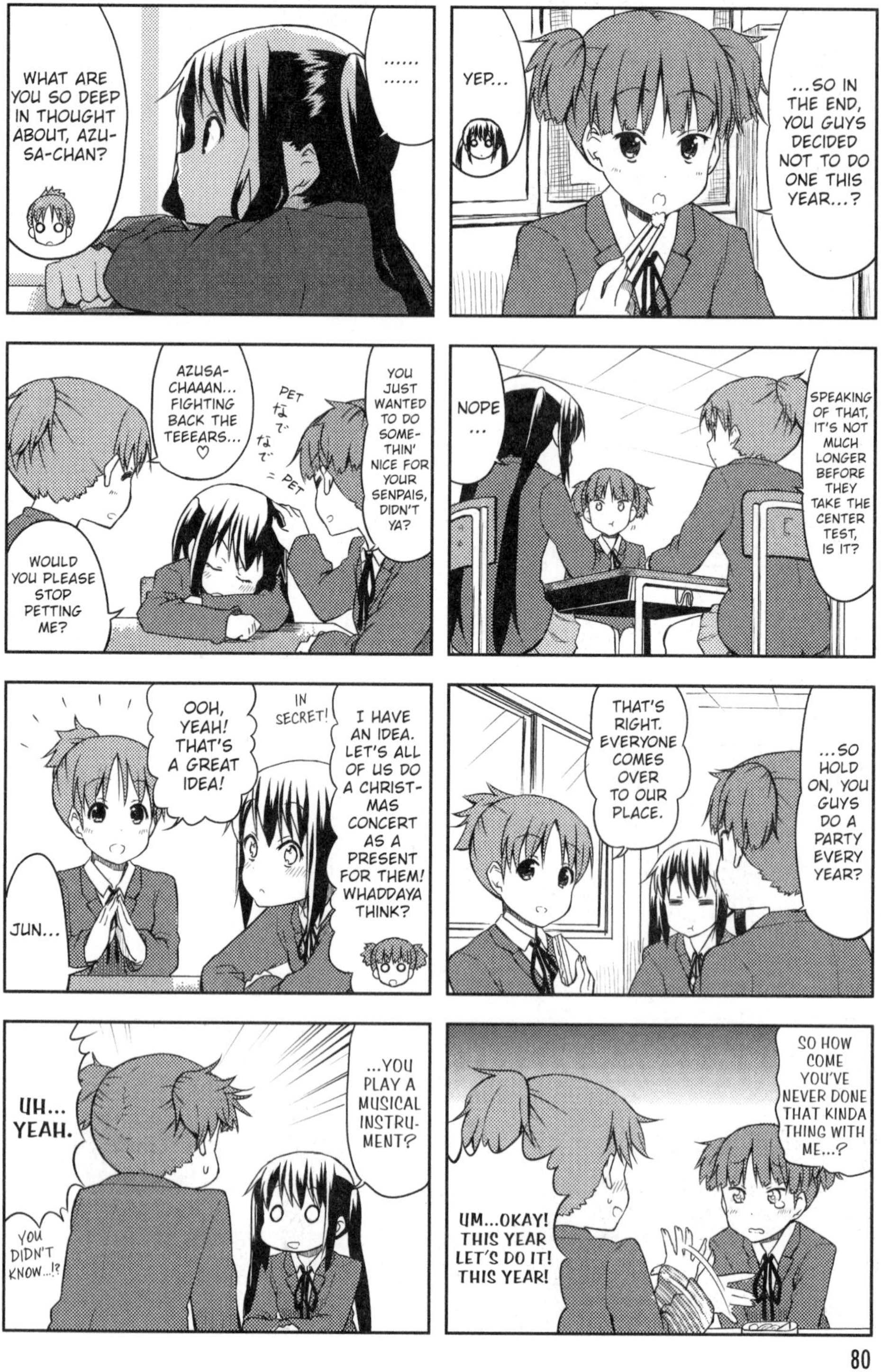
...SO IN THE END, YOU GUYS DECIDED NOT TO DO ONE THIS YEAR...?
YEP...
SPEAKING OF THAT, IT'S NOT MUCH LONGER BEFORE THEY TAKE THE CENTER TEST, IS IT?
NOPE...
...SO HOLD ON, YOU GUYS DO A PARTY EVERY YEAR?
THAT'S RIGHT. EVERYONE COMES OVER TO OUR PLACE.
SO HOW COME YOU'VE NEVER DONE THAT KINDA THING WITH ME...?
UM...OKAY! THIS YEAR LET'S DO IT! THIS YEAR!
......
......
WHAT ARE YOU SO DEEP IN THOUGHT ABOUT, AZUSA-CHAN?
YOU JUST WANTED TO DO SOME-THIN' NICE FOR YOUR SENPAIS, DIDN'T YA?
PET なで なで PET
AZUSA-CHAAAN... FIGHTING BACK THE TEEEARS...♡
WOULD YOU PLEASE STOP PETTING ME?
I HAVE AN IDEA. LET'S ALL OF US DO A CHRIST-MAS CONCERT AS A PRESENT FOR THEM! WHADDAYA THINK?
IN SECRET!
OOH, YEAH! THAT'S A GREAT IDEA!
JUN...
...YOU PLAY A MUSICAL INSTRU-MENT?
UH... YEAH.
YOU DIDN'T KNOW...!?

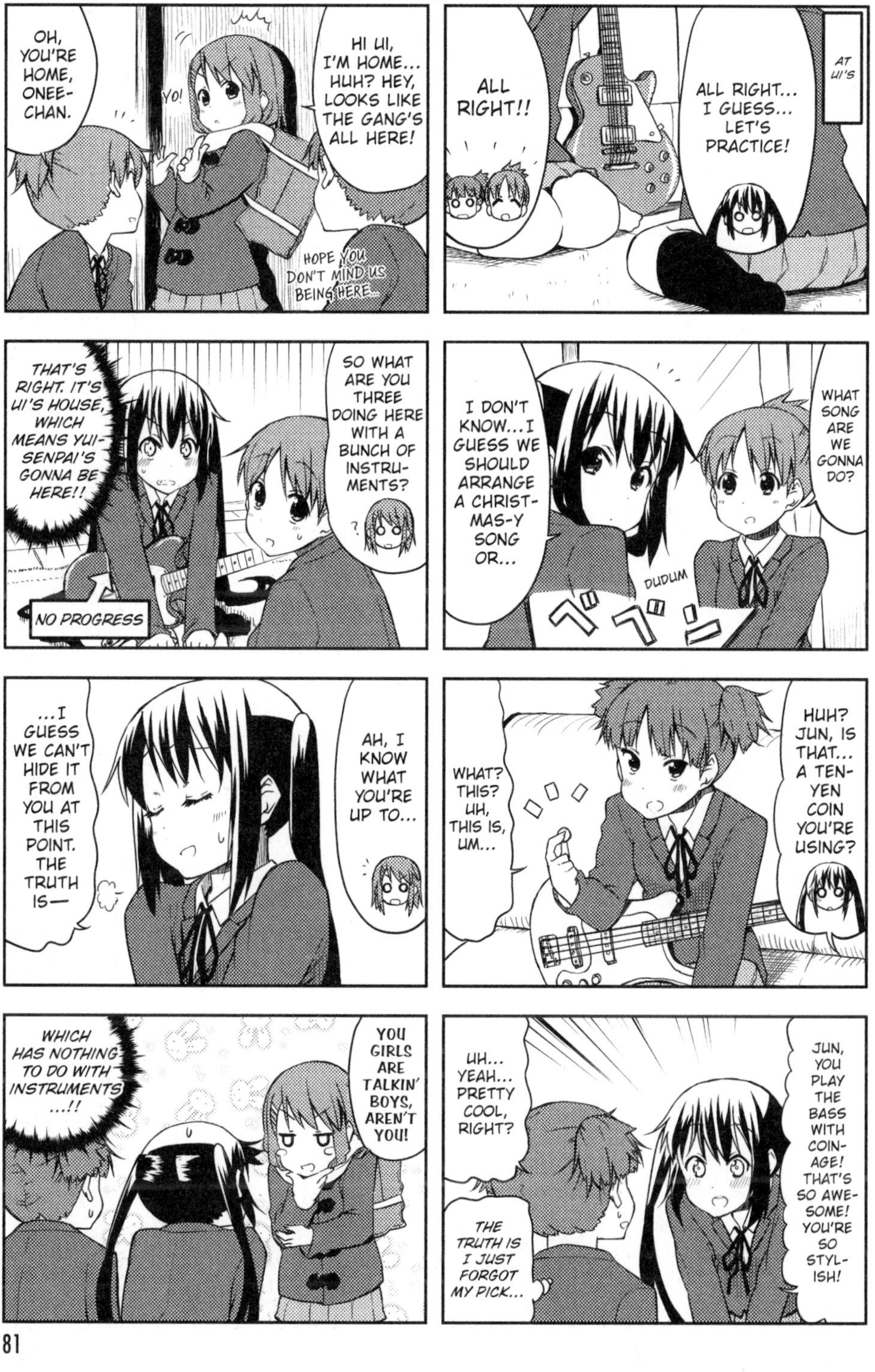
AT UI'S
ALL RIGHT... I GUESS... LET'S PRACTICE!
ALL RIGHT!!
WHAT SONG ARE WE GONNA DO?
I DON'T KNOW...I GUESS WE SHOULD ARRANGE A CHRISTMAS-Y SONG OR...
DUDUM
HUH? JUN, IS THAT... A TEN-YEN COIN YOU'RE USING?
WHAT? THIS? UH, THIS IS, UM...
JUN, YOU PLAY THE BASS WITH COINAGE! THAT'S SO AWESOME! YOU'RE SO STYLISH!
UH... YEAH... PRETTY COOL, RIGHT?
THE TRUTH IS I JUST FORGOT MY PICK...
HI UI, I'M HOME... HUH? HEY, LOOKS LIKE THE GANG'S ALL HERE!
YO!
OH, YOU'RE HOME, ONEE-CHAN.
HOPE YOU DON'T MIND US BEING HERE...
SO WHAT ARE YOU THREE DOING HERE WITH A BUNCH OF INSTRUMENTS?
THAT'S RIGHT. IT'S UI'S HOUSE, WHICH MEANS YUI-SENPAI'S GONNA BE HERE!!
NO PROGRESS
AH, I KNOW WHAT YOU'RE UP TO...
...I GUESS WE CAN'T HIDE IT FROM YOU AT THIS POINT. THE TRUTH IS—
YOU GIRLS ARE TALKIN' BOYS, AREN'T YOU!
WHICH HAS NOTHING TO DO WITH INSTRUMENTS...!!

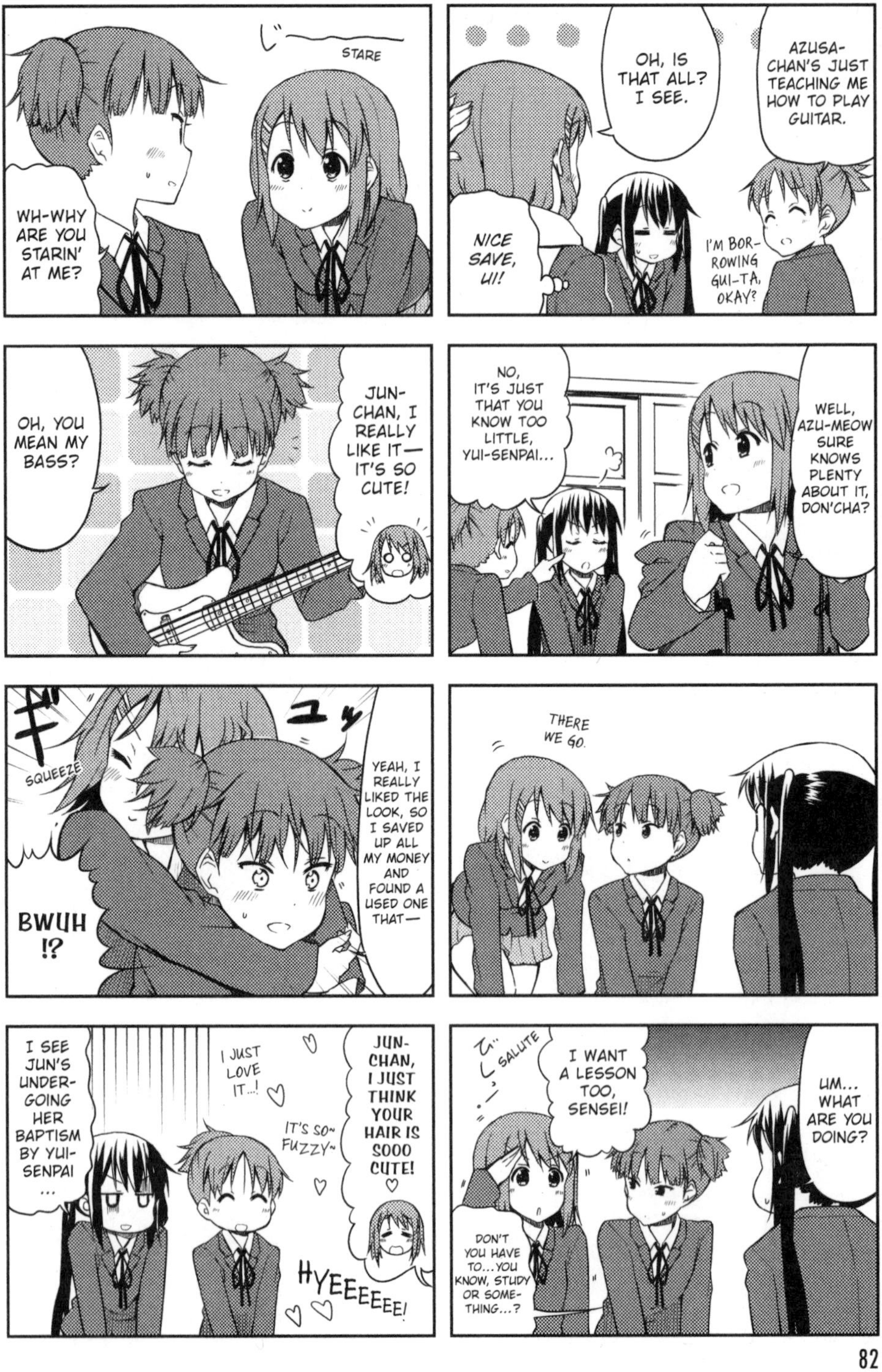
AZUSA-CHAN'S JUST TEACHING ME HOW TO PLAY GUITAR.
OH, IS THAT ALL? I SEE.
I'M BORROWING GUI-TA, OKAY?
NICE SAVE, UI!
WELL, AZU-MEOW SURE KNOWS PLENTY ABOUT IT, DON'CHA?
NO, IT'S JUST THAT YOU KNOW TOO LITTLE, YUI-SENPAI...
THERE WE GO.
UM... WHAT ARE YOU DOING?
I WANT A LESSON TOO, SENSEI!
SALUTE
DON'T YOU HAVE TO...YOU KNOW, STUDY OR SOMETHING...?
STARE
WH-WHY ARE YOU STARIN' AT ME?
JUN-CHAN, I REALLY LIKE IT—IT'S SO CUTE!
OH, YOU MEAN MY BASS?
YEAH, I REALLY LIKED THE LOOK, SO I SAVED UP ALL MY MONEY AND FOUND A USED ONE THAT—
SQUEEZE
BWUH !?
JUN-CHAN, I JUST THINK YOUR HAIR IS SOOO CUTE!
I JUST LOVE IT..!
IT'S SO~ FUZZY~
HYEEEEEEE!
I SEE JUN'S UNDERGOING HER BAPTISM BY YUI-SENPAI ...

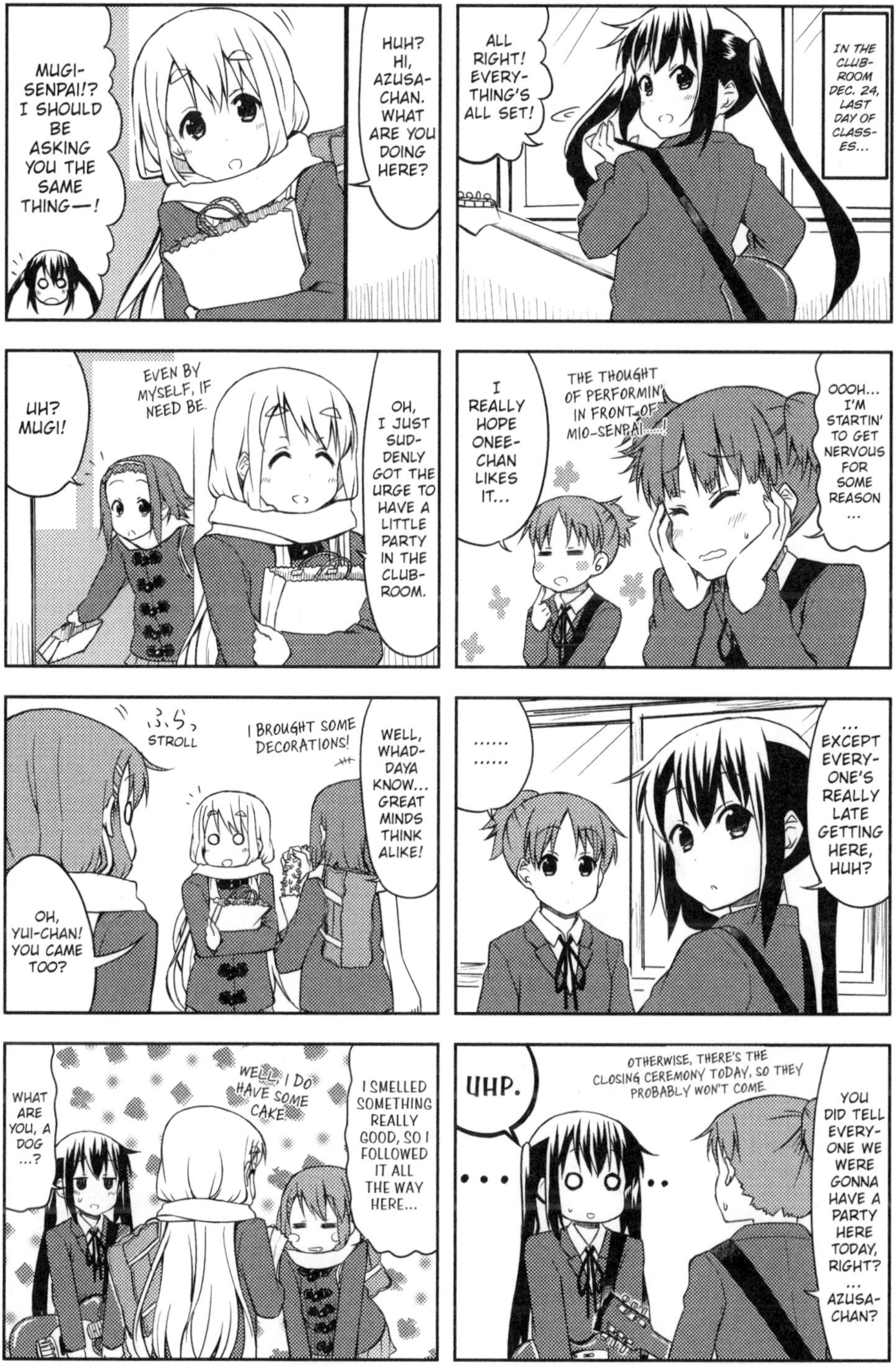
IN THE CLUBROOM DEC. 24, LAST DAY OF CLASSES...
ALL RIGHT! EVERYTHING'S ALL SET!
OOOH... I'M STARTIN' TO GET NERVOUS FOR SOME REASON...
THE THOUGHT OF PERFORMIN' IN FRONT OF MIO-SENPAI......!
I REALLY HOPE ONEE-CHAN LIKES IT...
...EXCEPT EVERYONE'S REALLY LATE GETTING HERE, HUH?
....
YOU DID TELL EVERYONE WE WERE GONNA HAVE A PARTY HERE TODAY, RIGHT? ...AZUSA-CHAN?
OTHERWISE, THERE'S THE CLOSING CEREMONY TODAY, SO THEY PROBABLY WON'T COME.
UHP.
...
..
HUH? HI, AZUSA-CHAN. WHAT ARE YOU DOING HERE?
MUGI-SENPAI!? I SHOULD BE ASKING YOU THE SAME THING—!
OH, I JUST SUDDENLY GOT THE URGE TO HAVE A LITTLE PARTY IN THE CLUBROOM.
EVEN BY MYSELF, IF NEED BE.
UH? MUGI!
WELL, WHADDAYA KNOW... GREAT MINDS THINK ALIKE!
I BROUGHT SOME DECORATIONS!
ふらっ STROLL
OH, YUI-CHAN! YOU CAME TOO?
I SMELLED SOMETHING REALLY GOOD, SO I FOLLOWED IT ALL THE WAY HERE...
WELL, I DO HAVE SOME CAKE.
WHAT ARE YOU, A DOG...?

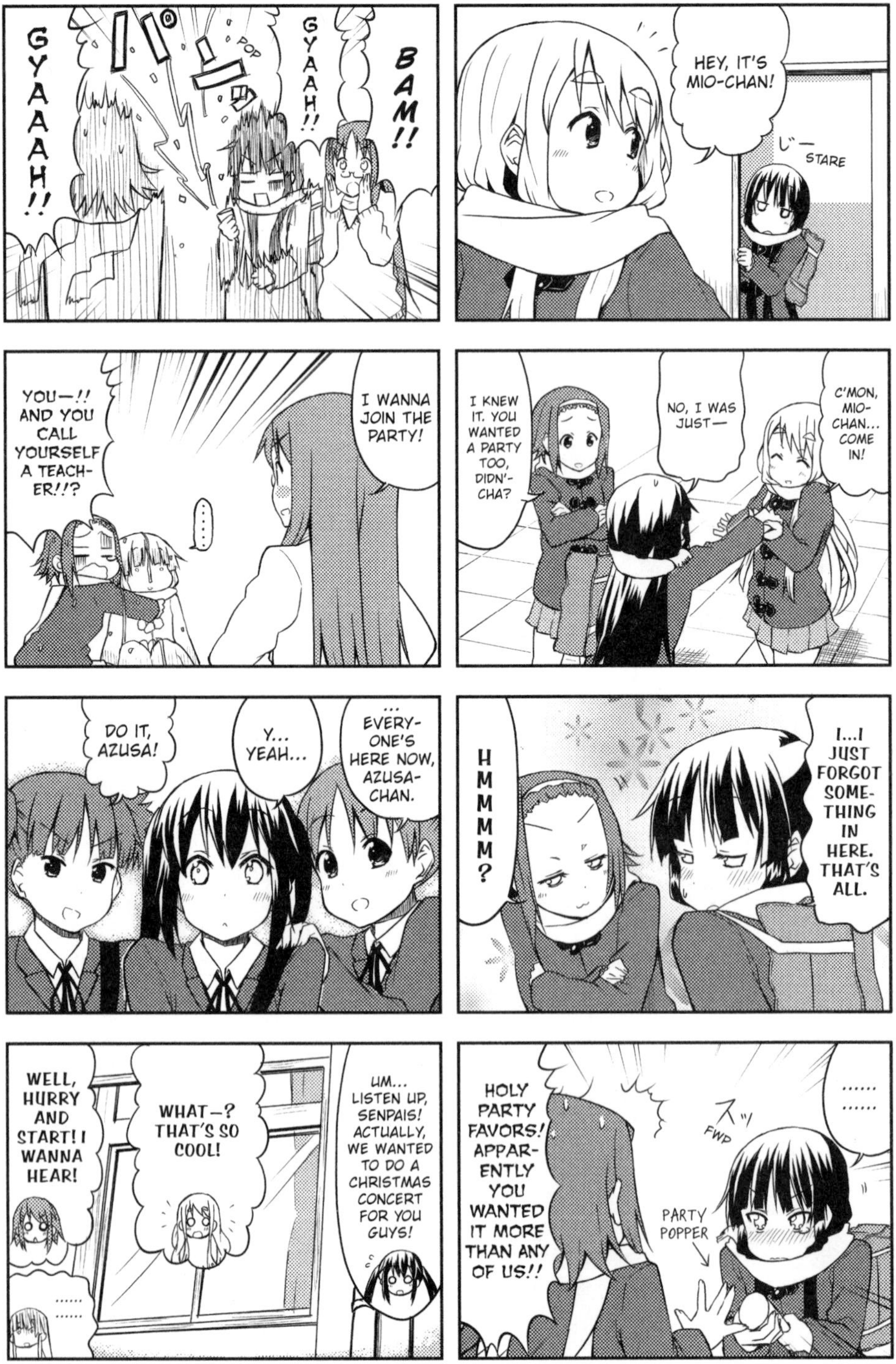
HEY, IT'S MIO-CHAN!
じー STARE
C'MON, MIO-CHAN... COME IN!
NO, I WAS JUST—
I KNEW IT. YOU WANTED A PARTY TOO, DIDN'CHA?
I...I JUST FORGOT SOMETHING IN HERE. THAT'S ALL.
HMMMM?
......
......
スッ FWP
HOLY PARTY FAVORS! APPARENTLY YOU WANTED IT MORE THAN ANY OF US!!
PARTY POPPER
BAM!!
GYAAAH!!
POP
GYAAAAH!!
I WANNA JOIN THE PARTY!
......
YOU—!! AND YOU CALL YOURSELF A TEACHER!!?
...EVERYONE'S HERE NOW, AZUSA-CHAN.
Y... YEAH...
DO IT, AZUSA!
UM... LISTEN UP, SENPAIS! ACTUALLY, WE WANTED TO DO A CHRISTMAS CONCERT FOR YOU GUYS!
WHAT—? THAT'S SO COOL!
WELL, HURRY AND START! I WANNA HEAR!
......
......

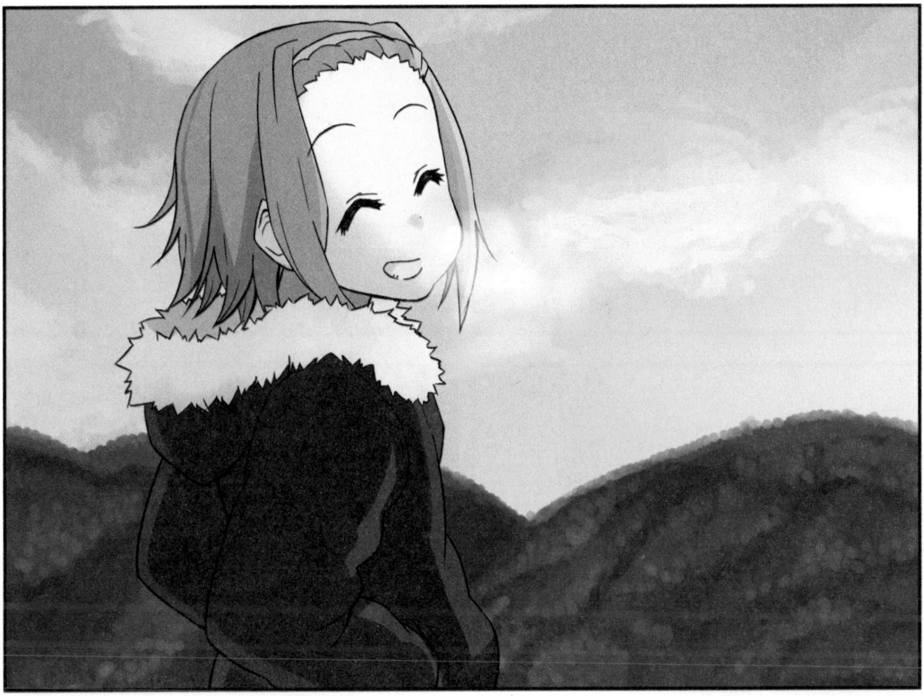

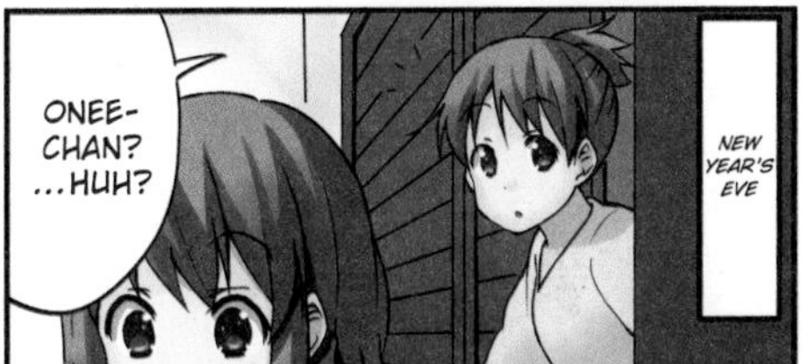
NEW YEAR'S EVE
ONEE-CHAN? ...HUH?
RUMMAGE
RUMMAGE

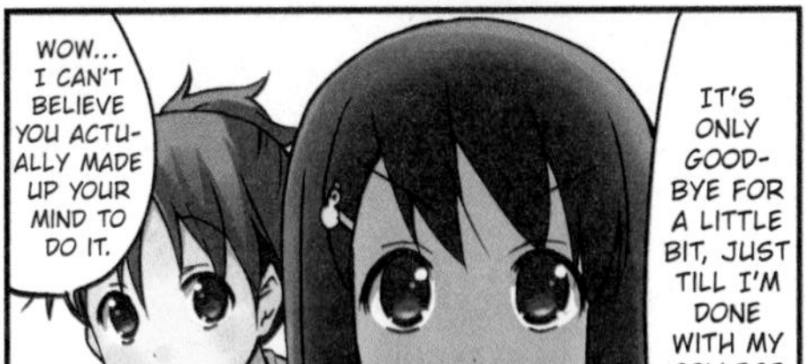
IT'S ONLY GOOD-BYE FOR A LITTLE BIT, JUST TILL I'M DONE WITH MY COLLEGE ENTRANCE EXAM... OKAY?
WOW... I CAN'T BELIEVE YOU ACTU-ALLY MADE UP YOUR MIND TO DO IT.

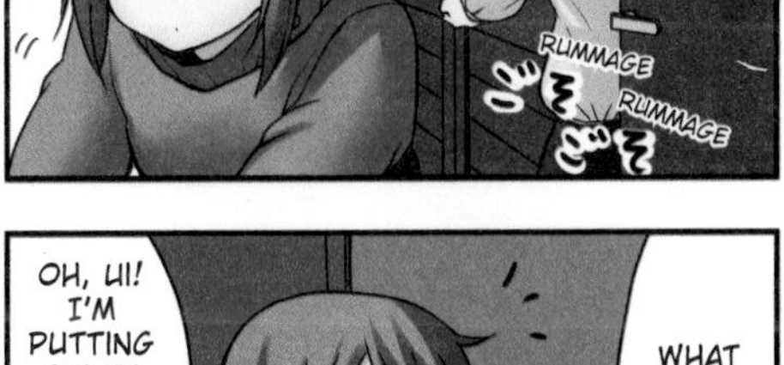
WHAT ARE YOU DOING?
OH, UI! I'M PUTTING GUI-TA AWAY IN THE CLOSET FOR NOW.

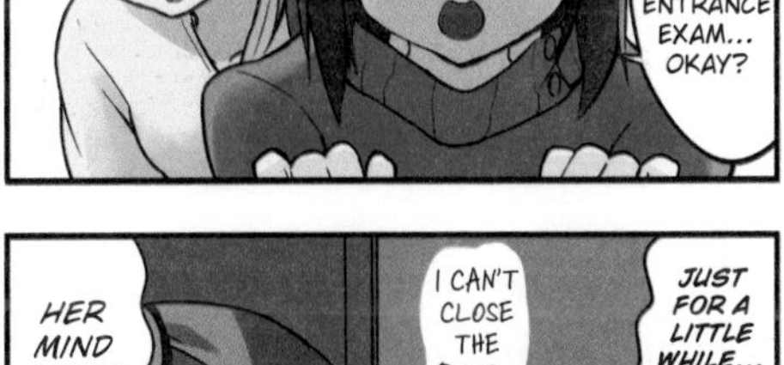
JUST FOR A LITTLE WHILE... IT'LL BE OVER BEFORE WE KNOW IT...
I CAN'T CLOSE THE DOOR...
HER MIND ISN'T MADE UP AT ALL!

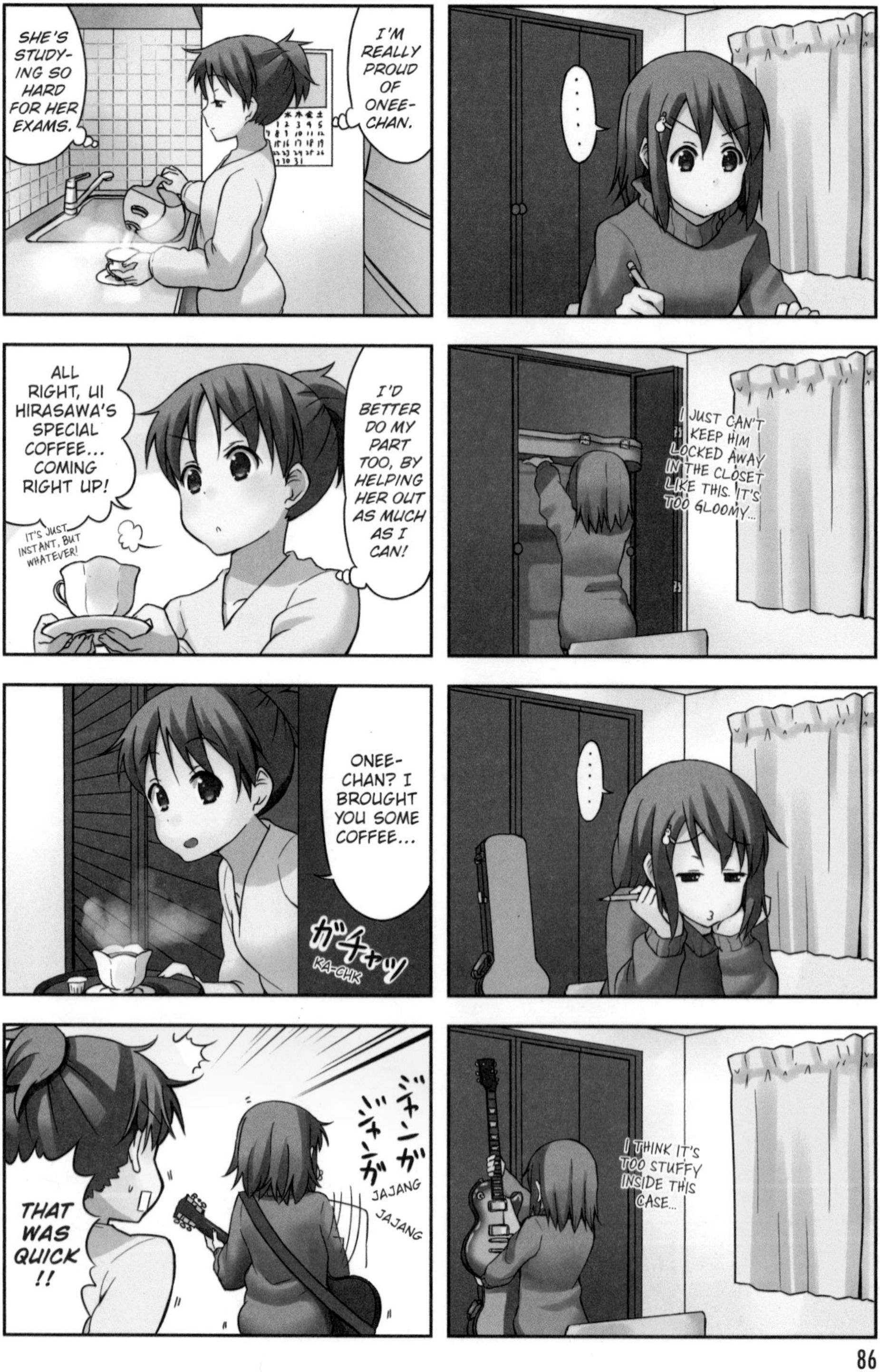
......
I JUST CAN'T KEEP HIM LOCKED AWAY IN THE CLOSET LIKE THIS. IT'S TOO GLOOMY...
......
I THINK IT'S TOO STUFFY INSIDE THIS CASE...
I'M REALLY PROUD OF ONEE-CHAN.
SHE'S STUDYING SO HARD FOR HER EXAMS.
I'D BETTER DO MY PART TOO, BY HELPING HER OUT AS MUCH AS I CAN!
ALL RIGHT, UI HIRASAWA'S SPECIAL COFFEE... COMING RIGHT UP!
IT'S JUST INSTANT, BUT WHATEVER!
ONEE-CHAN? I BROUGHT YOU SOME COFFEE...
ガチャッ
KA-CHK
ジャンガ ジャンガ
JAJANG JAJANG
THAT WAS QUICK!!

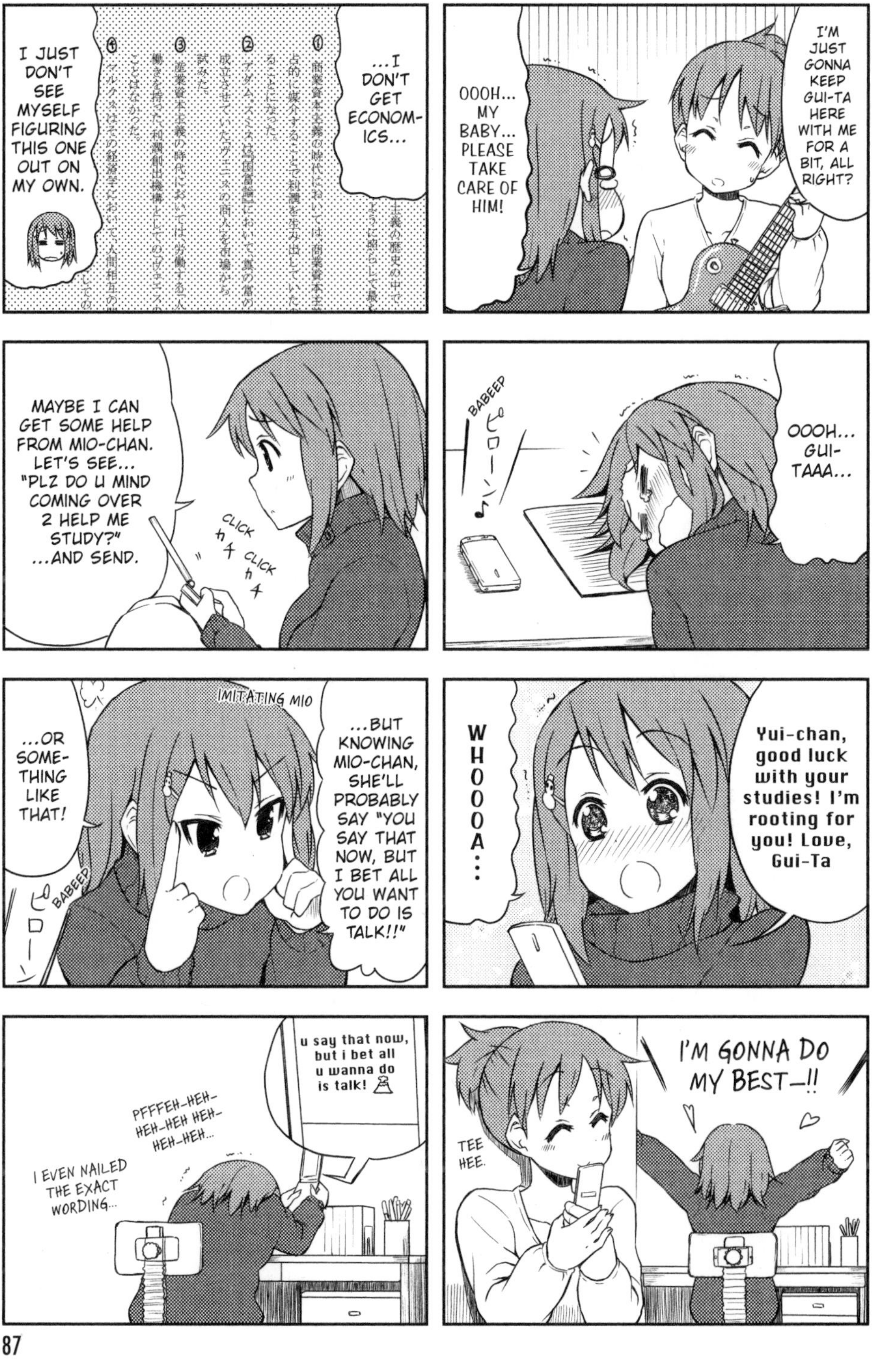
I'M JUST GONNA KEEP GUI-TA HERE WITH ME FOR A BIT, ALL RIGHT?
OOOH... MY BABY... PLEASE TAKE CARE OF HIM!
BABEEP
OOOH... GUI-TAAA...
Yui-chan, good luck with your studies! I'm rooting for you! Love, Gui-Ta
WHOOOOA...
I'M GONNA DO MY BEST-!!
TEE HEE.
...I DON'T GET ECONOMICS...
I JUST DON'T SEE MYSELF FIGURING THIS ONE OUT ON MY OWN.
MAYBE I CAN GET SOME HELP FROM MIO-CHAN. LET'S SEE... "PLZ DO U MIND COMING OVER 2 HELP ME STUDY?" ...AND SEND.
CLICK
CLICK
IMITATING MIO
...BUT KNOWING MIO-CHAN, SHE'LL PROBABLY SAY "YOU SAY THAT NOW, BUT I BET ALL YOU WANT TO DO IS TALK!!"
...OR SOMETHING LIKE THAT!
BABEEP
u say that now, but i bet all u wanna do is talk!
PFFFEH-HEH-HEH-HEH HEH-HEH-HEH...
I EVEN NAILED THE EXACT WORDING...

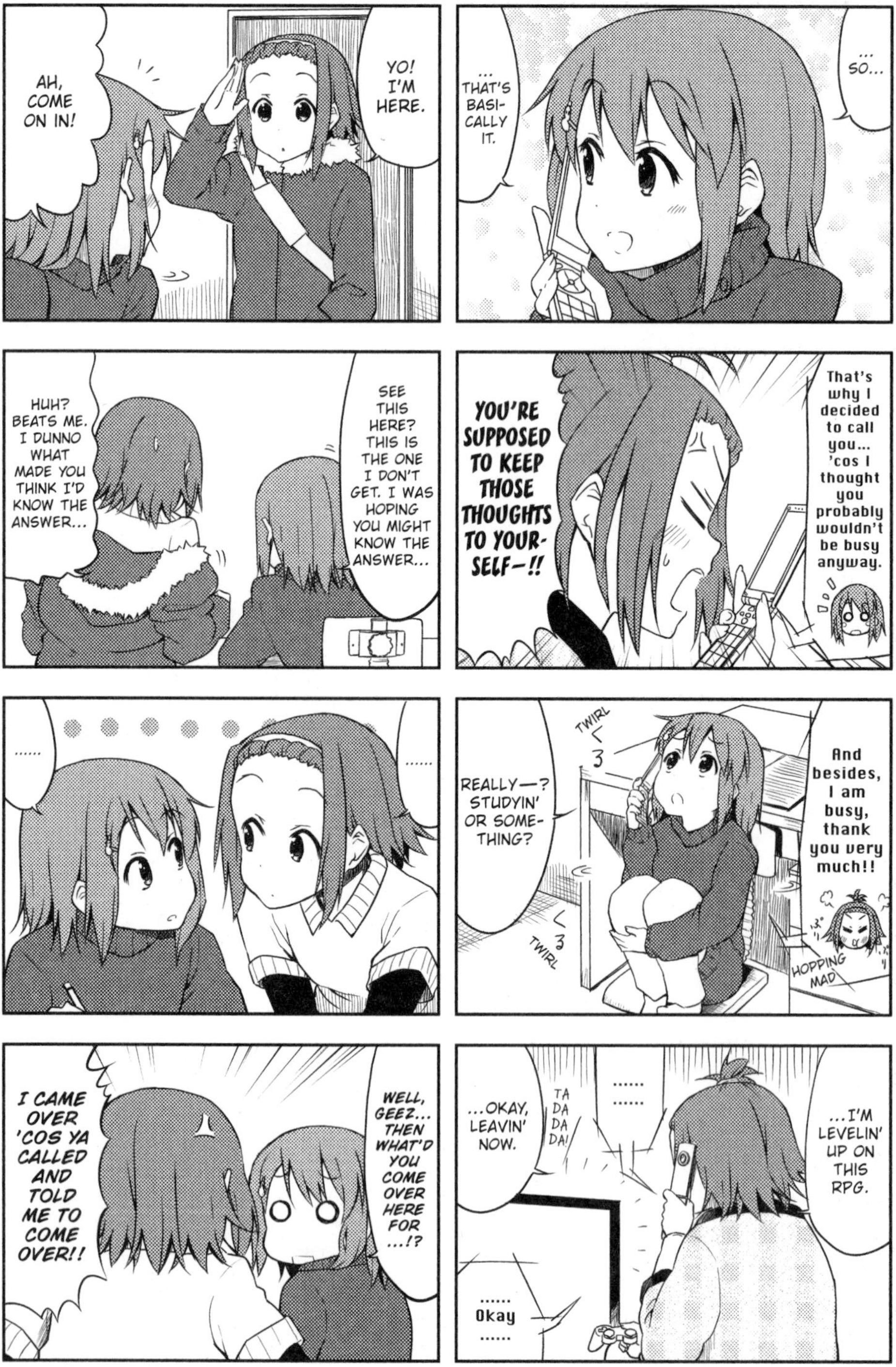
... SO...
... THAT'S BASI-CALLY IT.
That's why I decided to call you... 'cos I thought you probably wouldn't be busy anyway.
YOU'RE SUPPOSED TO KEEP THOSE THOUGHTS TO YOUR-SELF—!!
And besides, I am busy, thank you very much!!
HOPPING MAD
TWIRL
REALLY—? STUDYIN' OR SOME-THING?
TWIRL
...I'M LEVELIN' UP ON THIS RPG.
......
......
TA DA DA DA!
...OKAY, LEAVIN' NOW.
......
Okay
......
YO! I'M HERE.
AH, COME ON IN!
SEE THIS HERE? THIS IS THE ONE I DON'T GET. I WAS HOPING YOU MIGHT KNOW THE ANSWER...
HUH? BEATS ME. I DUNNO WHAT MADE YOU THINK I'D KNOW THE ANSWER...
......
......
WELL, GEEZ... THEN WHAT'D YOU COME OVER HERE FOR ...!?
I CAME OVER 'COS YA CALLED AND TOLD ME TO COME OVER!!

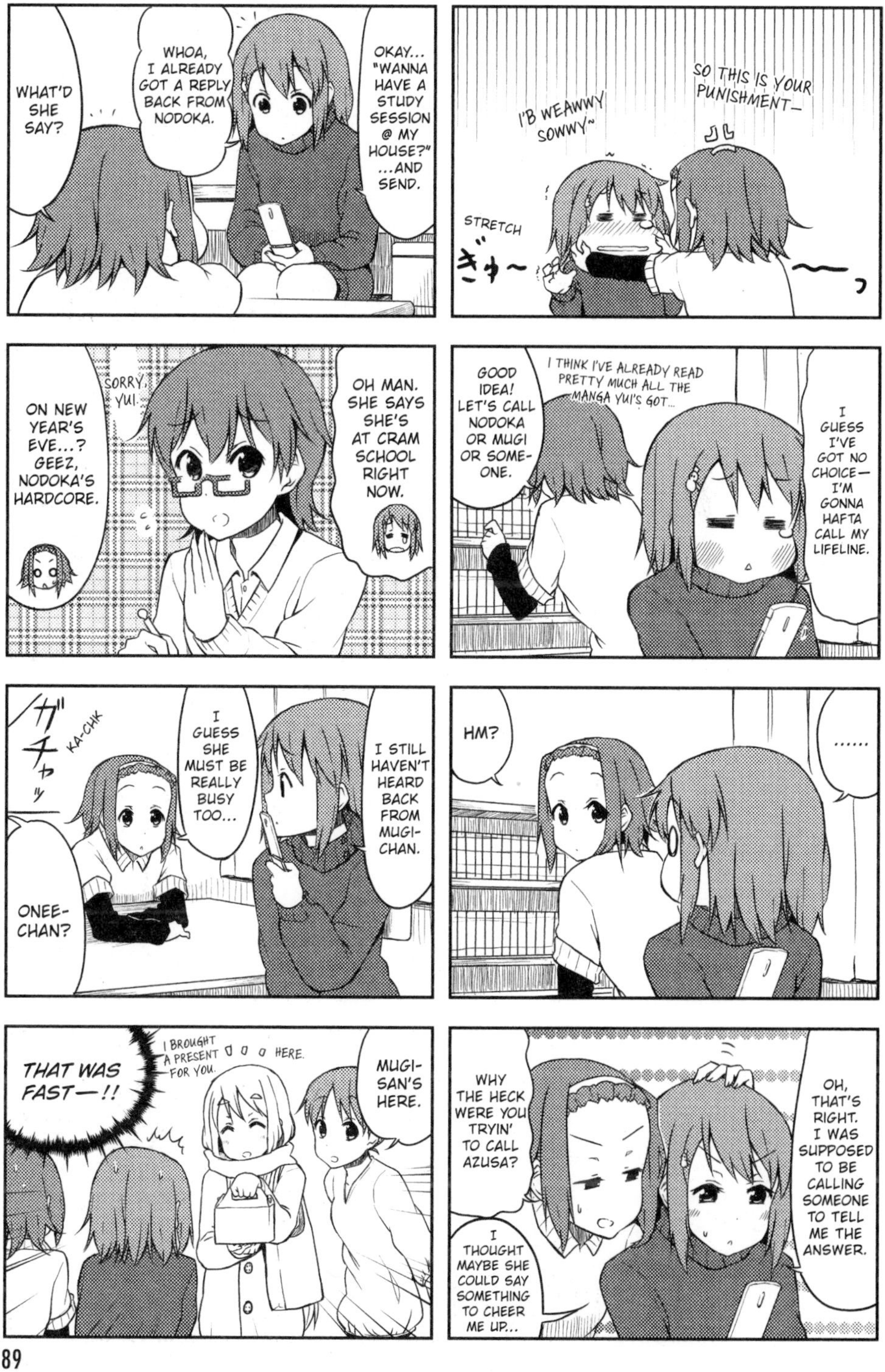
SO THIS IS YOUR PUNISHMENT—
I'B WEAWWY SOWWY~
STRETCH
ぎゅ~
I GUESS I'VE GOT NO CHOICE— I'M GONNA HAFTA CALL MY LIFELINE.
I THINK I'VE ALREADY READ PRETTY MUCH ALL THE MANGA YUI'S GOT...
GOOD IDEA! LET'S CALL NODOKA OR MUGI OR SOME-ONE.
......
HM?
OH, THAT'S RIGHT. I WAS SUPPOSED TO BE CALLING SOMEONE TO TELL ME THE ANSWER.
WHY THE HECK WERE YOU TRYIN' TO CALL AZUSA?
I THOUGHT MAYBE SHE COULD SAY SOMETHING TO CHEER ME UP...
OKAY... "WANNA HAVE A STUDY SESSION @ MY HOUSE?" ...AND SEND.
WHOA, I ALREADY GOT A REPLY BACK FROM NODOKA.
WHAT'D SHE SAY?
OH MAN. SHE SAYS SHE'S AT CRAM SCHOOL RIGHT NOW.
SORRY, YUI.
ON NEW YEAR'S EVE...? GEEZ, NODOKA'S HARDCORE.
I STILL HAVEN'T HEARD BACK FROM MUGI-CHAN.
I GUESS SHE MUST BE REALLY BUSY TOO...
ガチャッ
KA-CHK
ONEE-CHAN?
MUGI-SAN'S HERE.
I BROUGHT A PRESENT FOR YOU.
HERE.
THAT WAS FAST—!!

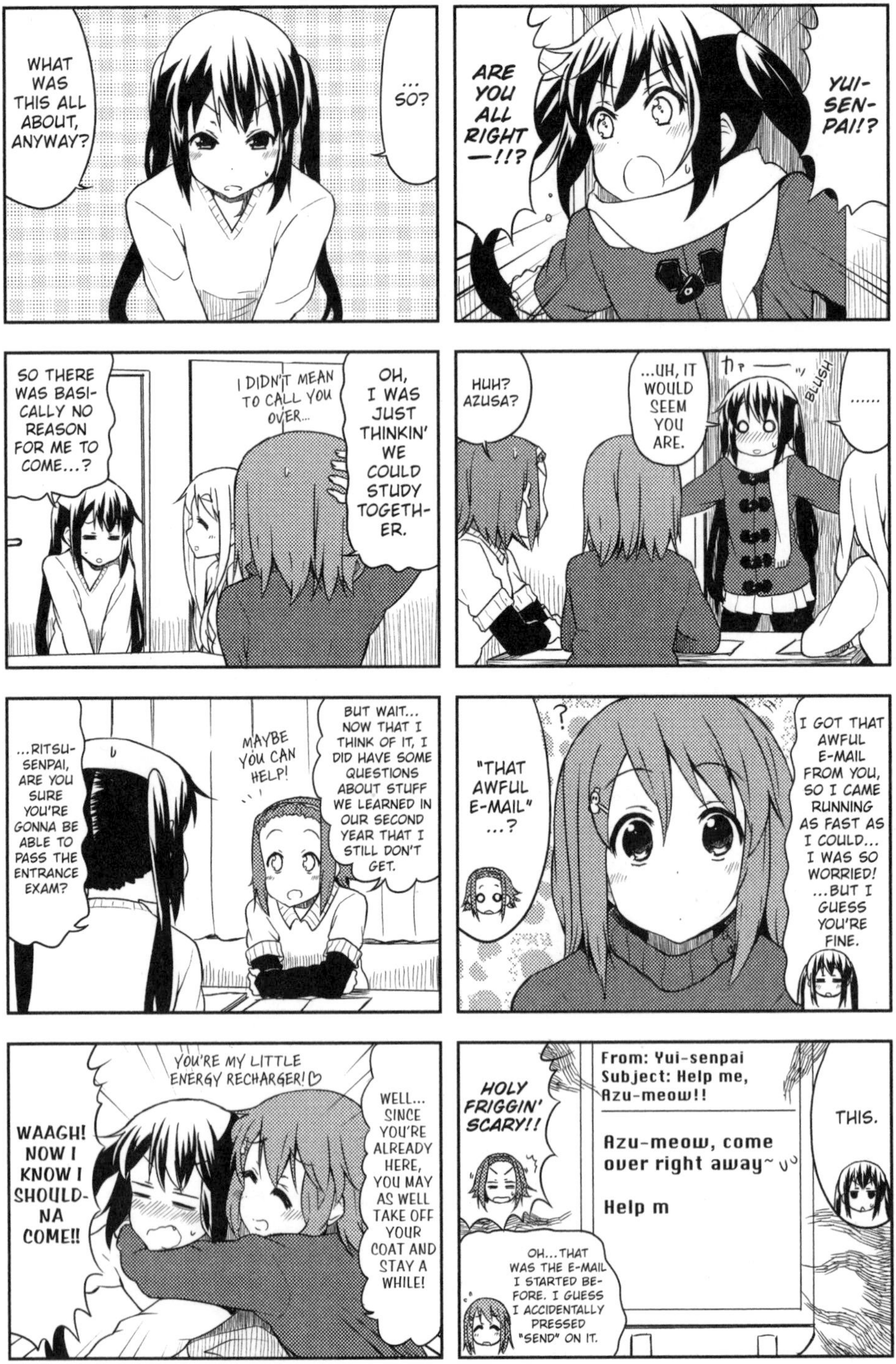
YUI-SENPAI!?
ARE YOU ALL RIGHT—!!?
......
BLUSH
...UH, IT WOULD SEEM YOU ARE.
HUH? AZUSA?
I GOT THAT AWFUL E-MAIL FROM YOU, SO I CAME RUNNING AS FAST AS I COULD... I WAS SO WORRIED! ...BUT I GUESS YOU'RE FINE.
"THAT AWFUL E-MAIL" ...?
THIS.
From: Yui-senpai
Subject: Help me, Azu-meow!!
Azu-meow, come over right away~
Help m
HOLY FRIGGIN' SCARY!!
OH...THAT WAS THE E-MAIL I STARTED BEFORE. I GUESS I ACCIDENTALLY PRESSED "SEND" ON IT.
...SO?
WHAT WAS THIS ALL ABOUT, ANYWAY?
OH, I WAS JUST THINKIN' WE COULD STUDY TOGETHER.
I DIDN'T MEAN TO CALL YOU OVER...
SO THERE WAS BASICALLY NO REASON FOR ME TO COME...?
BUT WAIT... NOW THAT I THINK OF IT, I DID HAVE SOME QUESTIONS ABOUT STUFF WE LEARNED IN OUR SECOND YEAR THAT I STILL DON'T GET.
MAYBE YOU CAN HELP!
...RITSU-SENPAI, ARE YOU SURE YOU'RE GONNA BE ABLE TO PASS THE ENTRANCE EXAM?
WELL... SINCE YOU'RE ALREADY HERE, YOU MAY AS WELL TAKE OFF YOUR COAT AND STAY A WHILE!
YOU'RE MY LITTLE ENERGY RECHARGER! ♡
WAAGH! NOW I KNOW I SHOULDNA COME!!

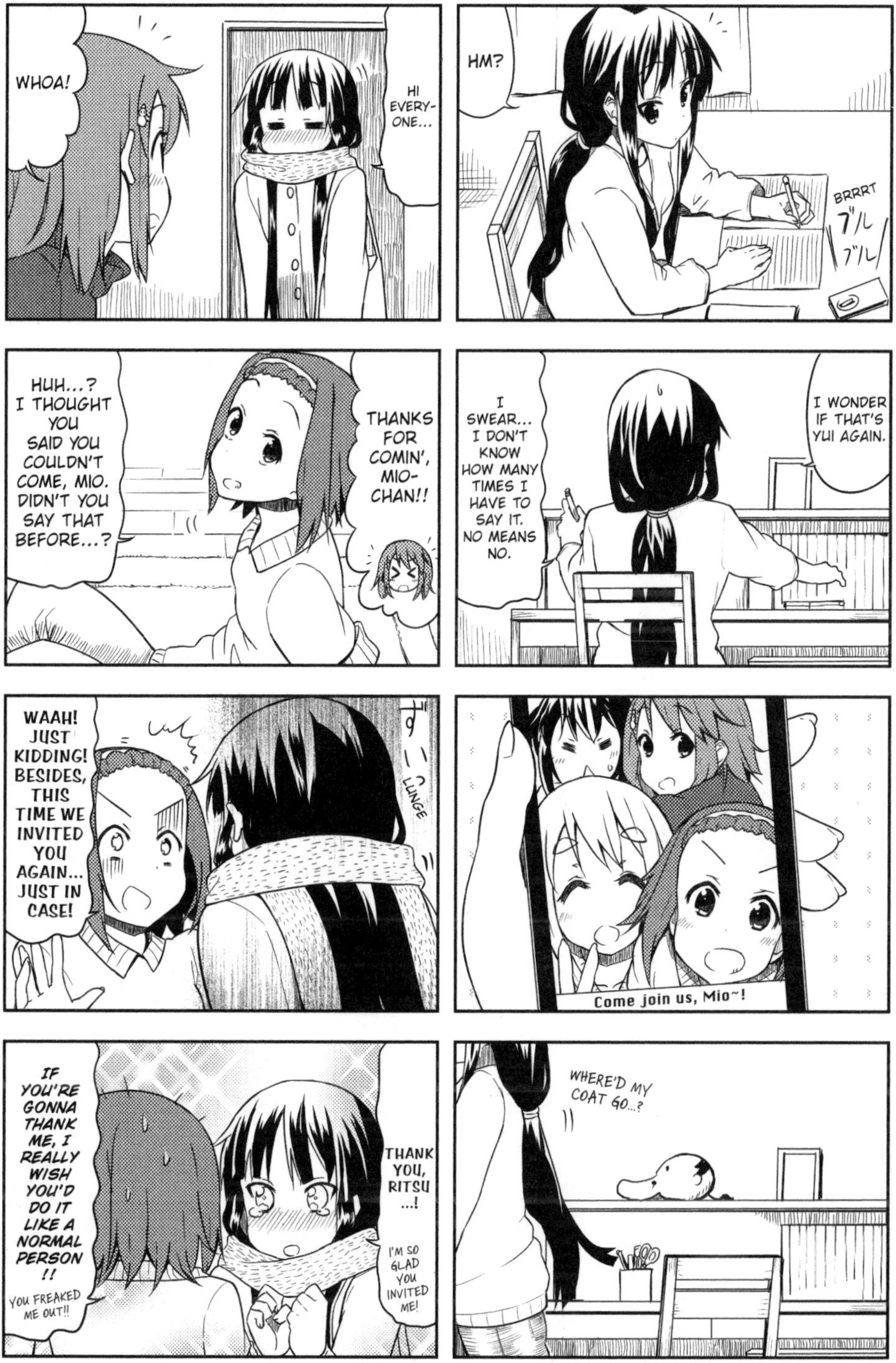
HM?
BRRRT
ブル ブル
I WONDER IF THAT'S YUI AGAIN.
I SWEAR... I DON'T KNOW HOW MANY TIMES I HAVE TO SAY IT. NO MEANS NO.
Come join us, Mio~!
WHERE'D MY COAT GO...?
HI EVERYONE...
WHOA!
THANKS FOR COMIN', MIO-CHAN!!
HUH...? I THOUGHT YOU SAID YOU COULDN'T COME, MIO. DIDN'T YOU SAY THAT BEFORE...?
LUNGE
WAAH! JUST KIDDING! BESIDES, THIS TIME WE INVITED YOU AGAIN... JUST IN CASE!
THANK YOU, RITSU...!
I'M SO GLAD YOU INVITED ME!
IF YOU'RE GONNA THANK ME, I REALLY WISH YOU'D DO IT LIKE A NORMAL PERSON!!
YOU FREAKED ME OUT!!

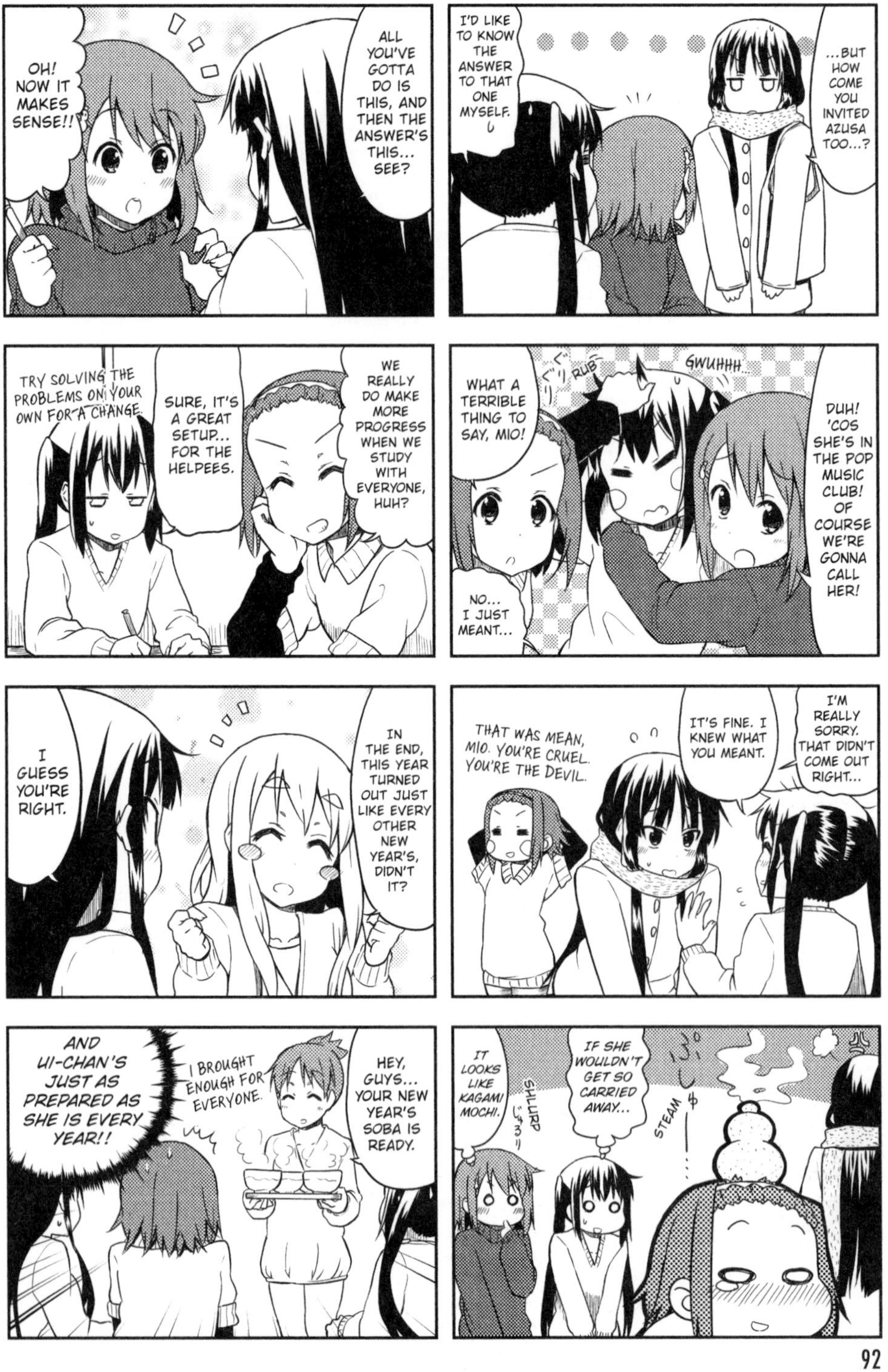
...BUT HOW COME YOU INVITED AZUSA TOO...?
I'D LIKE TO KNOW THE ANSWER TO THAT ONE MYSELF.
DUH! 'COS SHE'S IN THE POP MUSIC CLUB! OF COURSE WE'RE GONNA CALL HER!
GWUHHH...
RUB
WHAT A TERRIBLE THING TO SAY, MIO!
NO... I JUST MEANT...
I'M REALLY SORRY. THAT DIDN'T COME OUT RIGHT...
IT'S FINE. I KNEW WHAT YOU MEANT.
THAT WAS MEAN, MIO. YOU'RE CRUEL. YOU'RE THE DEVIL.
IF SHE WOULDN'T GET SO CARRIED AWAY...
STEAM
IT LOOKS LIKE KAGAMI MOCHI.
SHLURP
ALL YOU'VE GOTTA DO IS THIS, AND THEN THE ANSWER'S THIS... SEE?
OH! NOW IT MAKES SENSE!!
WE REALLY DO MAKE MORE PROGRESS WHEN WE STUDY WITH EVERYONE, HUH?
SURE, IT'S A GREAT SETUP... FOR THE HELPEES.
TRY SOLVING THE PROBLEMS ON YOUR OWN FOR A CHANGE.
IN THE END, THIS YEAR TURNED OUT JUST LIKE EVERY OTHER NEW YEAR'S, DIDN'T IT?
I GUESS YOU'RE RIGHT.
HEY, GUYS... YOUR NEW YEAR'S SOBA IS READY.
I BROUGHT ENOUGH FOR EVERYONE.
AND UI-CHAN'S JUST AS PREPARED AS SHE IS EVERY YEAR!!

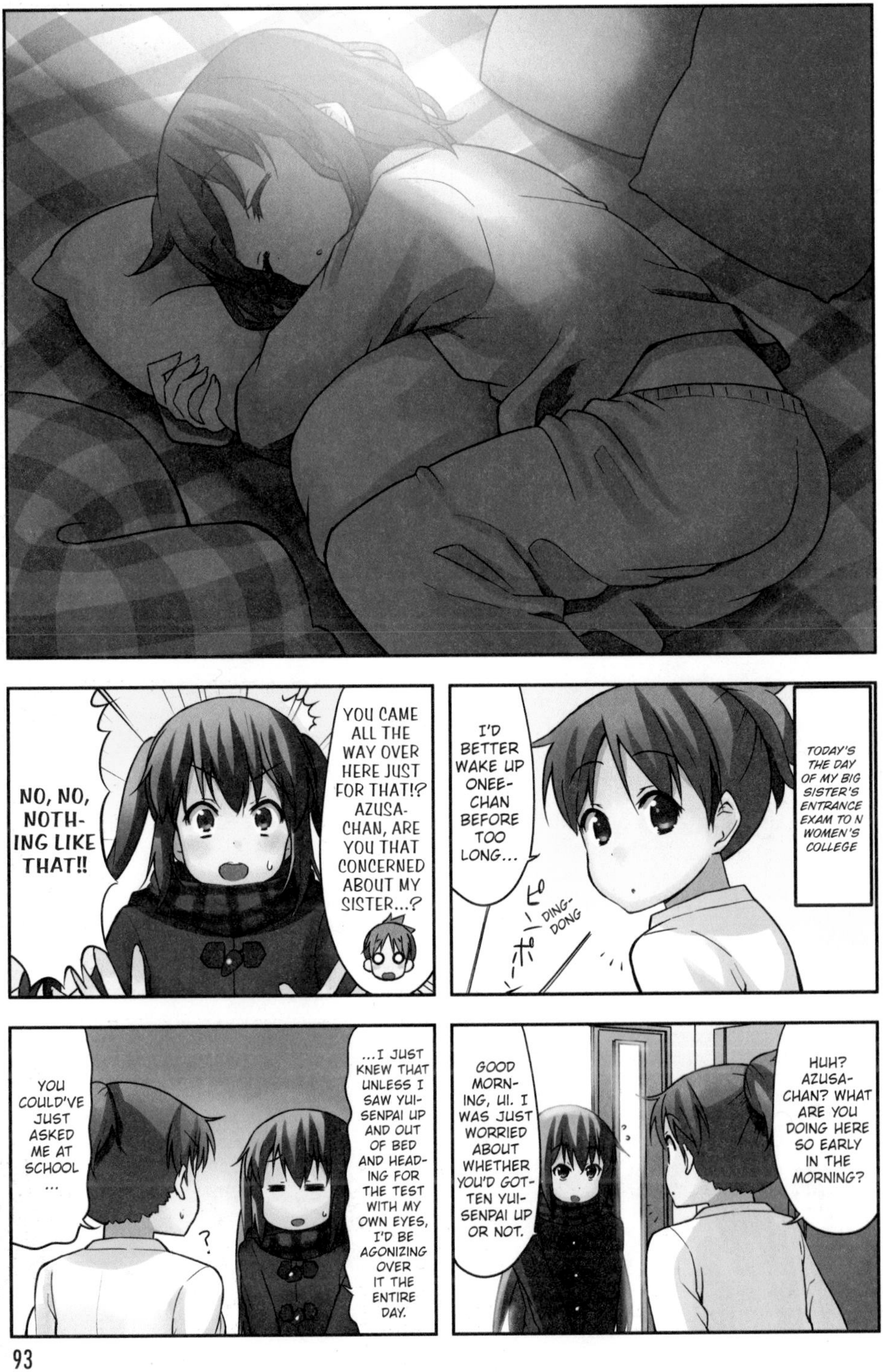
TODAY'S THE DAY OF MY BIG SISTER'S ENTRANCE EXAM TO N WOMEN'S COLLEGE
I'D BETTER WAKE UP ONEE-CHAN BEFORE TOO LONG...
DING-DONG
HUH? AZUSA-CHAN? WHAT ARE YOU DOING HERE SO EARLY IN THE MORNING?
GOOD MORNING, UI. I WAS JUST WORRIED ABOUT WHETHER YOU'D GOTTEN YUI-SENPAI UP OR NOT.
YOU CAME ALL THE WAY OVER HERE JUST FOR THAT!? AZUSA-CHAN, ARE YOU THAT CONCERNED ABOUT MY SISTER...?
NO, NO, NOTHING LIKE THAT!!
...I JUST KNEW THAT UNLESS I SAW YUI-SENPAI UP AND OUT OF BED AND HEADING FOR THE TEST WITH MY OWN EYES, I'D BE AGONIZING OVER IT THE ENTIRE DAY.
YOU COULD'VE JUST ASKED ME AT SCHOOL...

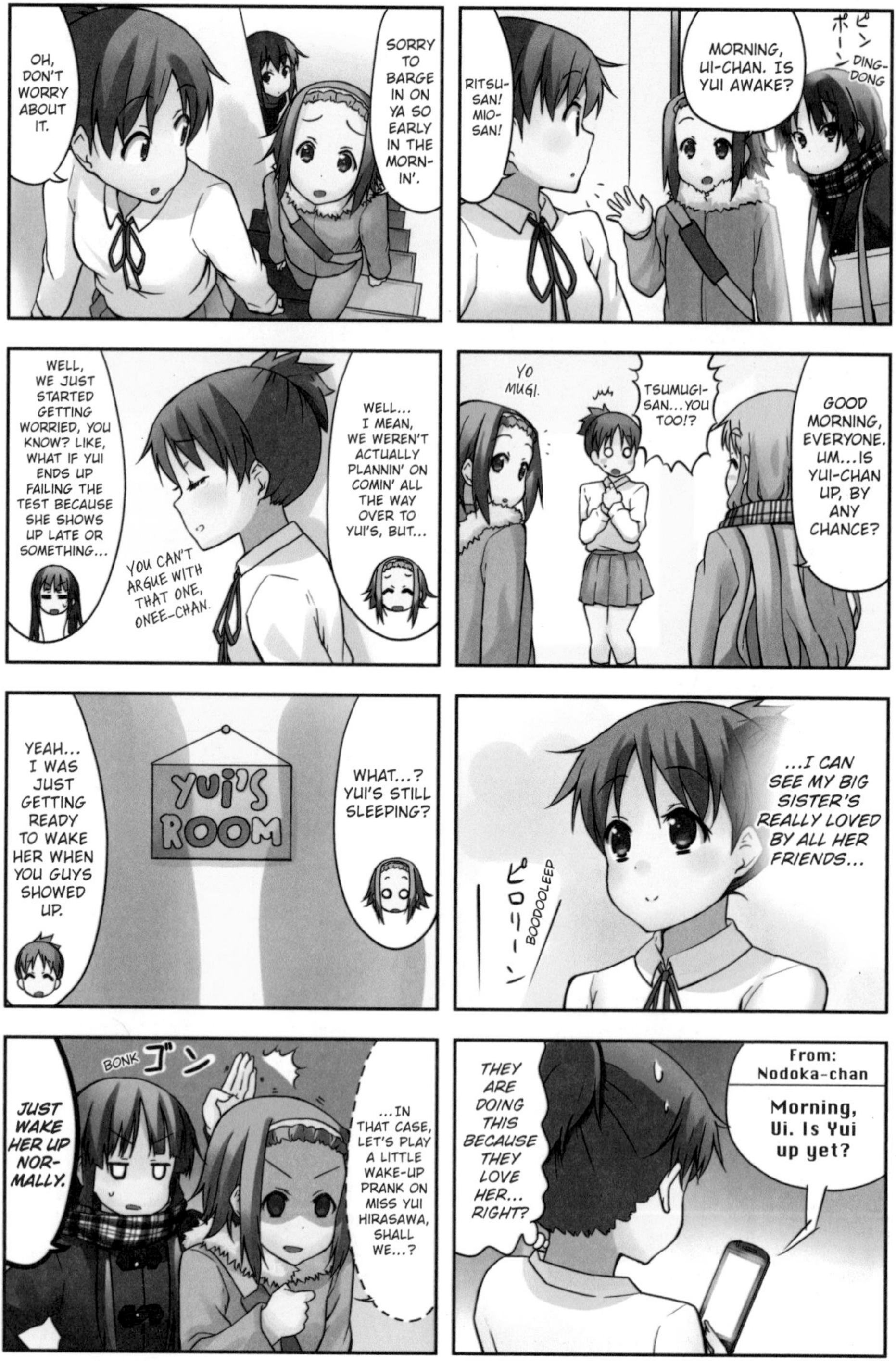
ピンポーン
DING-DONG
MORNING, UI-CHAN. IS YUI AWAKE?
RITSU-SAN! MIO-SAN!
GOOD MORNING, EVERYONE. UM...IS YUI-CHAN UP, BY ANY CHANCE?
TSUMUGI-SAN...YOU TOO!?
YO MUGI.
...I CAN SEE MY BIG SISTER'S REALLY LOVED BY ALL HER FRIENDS...
ピロリーン
BOODOOLEEP
From: Nodoka-chan
Morning, Ui. Is Yui up yet?
THEY ARE DOING THIS BECAUSE THEY LOVE HER... RIGHT?
SORRY TO BARGE IN ON YA SO EARLY IN THE MORNIN'.
OH, DON'T WORRY ABOUT IT.
WELL... I MEAN, WE WEREN'T ACTUALLY PLANNIN' ON COMIN' ALL THE WAY OVER TO YUI'S, BUT...
WELL, WE JUST STARTED GETTING WORRIED, YOU KNOW? LIKE, WHAT IF YUI ENDS UP FAILING THE TEST BECAUSE SHE SHOWS UP LATE OR SOMETHING...
YOU CAN'T ARGUE WITH THAT ONE, ONEE-CHAN.
WHAT...? YUI'S STILL SLEEPING?
YUI'S ROOM
YEAH... I WAS JUST GETTING READY TO WAKE HER WHEN YOU GUYS SHOWED UP.
...IN THAT CASE, LET'S PLAY A LITTLE WAKE-UP PRANK ON MISS YUI HIRASAWA, SHALL WE...?
ゴン
BONK
JUST WAKE HER UP NOR-MALLY.

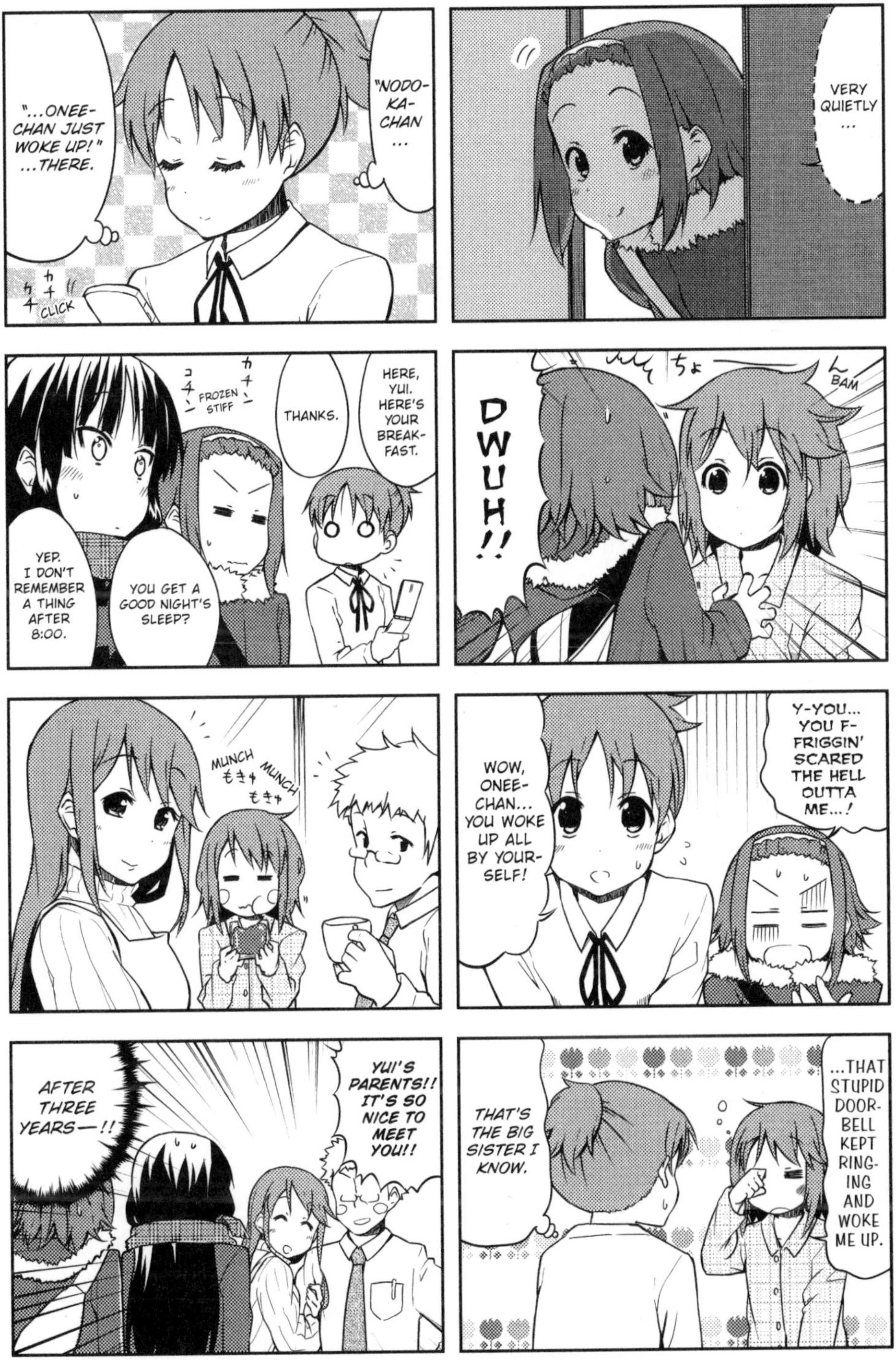
VERY QUIETLY...
DWUH!!
ちょ
ん
BAM
Y-YOU... YOU F-FRIGGIN' SCARED THE HELL OUTTA ME...!
WOW, ONEE-CHAN... YOU WOKE UP ALL BY YOURSELF!
...THAT STUPID DOORBELL KEPT RINGING AND WOKE ME UP.
THAT'S THE BIG SISTER I KNOW.
"NODOKA-CHAN...
"...ONEE-CHAN JUST WOKE UP!" ...THERE.
カチカチ
CLICK
HERE, YUI. HERE'S YOUR BREAKFAST.
THANKS.
カチーン
コチーン
FROZEN STIFF
YOU GET A GOOD NIGHT'S SLEEP?
YEP. I DON'T REMEMBER A THING AFTER 8:00.
MUNCH
もきゅ
MUNCH
もきゅ
YUI'S PARENTS!! IT'S SO NICE TO MEET YOU!!
AFTER THREE YEARS—!!

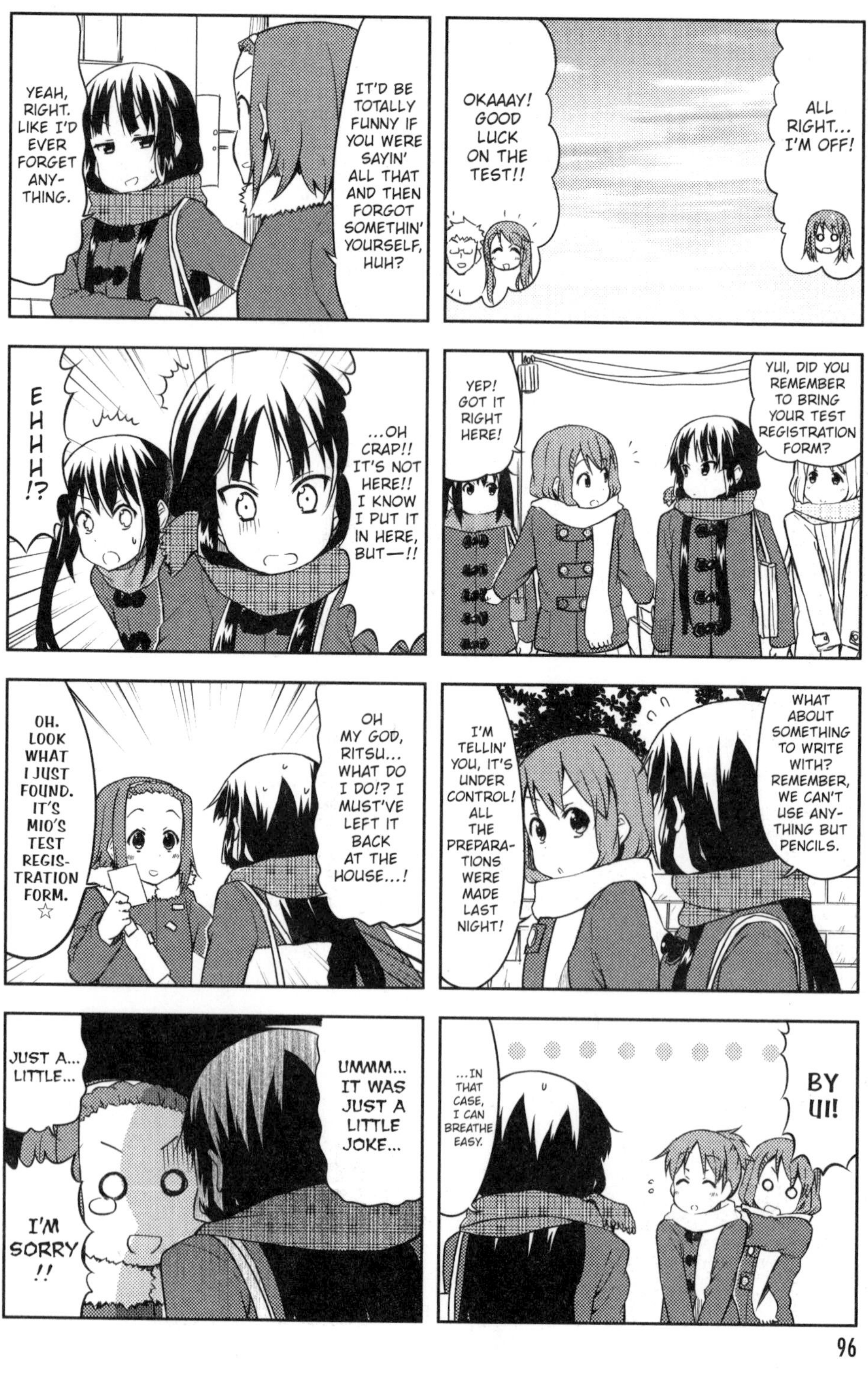
ALL RIGHT... I'M OFF!
OKAAAY! GOOD LUCK ON THE TEST!!
YUI, DID YOU REMEMBER TO BRING YOUR TEST REGISTRATION FORM?
YEP! GOT IT RIGHT HERE!
WHAT ABOUT SOMETHING TO WRITE WITH? REMEMBER, WE CAN'T USE ANYTHING BUT PENCILS.
I'M TELLIN' YOU, IT'S UNDER CONTROL! ALL THE PREPARATIONS WERE MADE LAST NIGHT!
BY UI!
...IN THAT CASE, I CAN BREATHE EASY.
IT'D BE TOTALLY FUNNY IF YOU WERE SAYIN' ALL THAT AND THEN FORGOT SOMETHIN' YOURSELF, HUH?
YEAH, RIGHT. LIKE I'D EVER FORGET ANYTHING.
...OH CRAP!! IT'S NOT HERE!! I KNOW I PUT IT IN HERE, BUT—!!
EHHHH!?
OH MY GOD, RITSU... WHAT DO I DO!? I MUST'VE LEFT IT BACK AT THE HOUSE...!
OH. LOOK WHAT I JUST FOUND. IT'S MIO'S TEST REGISTRATION FORM. ☆
UMMM... IT WAS JUST A LITTLE JOKE...
JUST A... LITTLE...
I'M SORRY!!

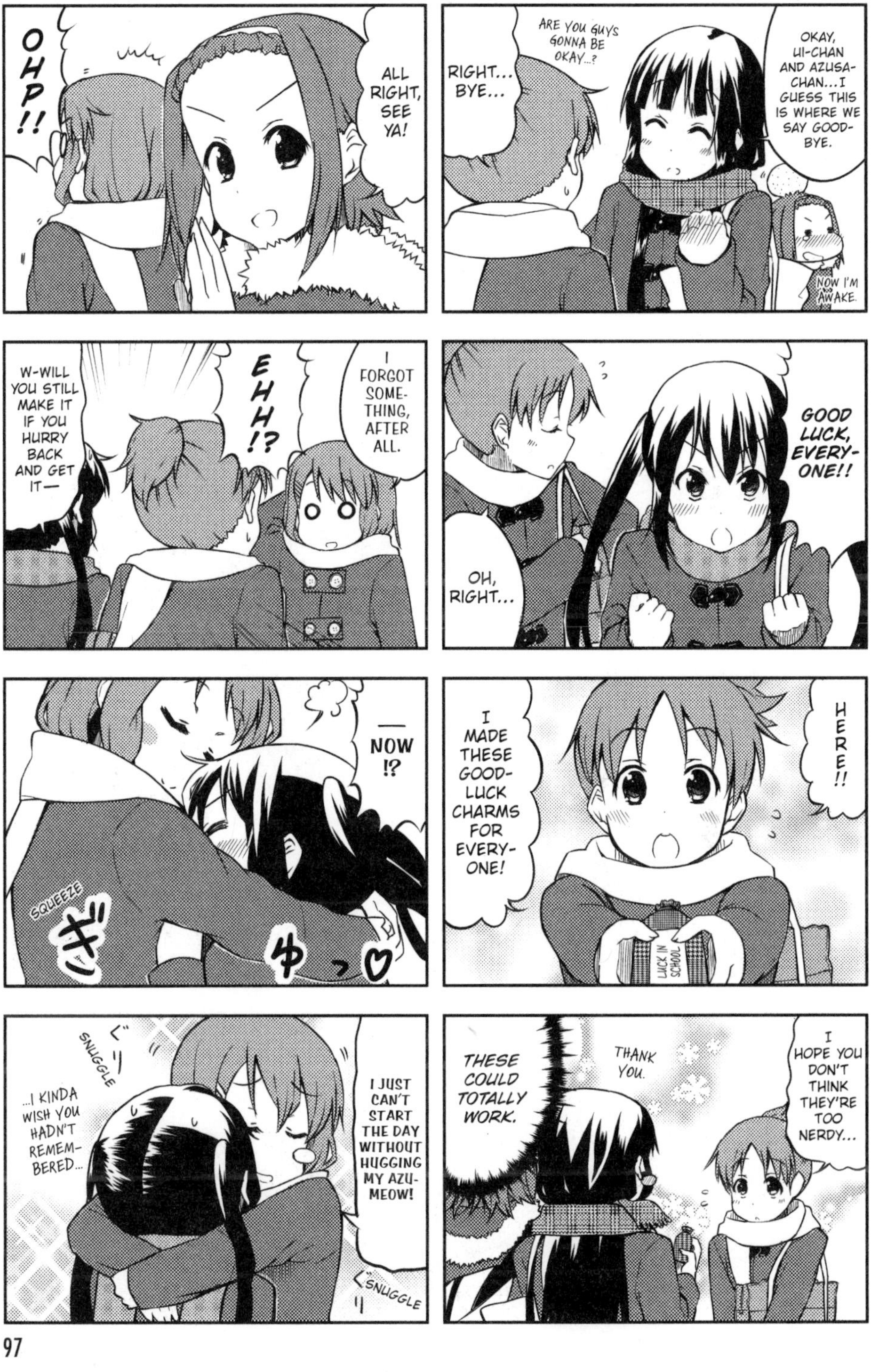
OKAY, UI-CHAN AND AZUSA-CHAN...I GUESS THIS IS WHERE WE SAY GOOD-BYE.
ARE YOU GUYS GONNA BE OKAY...?
RIGHT... BYE...
NOW I'M AWAKE.
GOOD LUCK, EVERYONE!!
OH, RIGHT...
HERE!!
I MADE THESE GOOD-LUCK CHARMS FOR EVERYONE!
LUCK IN SCHOOL
I HOPE YOU DON'T THINK THEY'RE TOO NERDY...
THANK YOU.
THESE COULD TOTALLY WORK.
ALL RIGHT, SEE YA!
OHP!!
I FORGOT SOMETHING, AFTER ALL.
EHH!?
W-WILL YOU STILL MAKE IT IF YOU HURRY BACK AND GET IT—
—NOW!?
SQUEEZE
I JUST CAN'T START THE DAY WITHOUT HUGGING MY AZU-MEOW!
SNUGGLE
...I KINDA WISH YOU HADN'T REMEMBERED...
SNUGGLE

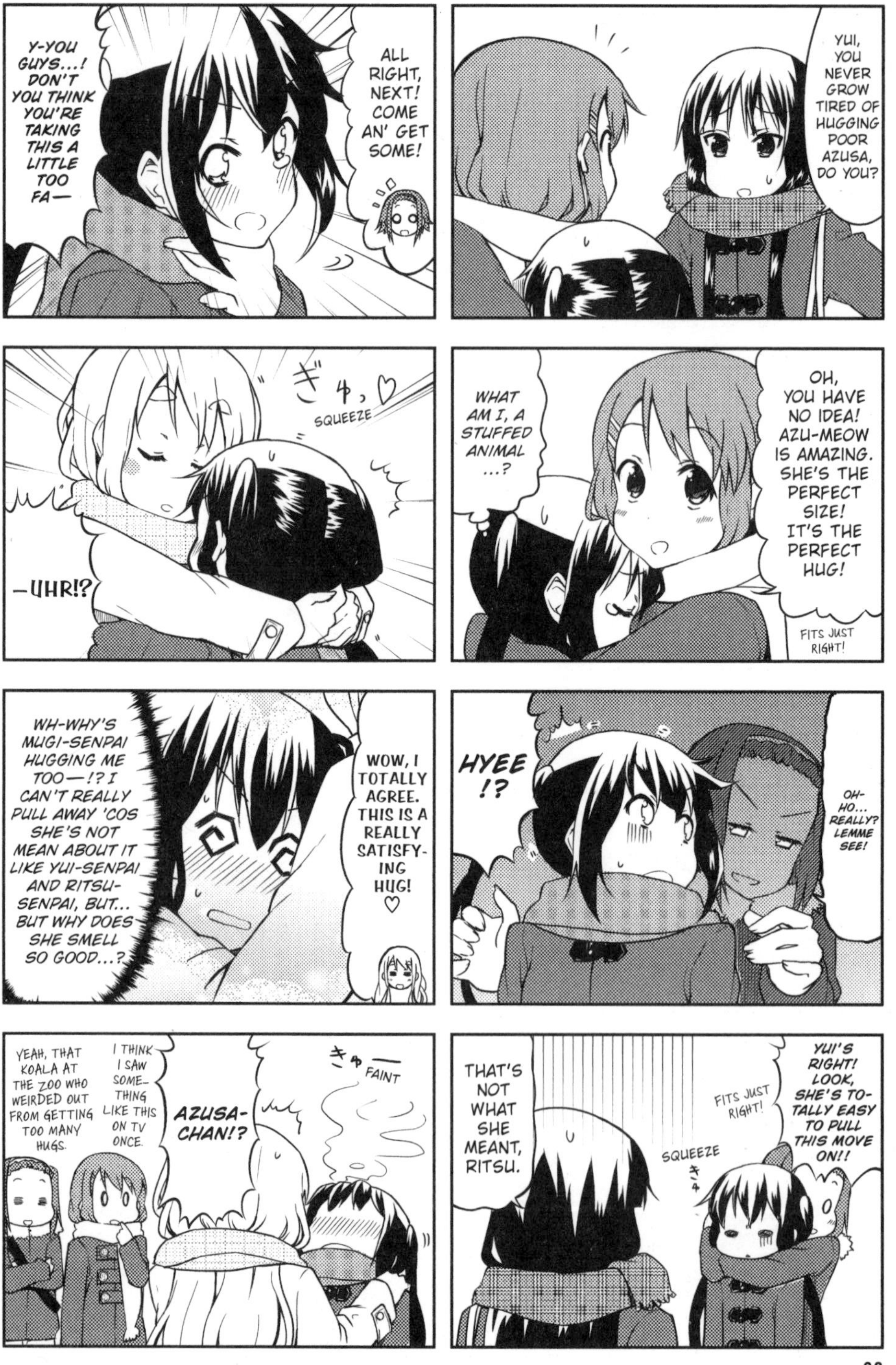
YUI, YOU NEVER GROW TIRED OF HUGGING POOR AZUSA, DO YOU?
OH, YOU HAVE NO IDEA! AZU-MEOW IS AMAZING. SHE'S THE PERFECT SIZE! IT'S THE PERFECT HUG!
WHAT AM I, A STUFFED ANIMAL...?
FITS JUST RIGHT!
OH-HO... REALLY? LEMME SEE!
HYEE !?
YUI'S RIGHT! LOOK, SHE'S TOTALLY EASY TO PULL THIS MOVE ON!!
FITS JUST RIGHT!
THAT'S NOT WHAT SHE MEANT, RITSU.
SQUEEZE
ALL RIGHT, NEXT! COME AN' GET SOME!
Y-YOU GUYS...! DON'T YOU THINK YOU'RE TAKING THIS A LITTLE TOO FA—
ぎゅっ♡
SQUEEZE
—UHR!?
WOW, I TOTALLY AGREE. THIS IS A REALLY SATISFYING HUG! ♡
WH-WHY'S MUGI-SENPAI HUGGING ME TOO—!? I CAN'T REALLY PULL AWAY 'COS SHE'S NOT MEAN ABOUT IT LIKE YUI-SENPAI AND RITSU-SENPAI, BUT... BUT WHY DOES SHE SMELL SO GOOD...?
きゅー
FAINT
AZUSA-CHAN!?
I THINK I SAW SOME-THING LIKE THIS ON TV ONCE.
YEAH, THAT KOALA AT THE ZOO WHO WEIRDED OUT FROM GETTING TOO MANY HUGS.

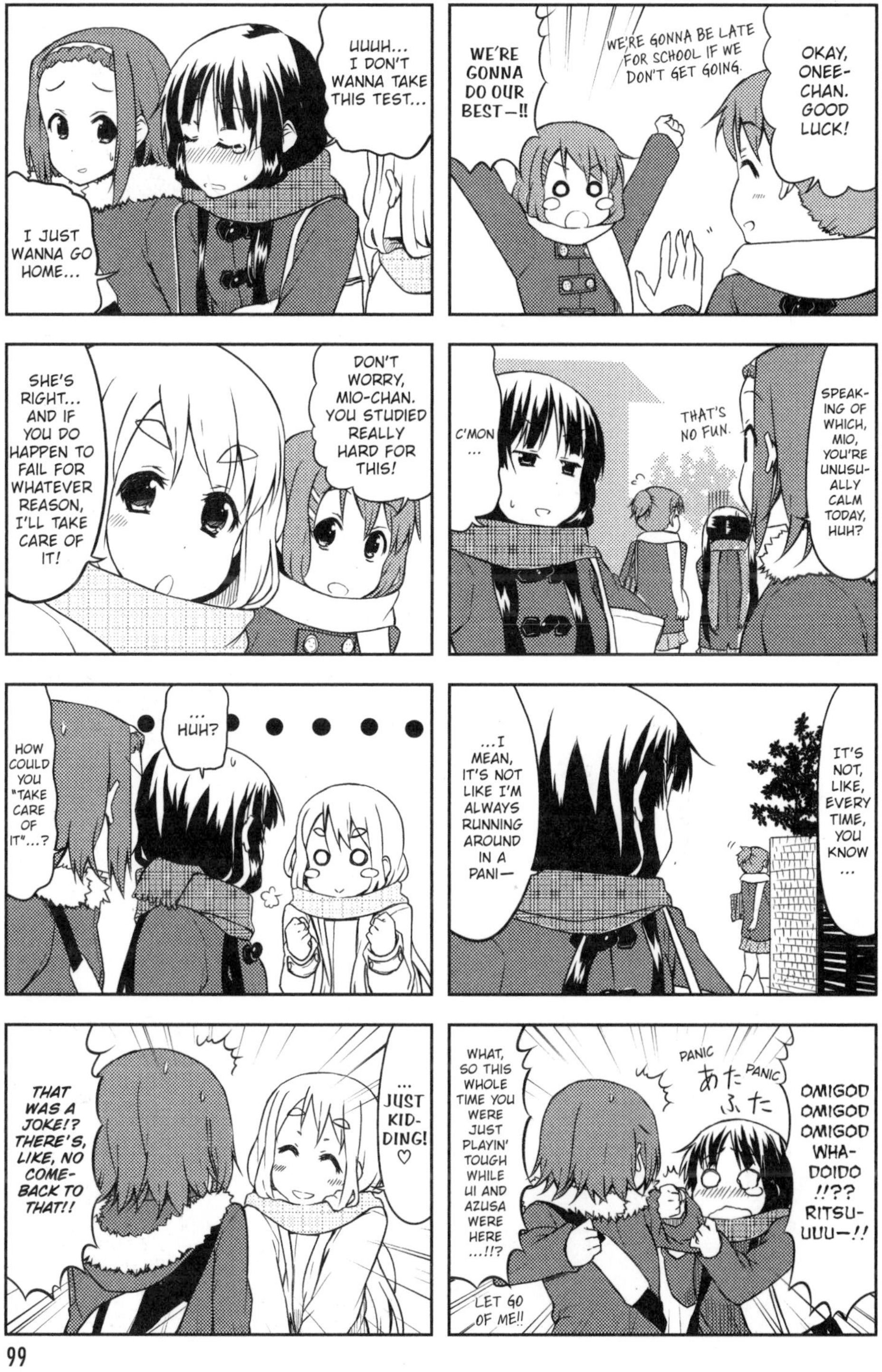
OKAY, ONEE-CHAN. GOOD LUCK!
WE'RE GONNA BE LATE FOR SCHOOL IF WE DON'T GET GOING.
WE'RE GONNA DO OUR BEST—!!
SPEAKING OF WHICH, MIO, YOU'RE UNUSUALLY CALM TODAY, HUH?
THAT'S NO FUN.
C'MON ...
IT'S NOT, LIKE, EVERY TIME, YOU KNOW ...
...I MEAN, IT'S NOT LIKE I'M ALWAYS RUNNING AROUND IN A PANI—
OMIGOD OMIGOD OMIGOD WHA-DOIDO !!?? RITSU-UUU—!!
PANIC
あたふた
PANIC
WHAT, SO THIS WHOLE TIME YOU WERE JUST PLAYIN' TOUGH WHILE UI AND AZUSA WERE HERE ...!!?
LET GO OF ME!!
UUUH... I DON'T WANNA TAKE THIS TEST...
I JUST WANNA GO HOME...
DON'T WORRY, MIO-CHAN. YOU STUDIED REALLY HARD FOR THIS!
SHE'S RIGHT... AND IF YOU DO HAPPEN TO FAIL FOR WHATEVER REASON, I'LL TAKE CARE OF IT!
... HUH?
HOW COULD YOU "TAKE CARE OF IT"...?
... JUST KID-DING! ♡
THAT WAS A JOKE!? THERE'S, LIKE, NO COME-BACK TO THAT!!

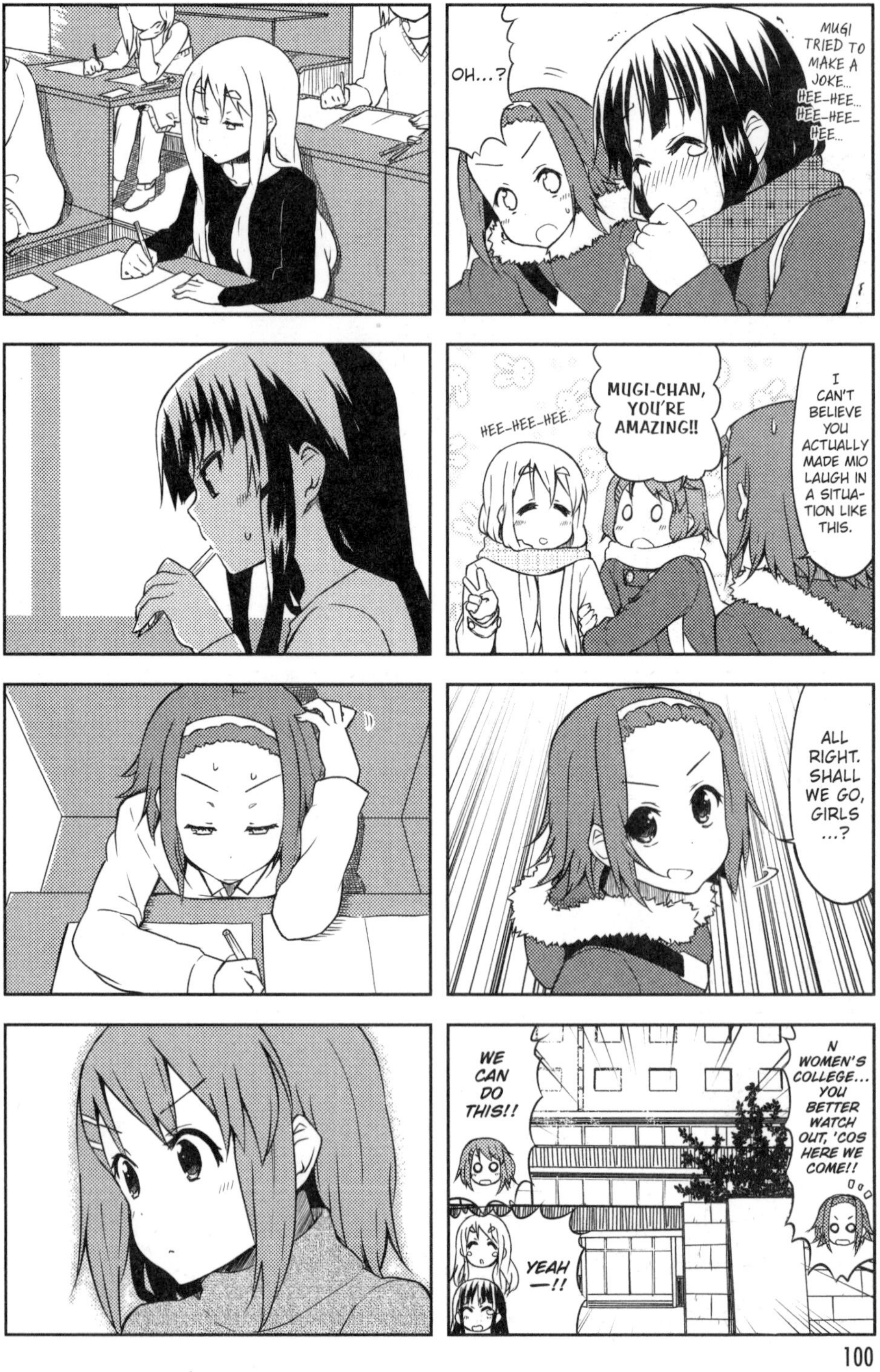
MUGI TRIED TO MAKE A JOKE... HEE-HEE... HEE-HEE-HEE...
OH...?
I CAN'T BELIEVE YOU ACTUALLY MADE MIO LAUGH IN A SITUATION LIKE THIS.
MUGI-CHAN, YOU'RE AMAZING!!
HEE-HEE-HEE.
ALL RIGHT. SHALL WE GO, GIRLS ...?
N WOMEN'S COLLEGE... YOU BETTER WATCH OUT, 'COS HERE WE COME!!
WE CAN DO THIS!!
YEAH—!!

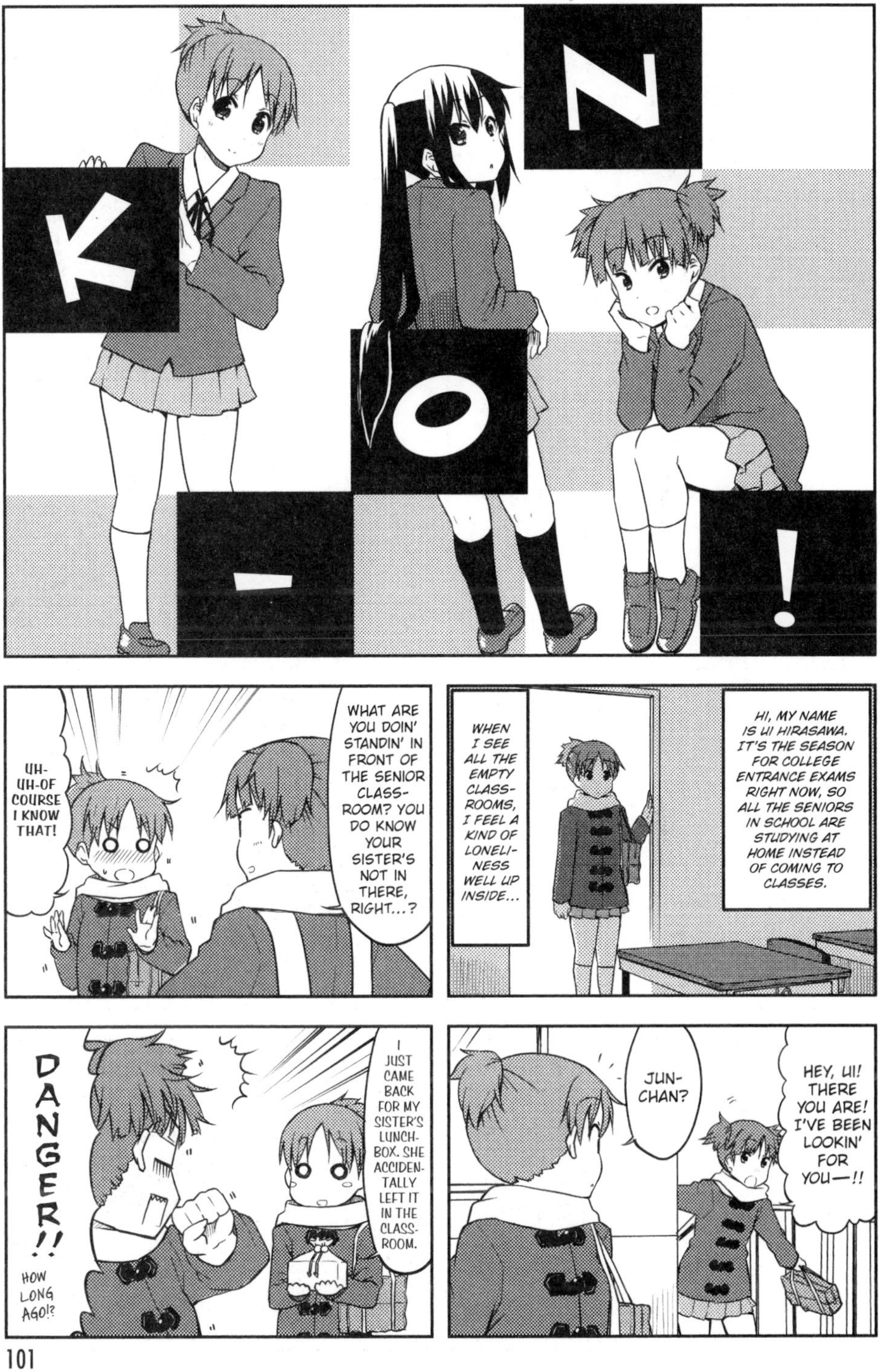
K-ON!
HI, MY NAME IS UI HIRASAWA. IT'S THE SEASON FOR COLLEGE ENTRANCE EXAMS RIGHT NOW, SO ALL THE SENIORS IN SCHOOL ARE STUDYING AT HOME INSTEAD OF COMING TO CLASSES.
WHEN I SEE ALL THE EMPTY CLASSROOMS, I FEEL A KIND OF LONELINESS WELL UP INSIDE...
WHAT ARE YOU DOIN' STANDIN' IN FRONT OF THE SENIOR CLASSROOM? YOU DO KNOW YOUR SISTER'S NOT IN THERE, RIGHT...?
UH-UH-OF COURSE I KNOW THAT!
HEY, UI! THERE YOU ARE! I'VE BEEN LOOKIN' FOR YOU—!!
JUN-CHAN?
I JUST CAME BACK FOR MY SISTER'S LUNCHBOX. SHE ACCIDENTALLY LEFT IT IN THE CLASSROOM.
DANGER!!
HOW LONG AGO!?

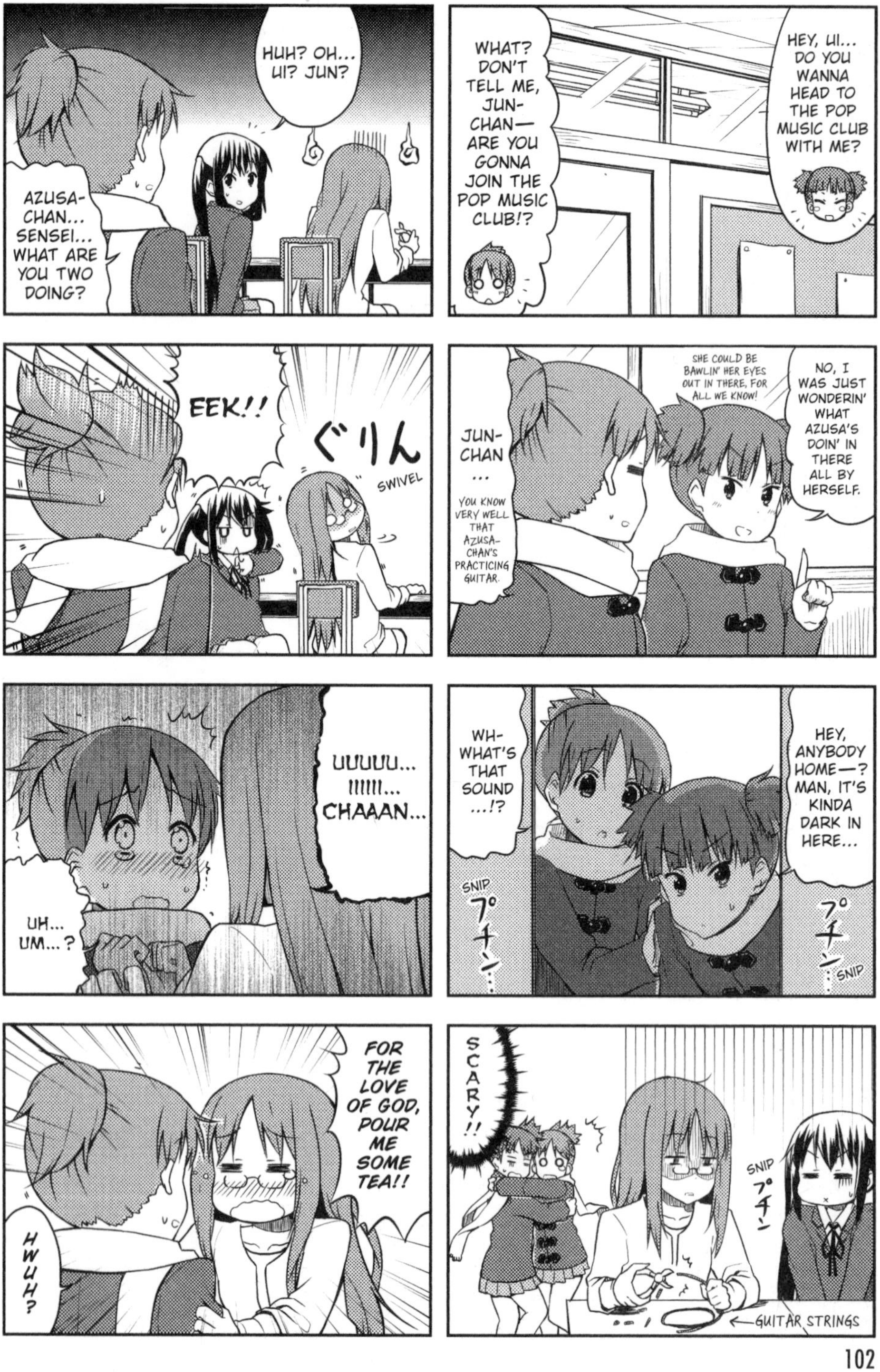
HEY, UI... DO YOU WANNA HEAD TO THE POP MUSIC CLUB WITH ME?
WHAT? DON'T TELL ME, JUN-CHAN—ARE YOU GONNA JOIN THE POP MUSIC CLUB!?
NO, I WAS JUST WONDERIN' WHAT AZUSA'S DOIN' IN THERE ALL BY HERSELF.
SHE COULD BE BAWLIN' HER EYES OUT IN THERE, FOR ALL WE KNOW!
JUN-CHAN...
YOU KNOW VERY WELL THAT AZUSA-CHAN'S PRACTICING GUITAR.
HEY, ANYBODY HOME—? MAN, IT'S KINDA DARK IN HERE...
プチン...
SNIP
WH-WHAT'S THAT SOUND...!?
SNIP
プチン...
SNIP
プチン
SCARY!!
GUITAR STRINGS
HUH? OH... UI? JUN?
AZUSA-CHAN... SENSEI... WHAT ARE YOU TWO DOING?
ぐりん
SWIVEL
EEK!!
UUUUU... IIIIII... CHAAAN...
UH... UM...?
FOR THE LOVE OF GOD, POUR ME SOME TEA!!
HWUH?

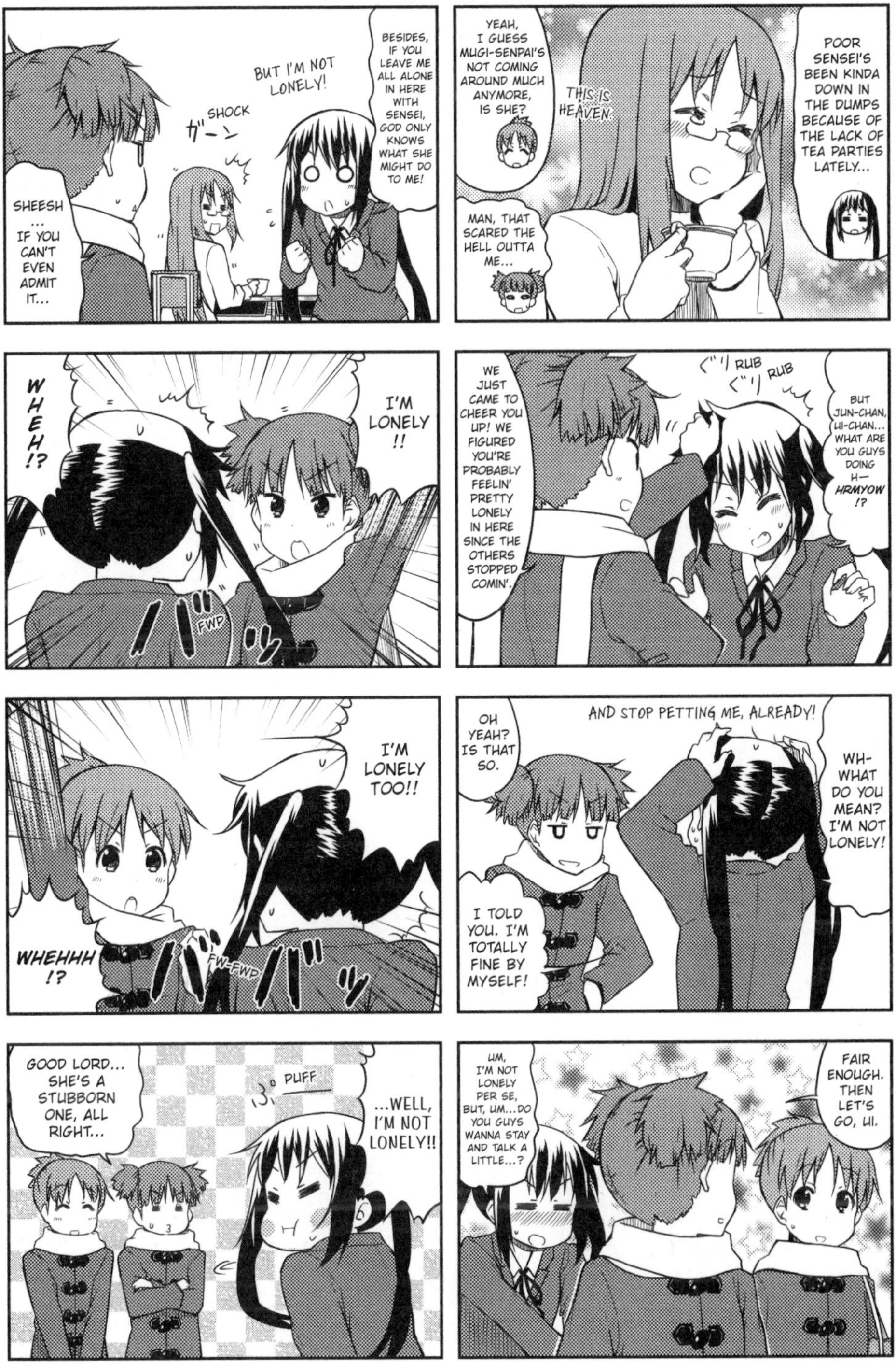
POOR SENSEI'S BEEN KINDA DOWN IN THE DUMPS BECAUSE OF THE LACK OF TEA PARTIES LATELY...
THIS IS HEAVEN.
YEAH, I GUESS MUGI-SENPAI'S NOT COMING AROUND MUCH ANYMORE, IS SHE?
MAN, THAT SCARED THE HELL OUTTA ME...
BUT JUN-CHAN, UI-CHAN... WHAT ARE YOU GUYS DOING H— HRMYOW!?
RUB RUB
WE JUST CAME TO CHEER YOU UP! WE FIGURED YOU'RE PROBABLY FEELIN' PRETTY LONELY IN HERE SINCE THE OTHERS STOPPED COMIN'.
WH- WHAT DO YOU MEAN? I'M NOT LONELY!
AND STOP PETTING ME, ALREADY!
OH YEAH? IS THAT SO.
I TOLD YOU. I'M TOTALLY FINE BY MYSELF!
FAIR ENOUGH. THEN LET'S GO, UI.
UM, I'M NOT LONELY PER SE, BUT, UM...DO YOU GUYS WANNA STAY AND TALK A LITTLE...?
BESIDES, IF YOU LEAVE ME ALL ALONE IN HERE WITH SENSEI, GOD ONLY KNOWS WHAT SHE MIGHT DO TO ME!
BUT I'M NOT LONELY!
SHOCK
SHEESH... IF YOU CAN'T EVEN ADMIT IT...
I'M LONELY!!
WHEH!?
FWP
I'M LONELY TOO!!
WHEHHH!?
FW-FWP
...WELL, I'M NOT LONELY!!
PUFF
GOOD LORD... SHE'S A STUBBORN ONE, ALL RIGHT...

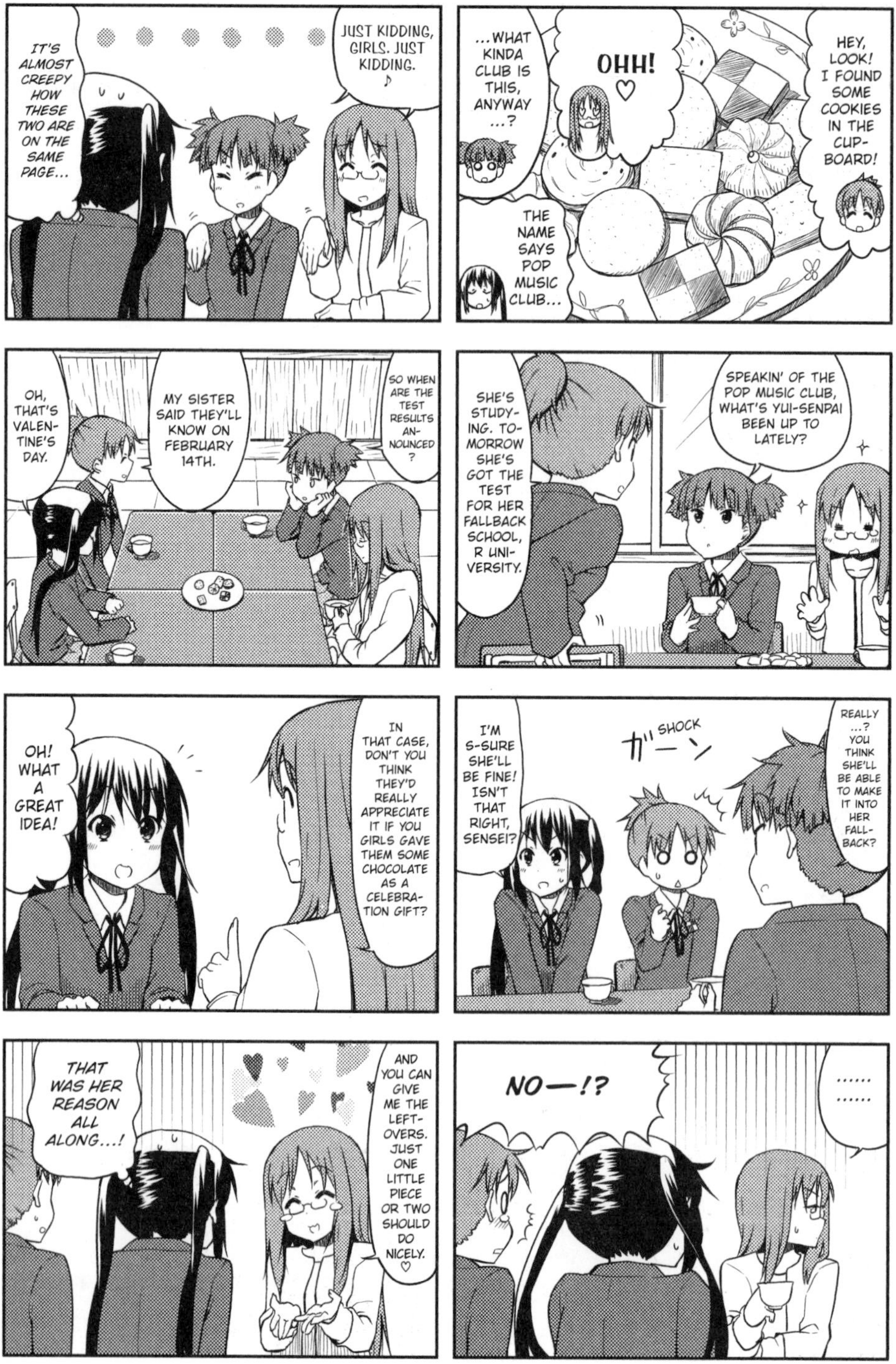
HEY, LOOK! I FOUND SOME COOKIES IN THE CUPBOARD!
OHH! ♡
...WHAT KINDA CLUB IS THIS, ANYWAY...?
THE NAME SAYS POP MUSIC CLUB...
SPEAKIN' OF THE POP MUSIC CLUB, WHAT'S YUI-SENPAI BEEN UP TO LATELY?
SHE'S STUDYING. TOMORROW SHE'S GOT THE TEST FOR HER FALLBACK SCHOOL, R UNIVERSITY.
REALLY...? YOU THINK SHE'LL BE ABLE TO MAKE IT INTO HER FALLBACK?
ガーン SHOCK
I'M S-SURE SHE'LL BE FINE! ISN'T THAT RIGHT, SENSEI?
......
......
NO—!?
JUST KIDDING, GIRLS. JUST KIDDING. ♪
IT'S ALMOST CREEPY HOW THESE TWO ARE ON THE SAME PAGE...
SO WHEN ARE THE TEST RESULTS ANNOUNCED?
MY SISTER SAID THEY'LL KNOW ON FEBRUARY 14TH.
OH, THAT'S VALENTINE'S DAY.
IN THAT CASE, DON'T YOU THINK THEY'D REALLY APPRECIATE IT IF YOU GIRLS GAVE THEM SOME CHOCOLATE AS A CELEBRATION GIFT?
OH! WHAT A GREAT IDEA!
AND YOU CAN GIVE ME THE LEFTOVERS. JUST ONE LITTLE PIECE OR TWO SHOULD DO NICELY. ♡
THAT WAS HER REASON ALL ALONG...!

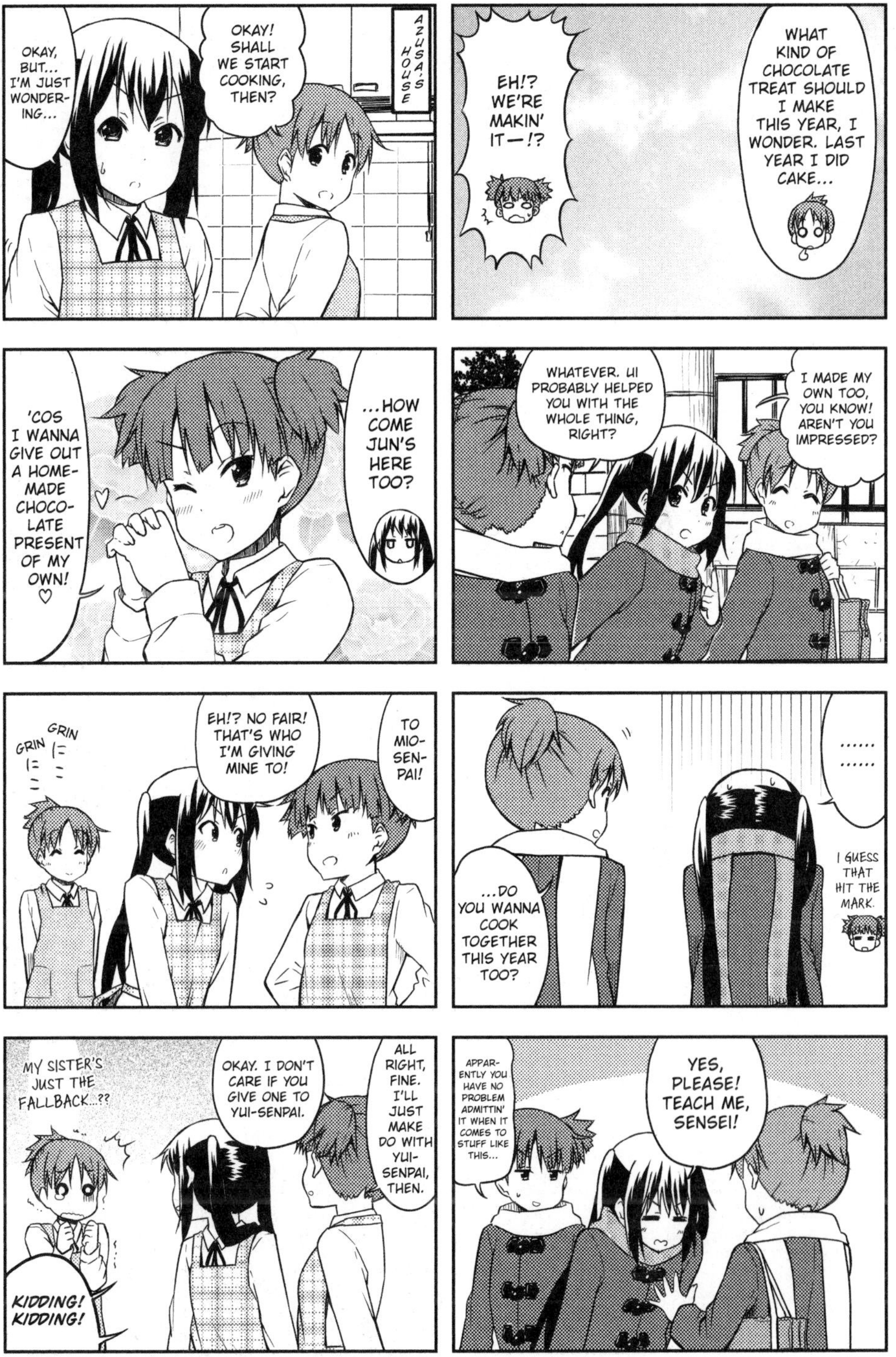
WHAT KIND OF CHOCOLATE TREAT SHOULD I MAKE THIS YEAR, I WONDER. LAST YEAR I DID CAKE...
EH!? WE'RE MAKIN' IT—!?
I MADE MY OWN TOO, YOU KNOW! AREN'T YOU IMPRESSED?
WHATEVER. UI PROBABLY HELPED YOU WITH THE WHOLE THING, RIGHT?
....
...DO YOU WANNA COOK TOGETHER THIS YEAR TOO?
I GUESS THAT HIT THE MARK.
YES, PLEASE! TEACH ME, SENSEI!
APPARENTLY YOU HAVE NO PROBLEM ADMITTIN' IT WHEN IT COMES TO STUFF LIKE THIS...
AZUSA'S HOUSE
OKAY! SHALL WE START COOKING, THEN?
OKAY, BUT... I'M JUST WONDERING...
...HOW COME JUN'S HERE TOO?
'COS I WANNA GIVE OUT A HOMEMADE CHOCOLATE PRESENT OF MY OWN! ♡
TO MIO-SENPAI!
EH!? NO FAIR! THAT'S WHO I'M GIVING MINE TO!
GRIN GRIN
ALL RIGHT, FINE. I'LL JUST MAKE DO WITH YUI-SENPAI, THEN.
OKAY. I DON'T CARE IF YOU GIVE ONE TO YUI-SENPAI.
MY SISTER'S JUST THE FALLBACK...??
KIDDING! KIDDING!

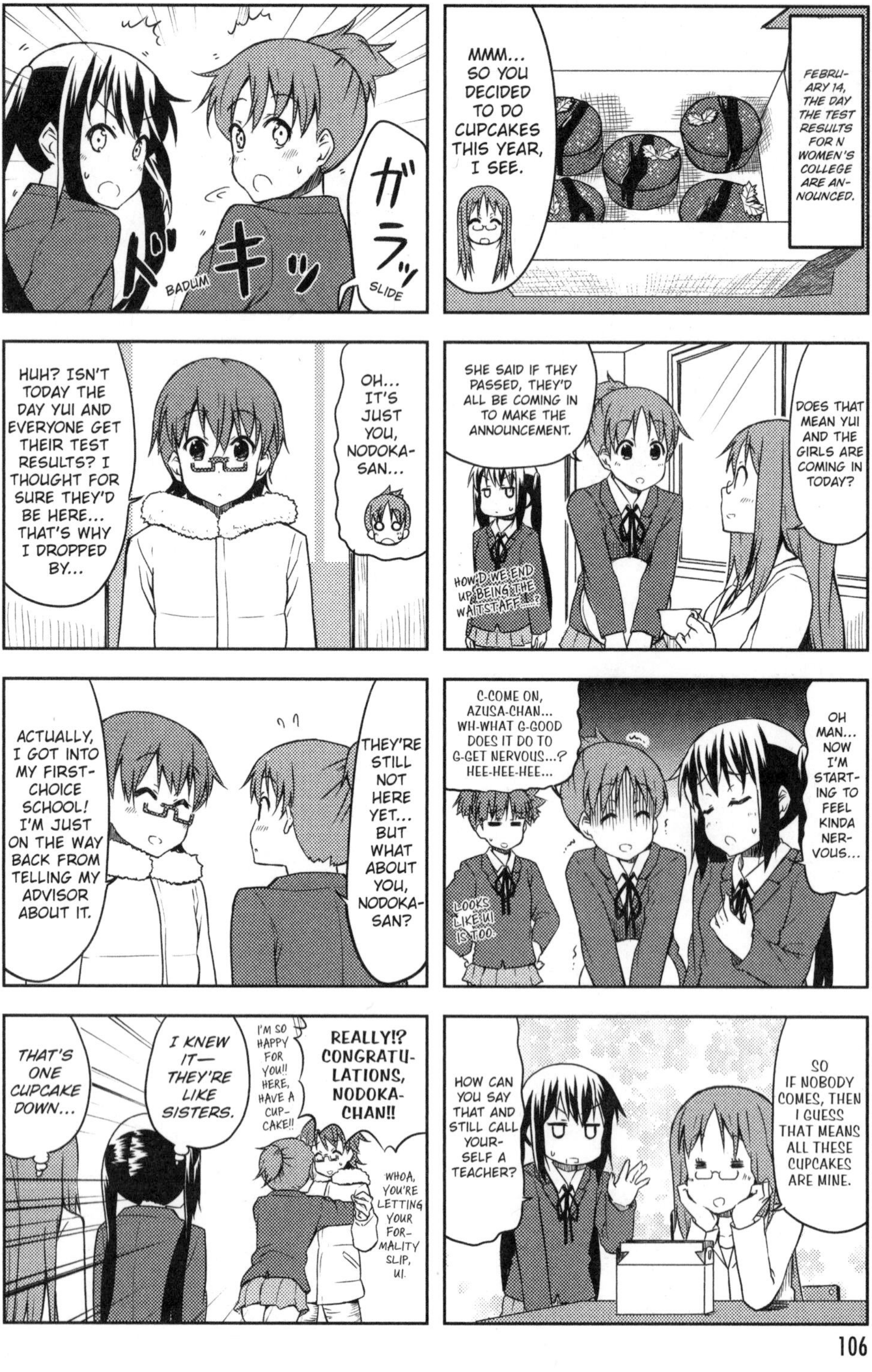
FEBRUARY 14, THE DAY THE TEST RESULTS FOR N WOMEN'S COLLEGE ARE ANNOUNCED.
MMM... SO YOU DECIDED TO DO CUPCAKES THIS YEAR, I SEE.
DOES THAT MEAN YUI AND THE GIRLS ARE COMING IN TODAY?
SHE SAID IF THEY PASSED, THEY'D ALL BE COMING IN TO MAKE THE ANNOUNCEMENT.
HOW'D WE END UP BEING THE WAITSTAFF...?
OH MAN... NOW I'M STARTING TO FEEL KINDA NERVOUS...
C-COME ON, AZUSA-CHAN... WH-WHAT G-GOOD DOES IT DO TO G-GET NERVOUS...? HEE-HEE-HEE...
LOOKS LIKE UI IS TOO.
SO IF NOBODY COMES, THEN I GUESS THAT MEANS ALL THESE CUPCAKES ARE MINE.
HOW CAN YOU SAY THAT AND STILL CALL YOURSELF A TEACHER?
ガラッ
SLIDE
ドキッ
BADUM
OH... IT'S JUST YOU, NODOKA-SAN...
HUH? ISN'T TODAY THE DAY YUI AND EVERYONE GET THEIR TEST RESULTS? I THOUGHT FOR SURE THEY'D BE HERE... THAT'S WHY I DROPPED BY...
THEY'RE STILL NOT HERE YET... BUT WHAT ABOUT YOU, NODOKA-SAN?
ACTUALLY, I GOT INTO MY FIRST-CHOICE SCHOOL! I'M JUST ON THE WAY BACK FROM TELLING MY ADVISOR ABOUT IT.
REALLY!? CONGRATULATIONS, NODOKA-CHAN!!
I'M SO HAPPY FOR YOU!! HERE, HAVE A CUPCAKE!!
WHOA, YOU'RE LETTING YOUR FORMALITY SLIP, UI.
I KNEW IT—THEY'RE LIKE SISTERS.
THAT'S ONE CUPCAKE DOWN...

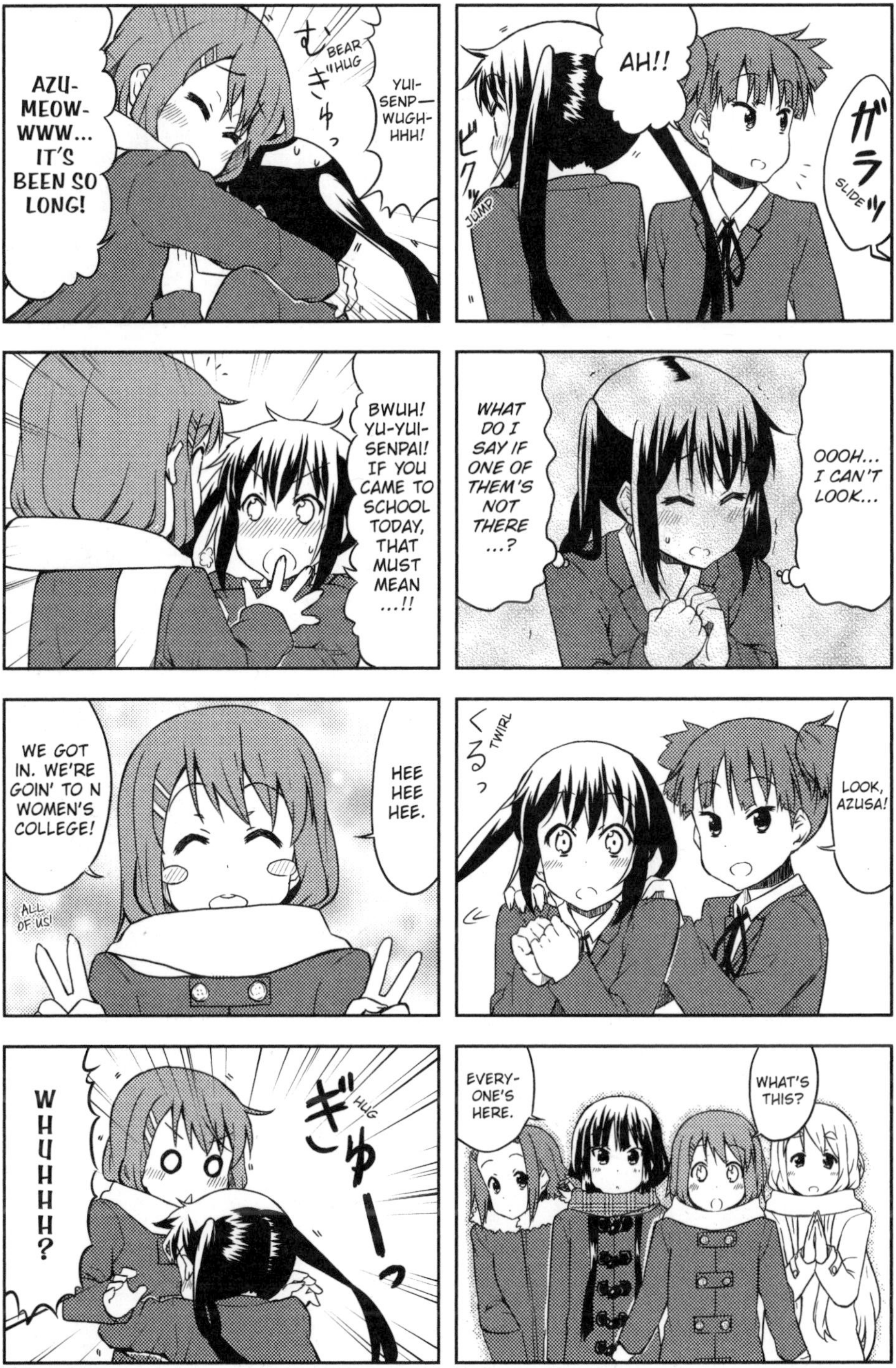
AH!!
ガラッ
SLIDE
ビクッ
JUMP
OOOH... I CAN'T LOOK...
WHAT DO I SAY IF ONE OF THEM'S NOT THERE ...?
LOOK, AZUSA!
くるっ
TWIRL
WHAT'S THIS?
EVERY-ONE'S HERE.
YUI-SENP— WUGH-HHH!
むぎゅっ
BEAR HUG
AZU-MEOW-WWW... IT'S BEEN SO LONG!
BWUH! YU-YUI-SENPAI! IF YOU CAME TO SCHOOL TODAY, THAT MUST MEAN ...!!
HEE HEE HEE.
WE GOT IN. WE'RE GOIN' TO N WOMEN'S COLLEGE!
ALL OF US!
ぎゅーっ
HUG
WHUHHHH?

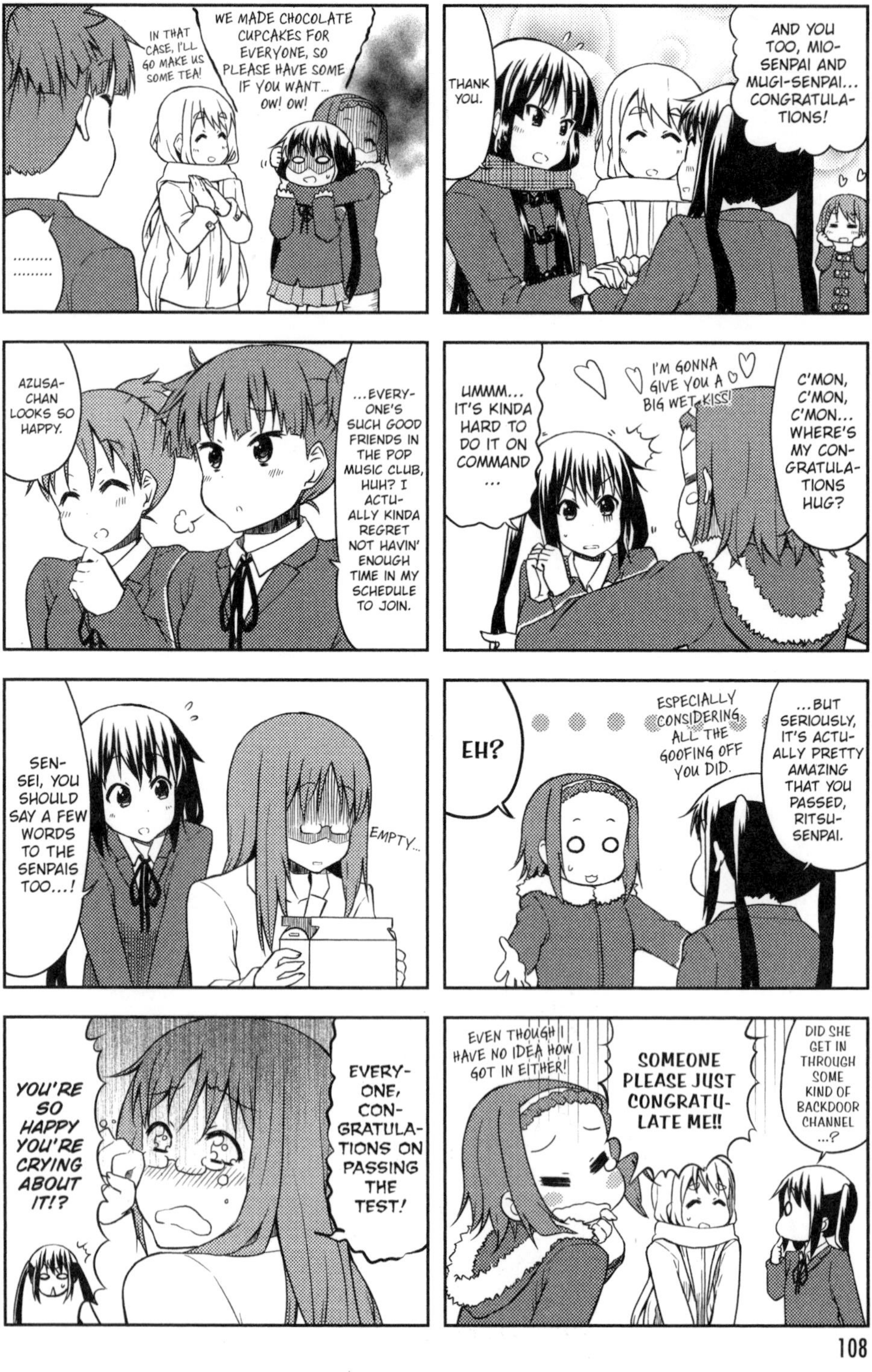
AND YOU TOO, MIO-SENPAI AND MUGI-SENPAI... CONGRATULATIONS!
THANK YOU.
C'MON, C'MON, C'MON... WHERE'S MY CONGRATULATIONS HUG?
I'M GONNA GIVE YOU A BIG WET KISS!
UMMM... IT'S KINDA HARD TO DO IT ON COMMAND...
...BUT SERIOUSLY, IT'S ACTUALLY PRETTY AMAZING THAT YOU PASSED, RITSU-SENPAI.
ESPECIALLY CONSIDERING ALL THE GOOFING OFF YOU DID.
EH?
DID SHE GET IN THROUGH SOME KIND OF BACKDOOR CHANNEL...?
SOMEONE PLEASE JUST CONGRATULATE ME!!
EVEN THOUGH I HAVE NO IDEA HOW I GOT IN EITHER!
WE MADE CHOCOLATE CUPCAKES FOR EVERYONE, SO PLEASE HAVE SOME IF YOU WANT... OW! OW!
IN THAT CASE, I'LL GO MAKE US SOME TEA!
....
....
...EVERYONE'S SUCH GOOD FRIENDS IN THE POP MUSIC CLUB, HUH? I ACTUALLY KINDA REGRET NOT HAVIN' ENOUGH TIME IN MY SCHEDULE TO JOIN.
AZUSA-CHAN LOOKS SO HAPPY.
EMPTY...
SENSEI, YOU SHOULD SAY A FEW WORDS TO THE SENPAIS TOO...!
EVERYONE, CONGRATULATIONS ON PASSING THE TEST!
YOU'RE SO HAPPY YOU'RE CRYING ABOUT IT!?

MY CHOCOLATE
CUPCAKES...

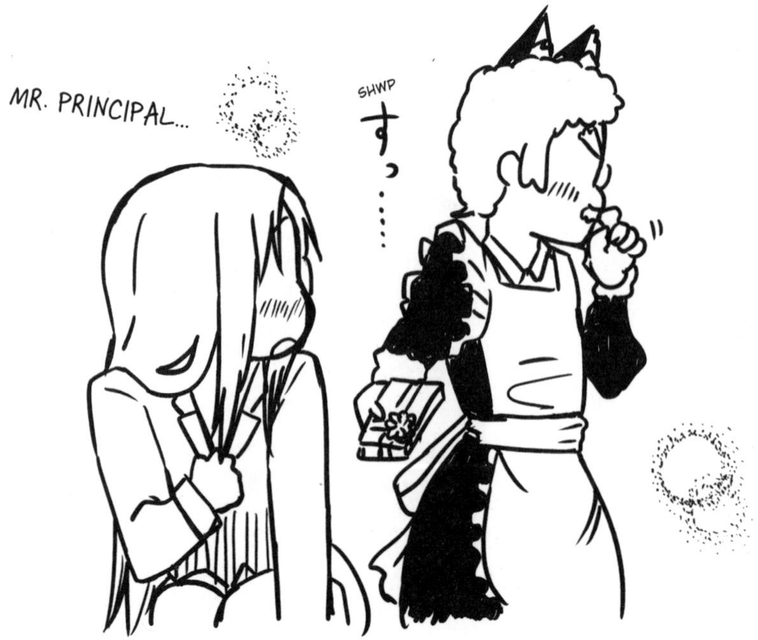
SHWP
すっ……
MR. PRINCIPAL...

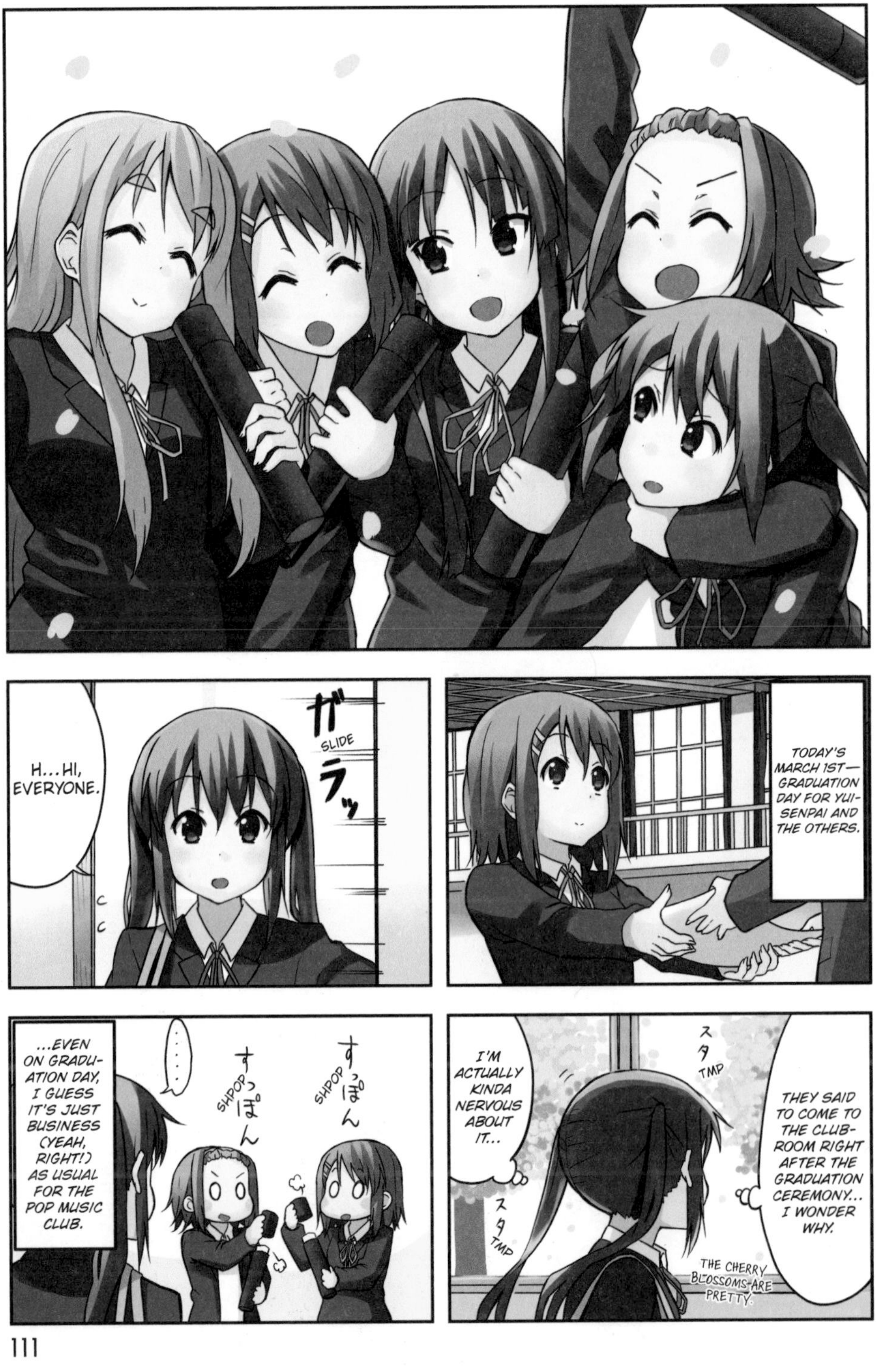
TODAY'S MARCH 1ST—GRADUATION DAY FOR YUI-SENPAI AND THE OTHERS.
スタ
TMP
THEY SAID TO COME TO THE CLUB-ROOM RIGHT AFTER THE GRADUATION CEREMONY... I WONDER WHY.
I'M ACTUALLY KINDA NERVOUS ABOUT IT...
スタ
TMP
THE CHERRY BLOSSOMS ARE PRETTY.
ガラッ
SLIDE
H...HI, EVERYONE.
すっぽん
SHPOP
すっぽん
SHPOP
...
...EVEN ON GRADUATION DAY, I GUESS IT'S JUST BUSINESS (YEAH, RIGHT!) AS USUAL FOR THE POP MUSIC CLUB.

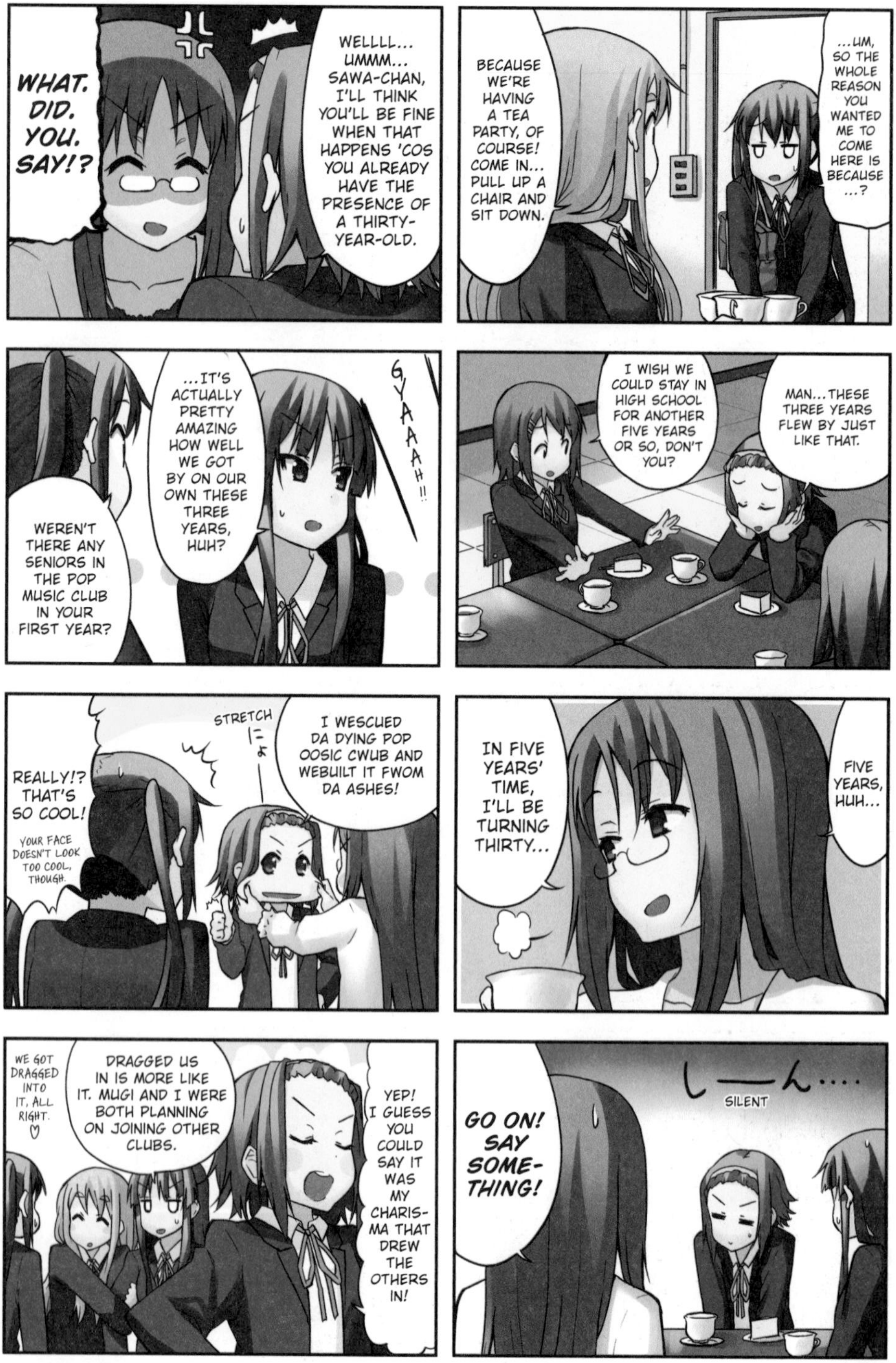
...UM, SO THE WHOLE REASON YOU WANTED ME TO COME HERE IS BECAUSE ...?
BECAUSE WE'RE HAVING A TEA PARTY, OF COURSE! COME IN... PULL UP A CHAIR AND SIT DOWN.
MAN... THESE THREE YEARS FLEW BY JUST LIKE THAT.
I WISH WE COULD STAY IN HIGH SCHOOL FOR ANOTHER FIVE YEARS OR SO, DON'T YOU?
FIVE YEARS, HUH...
IN FIVE YEARS' TIME, I'LL BE TURNING THIRTY...
しーん....
SILENT
GO ON! SAY SOME-THING!
WELLLL... UMMM... SAWA-CHAN, I'LL THINK YOU'LL BE FINE WHEN THAT HAPPENS 'COS YOU ALREADY HAVE THE PRESENCE OF A THIRTY-YEAR-OLD.
WHAT. DID. YOU. SAY!?
...IT'S ACTUALLY PRETTY AMAZING HOW WELL WE GOT BY ON OUR OWN THESE THREE YEARS, HUH?
GYAAAAH!!
WEREN'T THERE ANY SENIORS IN THE POP MUSIC CLUB IN YOUR FIRST YEAR?
STRETCH
I WESCUED DA DYING POP OOSIC CWUB AND WEBUILT IT FWOM DA ASHES!
REALLY!? THAT'S SO COOL!
YOUR FACE DOESN'T LOOK TOO COOL, THOUGH.
YEP! I GUESS YOU COULD SAY IT WAS MY CHARIS-MA THAT DREW THE OTHERS IN!
DRAGGED US IN IS MORE LIKE IT. MUGI AND I WERE BOTH PLANNING ON JOINING OTHER CLUBS.
WE GOT DRAGGED INTO IT, ALL RIGHT. ♡

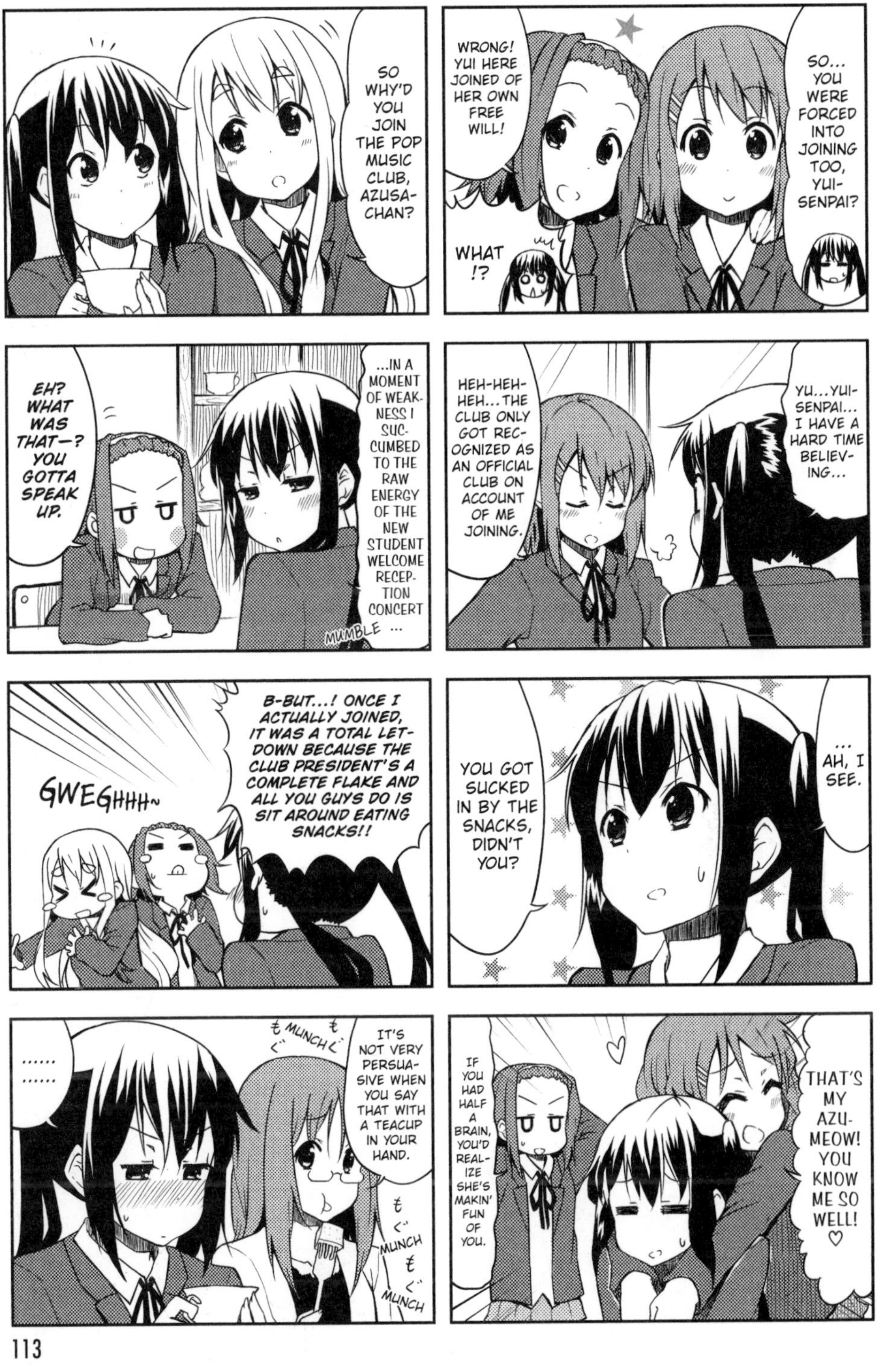

SO WHY'D YOU JOIN THE POP MUSIC CLUB, AZUSA-CHAN?
...IN A MOMENT OF WEAKNESS I SUCCUMBED TO THE RAW ENERGY OF THE NEW STUDENT WELCOME RECEPTION CONCERT
MUMBLE ...
EH? WHAT WAS THAT—? YOU GOTTA SPEAK UP.
B-BUT...! ONCE I ACTUALLY JOINED, IT WAS A TOTAL LET-DOWN BECAUSE THE CLUB PRESIDENT'S A COMPLETE FLAKE AND ALL YOU GUYS DO IS SIT AROUND EATING SNACKS!!
GWEGHHH~
......
......
IT'S NOT VERY PERSUASIVE WHEN YOU SAY THAT WITH A TEACUP IN YOUR HAND.
MUNCH
MUNCH
MUNCH
SO... YOU WERE FORCED INTO JOINING TOO, YUI-SENPAI?
WRONG! YUI HERE JOINED OF HER OWN FREE WILL!
WHAT !?
HEH-HEH-HEH...THE CLUB ONLY GOT RECOGNIZED AS AN OFFICIAL CLUB ON ACCOUNT OF ME JOINING.
YU...YUI-SENPAI... I HAVE A HARD TIME BELIEVING...
... AH, I SEE.
YOU GOT SUCKED IN BY THE SNACKS, DIDN'T YOU?
THAT'S MY AZU-MEOW! YOU KNOW ME SO WELL! ♡
IF YOU HAD HALF A BRAIN, YOU'D REALIZE SHE'S MAKIN' FUN OF YOU.

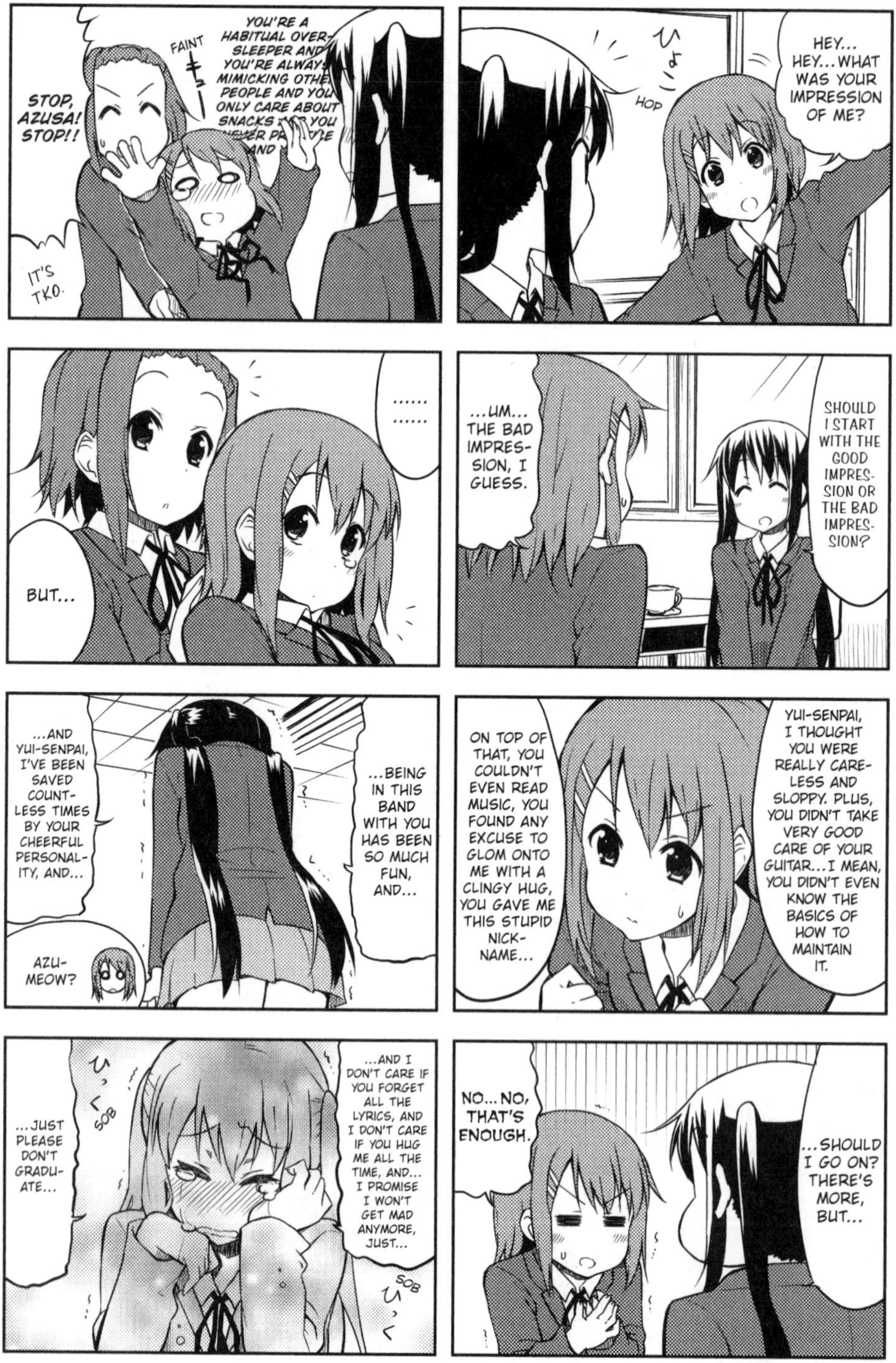
ひょ
HOP
HEY... HEY...WHAT WAS YOUR IMPRESSION OF ME?
SHOULD I START WITH THE GOOD IMPRESSION OR THE BAD IMPRESSION?
...UM... THE BAD IMPRESSION, I GUESS.
YUI-SENPAI, I THOUGHT YOU WERE REALLY CARELESS AND SLOPPY. PLUS, YOU DIDN'T TAKE VERY GOOD CARE OF YOUR GUITAR...I MEAN, YOU DIDN'T EVEN KNOW THE BASICS OF HOW TO MAINTAIN IT.
ON TOP OF THAT, YOU COULDN'T EVEN READ MUSIC, YOU FOUND ANY EXCUSE TO GLOM ONTO ME WITH A CLINGY HUG, YOU GAVE ME THIS STUPID NICKNAME...
...SHOULD I GO ON? THERE'S MORE, BUT...
NO...NO, THAT'S ENOUGH.
YOU'RE A HABITUAL OVER-SLEEPER AND YOU'RE ALWAYS MIMICKING OTHER PEOPLE AND YOU ONLY CARE ABOUT SNACKS
FAINT
STOP, AZUSA! STOP!!
IT'S TKO.
....
BUT...
...BEING IN THIS BAND WITH YOU HAS BEEN SO MUCH FUN, AND...
...AND YUI-SENPAI, I'VE BEEN SAVED COUNTLESS TIMES BY YOUR CHEERFUL PERSONALITY, AND...
AZU-MEOW?
...AND I DON'T CARE IF YOU FORGET ALL THE LYRICS, AND I DON'T CARE IF YOU HUG ME ALL THE TIME, AND... I PROMISE I WON'T GET MAD ANYMORE, JUST...
ひっく
SOB
...JUST PLEASE DON'T GRADUATE...

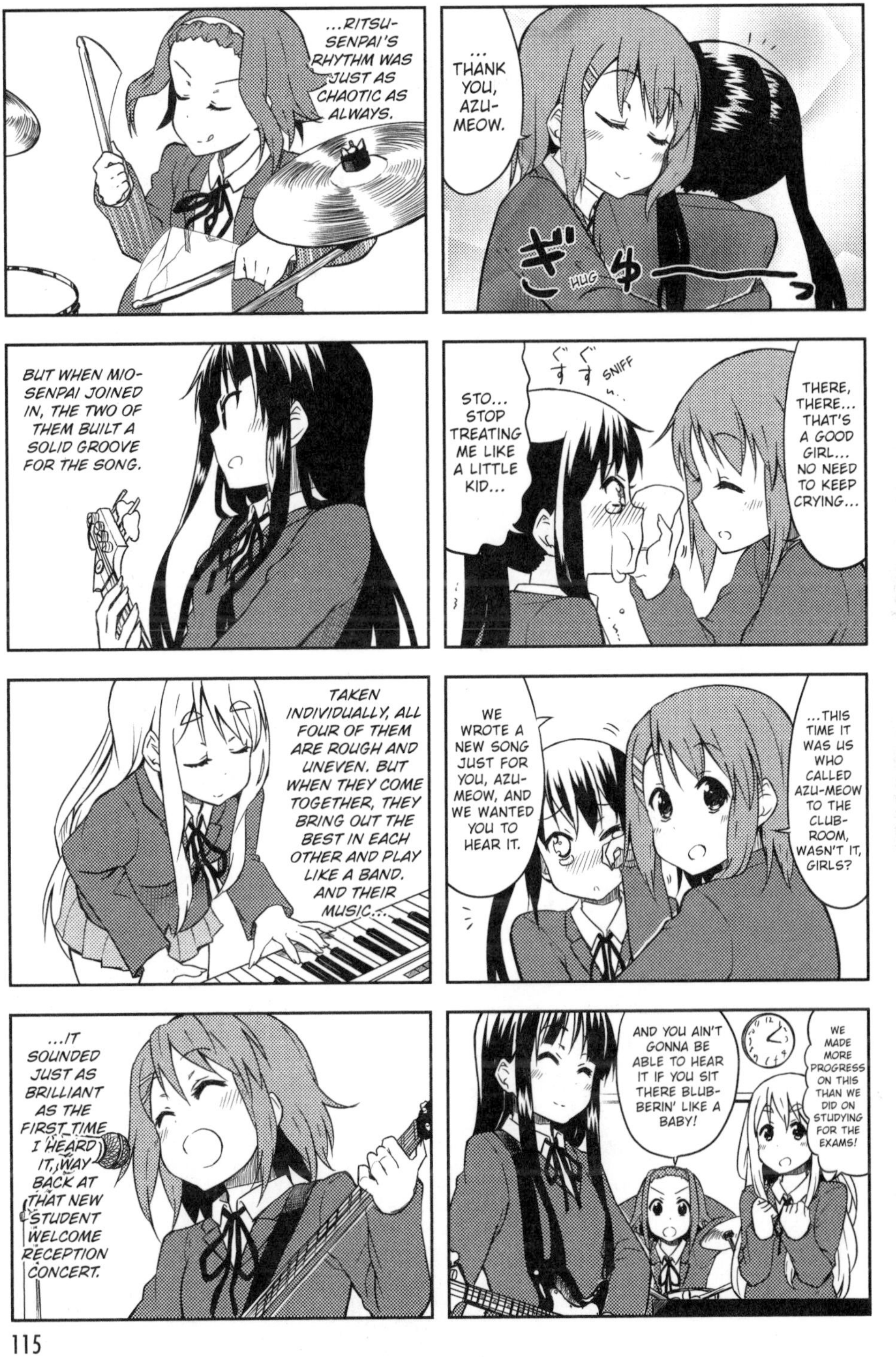
...THANK YOU, AZU-MEOW.
ぎゅーっ
HUG
THERE, THERE... THAT'S A GOOD GIRL... NO NEED TO KEEP CRYING...
ぐすぐす
SNIFF
STO... STOP TREATING ME LIKE A LITTLE KID...
...THIS TIME IT WAS US WHO CALLED AZU-MEOW TO THE CLUB-ROOM, WASN'T IT, GIRLS?
WE WROTE A NEW SONG JUST FOR YOU, AZU-MEOW, AND WE WANTED YOU TO HEAR IT.
WE MADE MORE PROGRESS ON THIS THAN WE DID ON STUDYING FOR THE EXAMS!
AND YOU AIN'T GONNA BE ABLE TO HEAR IT IF YOU SIT THERE BLUBBERIN' LIKE A BABY!
...RITSU-SENPAI'S RHYTHM WAS JUST AS CHAOTIC AS ALWAYS.
BUT WHEN MIO-SENPAI JOINED IN, THE TWO OF THEM BUILT A SOLID GROOVE FOR THE SONG.
TAKEN INDIVIDUALLY, ALL FOUR OF THEM ARE ROUGH AND UNEVEN. BUT WHEN THEY COME TOGETHER, THEY BRING OUT THE BEST IN EACH OTHER AND PLAY LIKE A BAND. AND THEIR MUSIC...
...IT SOUNDED JUST AS BRILLIANT AS THE FIRST TIME I HEARD IT, WAY BACK AT THAT NEW STUDENT WELCOME RECEPTION CONCERT.

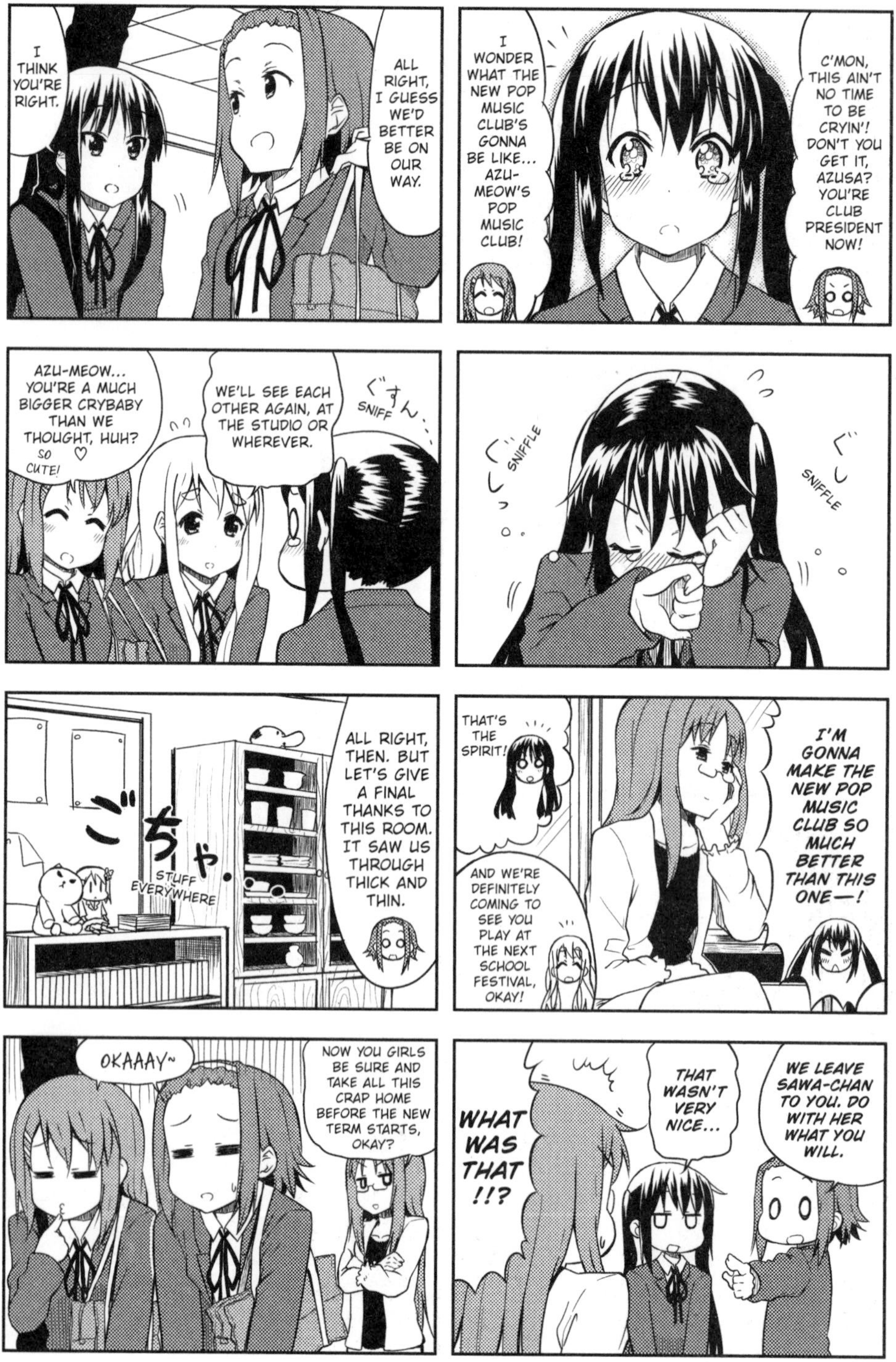
C'MON, THIS AIN'T NO TIME TO BE CRYIN'! DON'T YOU GET IT, AZUSA? YOU'RE CLUB PRESIDENT NOW!
I WONDER WHAT THE NEW POP MUSIC CLUB'S GONNA BE LIKE... AZU-MEOW'S POP MUSIC CLUB!
ALL RIGHT, I GUESS WE'D BETTER BE ON OUR WAY.
I THINK YOU'RE RIGHT.
じ SNIFFLE
じ SNIFFLE
ぐすん SNIFF
WE'LL SEE EACH OTHER AGAIN, AT THE STUDIO OR WHEREVER.
AZU-MEOW... YOU'RE A MUCH BIGGER CRYBABY THAN WE THOUGHT, HUH? ♡
SO CUTE!
I'M GONNA MAKE THE NEW POP MUSIC CLUB SO MUCH BETTER THAN THIS ONE—!
THAT'S THE SPIRIT!
AND WE'RE DEFINITELY COMING TO SEE YOU PLAY AT THE NEXT SCHOOL FESTIVAL, OKAY!
ALL RIGHT, THEN. BUT LET'S GIVE A FINAL THANKS TO THIS ROOM. IT SAW US THROUGH THICK AND THIN.
ごちゃ STUFF EVERYWHERE
WE LEAVE SAWA-CHAN TO YOU. DO WITH HER WHAT YOU WILL.
THAT WASN'T VERY NICE...
WHAT WAS THAT!!?
NOW YOU GIRLS BE SURE AND TAKE ALL THIS CRAP HOME BEFORE THE NEW TERM STARTS, OKAY?
OKAAAY~

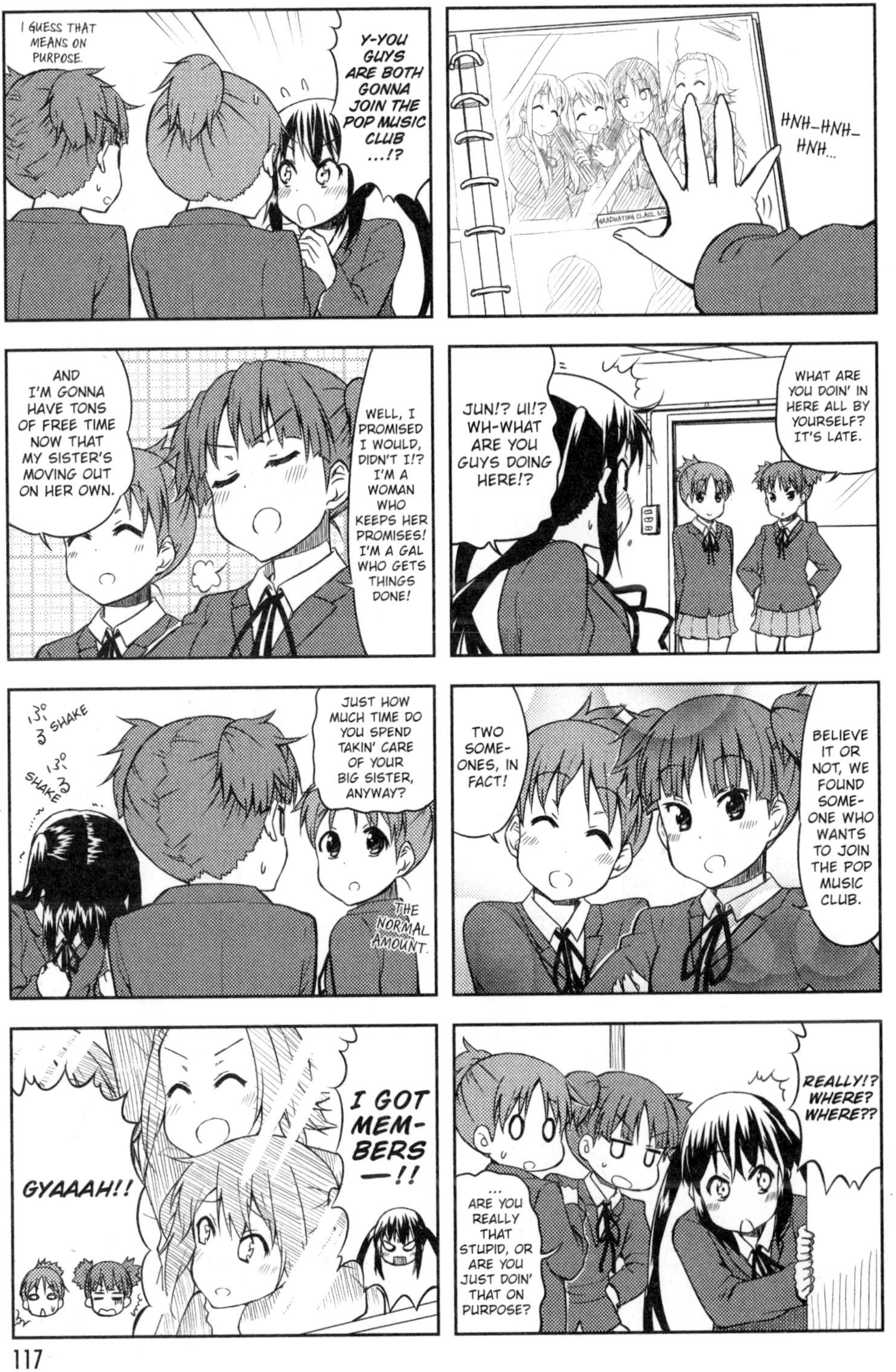
HNH-HNH-HNH...
WHAT ARE YOU DOIN' IN HERE ALL BY YOURSELF? IT'S LATE.
JUN!? UI!? WH-WHAT ARE YOU GUYS DOING HERE!?
BELIEVE IT OR NOT, WE FOUND SOME-ONE WHO WANTS TO JOIN THE POP MUSIC CLUB.
TWO SOME-ONES, IN FACT!
REALLY!? WHERE? WHERE??
...ARE YOU REALLY THAT STUPID, OR ARE YOU JUST DOIN' THAT ON PURPOSE?
Y-YOU GUYS ARE BOTH GONNA JOIN THE POP MUSIC CLUB ...!?
I GUESS THAT MEANS ON PURPOSE.
WELL, I PROMISED I WOULD, DIDN'T I!? I'M A WOMAN WHO KEEPS HER PROMISES! I'M A GAL WHO GETS THINGS DONE!
AND I'M GONNA HAVE TONS OF FREE TIME NOW THAT MY SISTER'S MOVING OUT ON HER OWN.
JUST HOW MUCH TIME DO YOU SPEND TAKIN' CARE OF YOUR BIG SISTER, ANYWAY?
SHAKE
SHAKE
THE NORMAL AMOUNT.
I GOT MEM-BERS—!!
GYAAAH!!

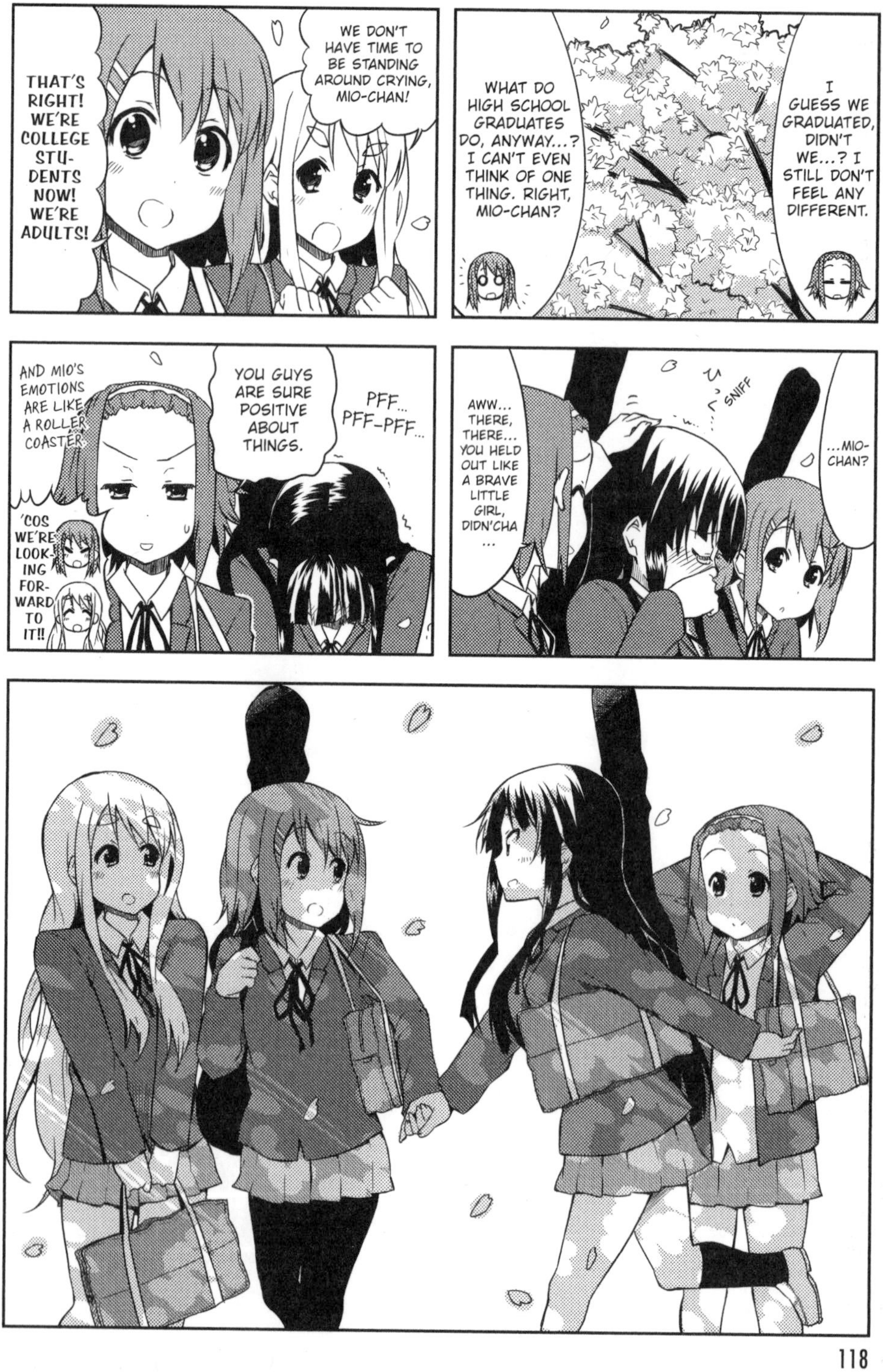
I GUESS WE GRADUATED, DIDN'T WE...? I STILL DON'T FEEL ANY DIFFERENT.
WHAT DO HIGH SCHOOL GRADUATES DO, ANYWAY...? I CAN'T EVEN THINK OF ONE THING. RIGHT, MIO-CHAN?
WE DON'T HAVE TIME TO BE STANDING AROUND CRYING, MIO-CHAN!
THAT'S RIGHT! WE'RE COLLEGE STU-DENTS NOW! WE'RE ADULTS!
...MIO-CHAN?
SNIFF
AWW... THERE, THERE... YOU HELD OUT LIKE A BRAVE LITTLE GIRL, DIDN'CHA...
PFF... PFF-PFF...
YOU GUYS ARE SURE POSITIVE ABOUT THINGS.
AND MIO'S EMOTIONS ARE LIKE A ROLLER COASTER.
'COS WE'RE LOOKING FORWARD TO IT!!

kakifly

C O M M E N T S

Hi, my name is kakifly. Recently I started my own oyster farm. (Just kidding.) Thank you so much for buying my manga.

THANKS FOR READING...

AFTERWORD

I'VE LEARNED SO MUCH ABOUT THE MANY DIFFICULTIES AND
RESPONSIBILITIES INVOLVED IN PRODUCING A MANGA SERIES,
ABOUT THE JOY OF SEEING THE WORK I'VE DONE BEING COMPILED
AND PRINTED IN BOUND VOLUMES, AND MOST IMPORTANTLY, ABOUT
RECEIVING REACTIONS AND FEEDBACK FROM MY READERS.

ALL THIS IS WHAT K-ON! HAS GIVEN ME OVER THE YEARS, EVER SINCE
HOUBUNSHA PICKED UP THE TITLE AND BROUGHT IT INTO THEIR FOLD.
AND NOW THAT I'VE SOMEHOW MANAGED TO COMPLETE THE SERIES—
WHICH MIRACULOUSLY STAYED AFLOAT DESPITE ALL THE FALSE STARTS,
BAD PLANNING, AND HAPHAZARD EXPERIMENTATION ON MY PART—
WHAT I'M FEELING MORE THAN ANYTHING ELSE RIGHT NOW IS RELIEF.

I FEAR THAT THE FLAWS AND MISSTEPS OF THIS SERIES HAVE
PROBABLY STOOD OUT MORE THAN ANY MEAGER VIRTUES IT MAY
POSSESS, BUT IF ANY OF YOU ARE ACTUALLY GLAD IN SOME SMALL
WAY THAT YOU READ IT, I CAN TELL YOU THERE'S NO GREATER JOY
FOR ME THAN KNOWING THAT.

K-ON! HAS ONLY MADE IT THIS FAR BECAUSE OF THE SUPPORT OF
COUNTLESS NUMBERS OF PEOPLE, AND I'D LIKE TO TAKE THIS
OPPORTUNITY TO EXPRESS MY HEARTFELT GRATITUDE TO ALL OF
THEM. TRULY, THANK YOU ALL SO VERY MUCH.

— KAKIFLY

BONUS COMICS

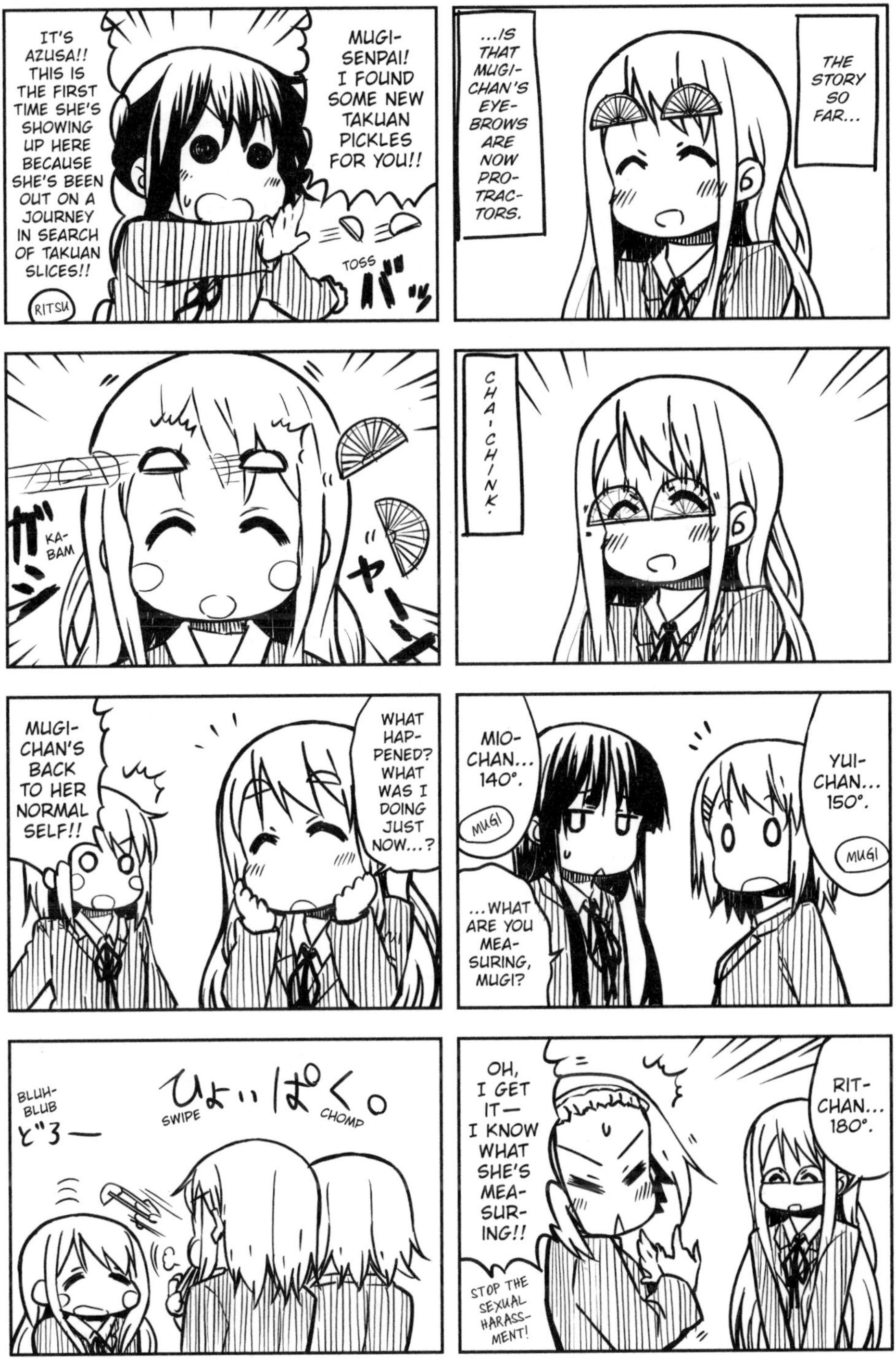
THE STORY SO FAR...
...IS THAT MUGI-CHAN'S EYEBROWS ARE NOW PROTRACTORS.
CHA-CHINK.
YUI-CHAN... 150°.
MUGI
MIO-CHAN... 140°.
MUGI
...WHAT ARE YOU MEASURING, MUGI?
RIT-CHAN... 180°.
OH, I GET IT— I KNOW WHAT SHE'S MEASURING!!
STOP THE SEXUAL HARASSMENT!
MUGI-SENPAI! I FOUND SOME NEW TAKUAN PICKLES FOR YOU!!
TOSS
バッ
IT'S AZUSA!! THIS IS THE FIRST TIME SHE'S SHOWING UP HERE BECAUSE SHE'S BEEN OUT ON A JOURNEY IN SEARCH OF TAKUAN SLICES!!
RITSU
KA-BAM
ガッ
WHAT HAPPENED? WHAT WAS I DOING JUST NOW...?
MUGI-CHAN'S BACK TO HER NORMAL SELF!!
ひょいぱく。
SWIPE
CHOMP
BLUH-BLUB
どろー

central region of the main island of Honshu). There's also a homonym pun in the song ("1, 2, 3, 4, GO-HAN!", where the prefix "go–" of "gohan" ("rice") doubles as the number 5, also "go") and a line in the Kansai dialect (*Donai ya nen*, which literally means "What's the deal?" but here is just used to give a nod to the region).

PAGE 30
Band T-shirts
The T-shirts that Sawako made for the girls' concert have English lettering on them, but the words are Japanese. "Ho-KaGo TeaTime" is the Japanese name for the girls' band—Afterschool (*hokago*) Tea Time—and "Sakura-Ko K-ON-BU" is short for Sakuragaoka High School (*koko*) Pop Music Club (*kei-on-gaku-bu*).

PAGE 35
Indoor Shoes
Japanese students are required to remove their outdoor shoes and wear indoor slippers while they're inside the school building. This follows the general Japanese cultural practice of not wearing outdoor shoes indoors (and requiring special shoes for "dirty" places like the bathroom) in order not to introduce filth into the home space.

PAGE 38
Studying for Entrance Exams
Most high school students in Japan devote their entire senior year to preparation for standardized college entrance exams. Doing well on these exams is a vital component of acceptance to a good school, so schools and parents put a lot of pressure on pre-test college-bound students to study intensively and avoid distractions.

PAGE 40
The Center Test
This is short for *Daigaku Nyushi Sentaa Shiken* (University Admissions Center Test), so named because it's administered by the National Center for University Entrance Examinations. It's a national standardized test that most universities in Japan rely on for making admissions decisions. Some universities also administer their own separate exams

in addition to the Center Test, but since Yui and Ritsu haven't decided on a particular college yet, Sawako suggests that they just focus on doing well on the Center Test (which they will almost certainly need) until they make a decision.

PAGE 40
Six-Sided Pencil
Ritsu is referring to an old (and idiotic) approach to multiple-choice tests: Write the numbers or letters of the possible choices on each face of the pencil, and then roll the pencil like a die, choosing the number or letter on the face that turns up.

PAGE 42
Admission Recommendation
Some Japanese universities allow a certain number of students to be admitted by recommendation of their high school (often paired with a "recommendation test" that usually amounts to little more than a simple interview). This path to admission is much easier than trying to get admitted through the general written admissions test, but the student needs to be a favorite of the high school faculty to get such a recommendation and also needs to commit to enrolling in the school to which the recommendation is directed.

PAGE 45
Cleaning Duty
In Japan it's common for students to perform many of the classroom duties (often on a rotating basis) that would normally be handled by the school faculty or staff in the US, such as taking roll and cleaning the classroom.

PAGE 58
Sneezing
There's a Japanese folk superstition that says you can get rid of a cold by giving it to someone else.

PAGE 61
Chance of Passing the Real Exam
The grades the girls get are not an absolute measure. The mock entrance examinations they're taking evaluate their performance *relative to other applicants* applying for the

TRANSLATION NOTES

COMMON HONORIFICS

no honorific: Indicates familiarity or closeness; if used without permission or reason, addressing someone in this manner would constitute an insult.

-san: The Japanese equivalent of Mr./Mrs./Miss. If a situation calls for politeness, this is the fail-safe honorific.

-sama: Conveys great respect; may also indicate that the social status of the speaker is lower than that of the addressee.

-kun: Used most often when referring to boys, this indicates affection or familiarity. Occasionally used by older men among their peers, but it may also be used by anyone referring to a person of lower standing.

-chan: An affectionate honorific indicating familiarity used mostly in reference to girls; also used in reference to cute persons or animals of either gender.

-senpai: Used to address upperclassmen or more experienced coworkers.

-sensei: A respectful term for teachers, artists, or high-level professionals.

K-ON!

The title K-ON! comes from the Japanese word "kei-ongaku," meaning "light music" in the sense of casual or easy listening (i.e., not serious or innovative as in serious classical or jazz). In the context of school clubs in Japan, the term "kei-ongaku-bu" ("light music club") usually contrasts with "ongaku-bu" ("music club") in that it focuses on popular forms of music (pop, rock, folk, etc.) where the latter focuses on symphonic and choral forms.

kakifly

The author's name, "kakifly," comes from the Japanese word "kaki-furai," meaning "fried oysters." It seems to be a running joke, as the author comments for this and future volumes reference his feelings toward oysters.

Yen Conversion

A general rule of thumb to use for converting Japanese yen to American dollars is ¥100 to 1 USD.

PAGE 4
JYAGUCHI T-shirt

Jyaguchi (normally romanized as "jaguchi")

means "faucet" (and sure enough, sports a picture of a dripping faucet). I believe it's making fun of Mari Yaguchi (of Morning Musume fame) goods, of which there are plenty.

Math, Level B

The "Level B" in this case means that it's a secondary-topics math textbook for second-year students. The typical mathematics curriculum in Japan is split into two broad groups of topics. The primary group is split into levels 1, 2, and 3 and includes analytic geometry and calculus, while the secondary group is divided into levels A, B, and C and presents topics in formal geometry, algebra, probability, statistics, and computer science. As this is a second-year textbook, third-year Yui should be familiar with the topics. (But she isn't, of course, because she's not a very good student.)

PAGE 9
Japanese School Terms

The Japanese school year is divided into three terms: the first starts in early April and ends in mid-July; the second begins in late August or early September and ends in late December; the third begins in early January and ends in late March.

PAGE 10
Yui and Ritsu

In Japanese, the silly song titles that Yui and Ritsu suggest are "Doki-Doki Bundoki" (literally, "Heart-pounding Protractor") and "Kaban no Bakaan" (a play on the fact that kaban "bag" in reverse syllable order sounds like bakan "bang").

PAGE 12
"Rice is the Dish"

Yui's "Rice is The Dish" ("Gohan wa Okazu" in Japanese) lyrics contain references to ramen (savory broth with vegetables, meat, and Chinese-style noodles), udon (similar to ramen, but with fatter noodles, simpler broth and less accompaniment), okonomiyaki (a kind of hearty pancake filled with meat and vegetables, and topped with mayonnaise and sweet Worcestershire-based BBQ sauce along with dried seaweed and fish flakes), as well as the region of Kansai (a western/south-the PlayStation 2. You can tell because one of the characters, Junpei Iori, always shouts "Ta da da da!" (*"terettette"* in the original Japanese version of the game) when leveling up. Because of this, Junpei has the nickname "Terette" among Japanese fans.

PAGE 89
Cram School
A cram school (*yobiko* in Japanese) is a paid tutoring course set up like a classroom but specifically targeting students preparing for entrance exams.

PAGE 92
Kagami Mochi
A traditional decorative New Year's dish, *kagami mochi* (literally "mirrored sweet-rice-cake") is made by stacking two *mochi* (rice cakes) one on top of the other and adorning the stack with an orange (and possibly additional garnishes). It's generally left up as a decoration for a couple of weeks, after which there is a small ceremony where the *mochi* is broken apart and eaten by the family.

PAGE 92
New Year's Soba
New Year's *soba* (*toshikoshi soba*, literally "year-spanning soba") is a simple noodle dish eaten on New Year's Eve. The long *soba* (buckwheat) noodles represent long life, and according to tradition, everyone has to finish their noodles completely by the time the new year rolls around.

PAGE 97
Good Luck Charms
Known as *omamori* in Japanese, there are various kinds of Shinto-themed amulets available in Japan for wishing success in all kinds of endeavors, from school to love. It's unusual (and endearing) that Ui made her own instead of buying them at a local shrine.

PAGE 111
Cherry Blossoms
Early spring is the time when flowering cherry trees bloom. The ephemeral beauty of the bright pink cherry blossoms and their association with the new growth of spring — and (when they begin to fall from the trees) with the fact that all glory eventually fades — has been a prominent and enduring theme in Japanese artistic sensibility for at least as long as Japan's written tradition (about 1500 years).

same programs at the same schools. Their scores are assigned an overall percentile (expressed as a letter grade "A" through "E," where "E" is essentially zero percent) reflecting how likely those scores would earn them acceptance to a specific program given the current state of competition.

Viewer Ratings

This might be a humorous nod to the *K-ON!* anime series. Viewer ratings in Japan are similar to Nielsen ratings in the US, listing what percentage of a sample of households was tuned in to a particular show. 20% would be a staggeringly high proportion.

PAGE 64
Heated Table

The "heated table" (*kotatsu*) is a typical piece of furniture in Japanese sitting rooms. It's a small coffee table with a space heater mounted to the underside and quilted material draped around the sides to trap the heat in the space underneath.

PAGE 65
Momotaro

Nodoka is reading the tale of Momotaro (The Peach Boy), a very famous children's story in Japan. It's about a boy who was found inside a peach. An elderly childless couple discovered the peach in a river and split it open to eat it, at which point Momotaro emerged. They take it as a sign from heaven and raise him as their own. Later he grows up and goes off heroically to fight demons with a number of talking animal friends.

PAGE 67
Humble Language

The distinction between honorific, neutral, and humble forms of speech is built right into Japanese grammar (meaning that every time you speak to someone, you're forced to make an overt assertion about your social status compared to them), and was even more pronounced in older forms of Japanese. Mio and Ritsu are studying classical Japanese, where frequently the identities of speakers and addressees are not explicitly given in dialogue but can be inferred by the relative usage of honorific language. The subject is

difficult even for modern Japanese speakers, because the modern language has diverged considerably from the classical one. (Sort of akin to modern English speakers' difficulty understanding Chaucer, or even worse, Alfred the Great.)

PAGE 68
Annual New Year's Sing-Off

This is a famous singing competition on Japanese TV called the *Kohaku Uta Gassen* (Red-White Song Battle). It's shown every year on New Year's Eve and receives almost universal viewership in Japan (much like the live New Year's countdown show hosted in Times Square in New York City that is watched by a large number of US households).

Pop-a-Point Pencil

The pop-a-point pencil (*roketto enpitsu* or "rocket pencil" in Japanese) is an old pencil fad. It was basically a stack of several plastic mini-pencil segments that fit together in a tube. When the lead got dull in front, you just popped that segment out and stuck it onto the back of the stack, which pushed the next sharp segment out.

PAGE 70
Castle

The mark Mio drew on Ritsu's forehead is a Chinese character that means "jut out" (and is also the spelling of the "*deko–*" part in the Japanese word "*dekoboko*" — "bumpy"), but here it's being used as a funny way to write the "*deko*" which is slang for "forehead," or for someone with a high, prominent forehead like Ritsu's. What Yui finds funny is that it also resembles the symbol for castle sites on Japanese maps.

PAGE 76
–dono

The suffix "*–dono*" (literally "lord") is an uncommon honorific form that's historically more formal and deferential than "*–sama*" but now is mostly used for humorous effect.

PAGE 88
Ritsu's RPG

Ritsu is playing *Shin Megami Tensei: Persona 3*, a high-school-themed RPG released for

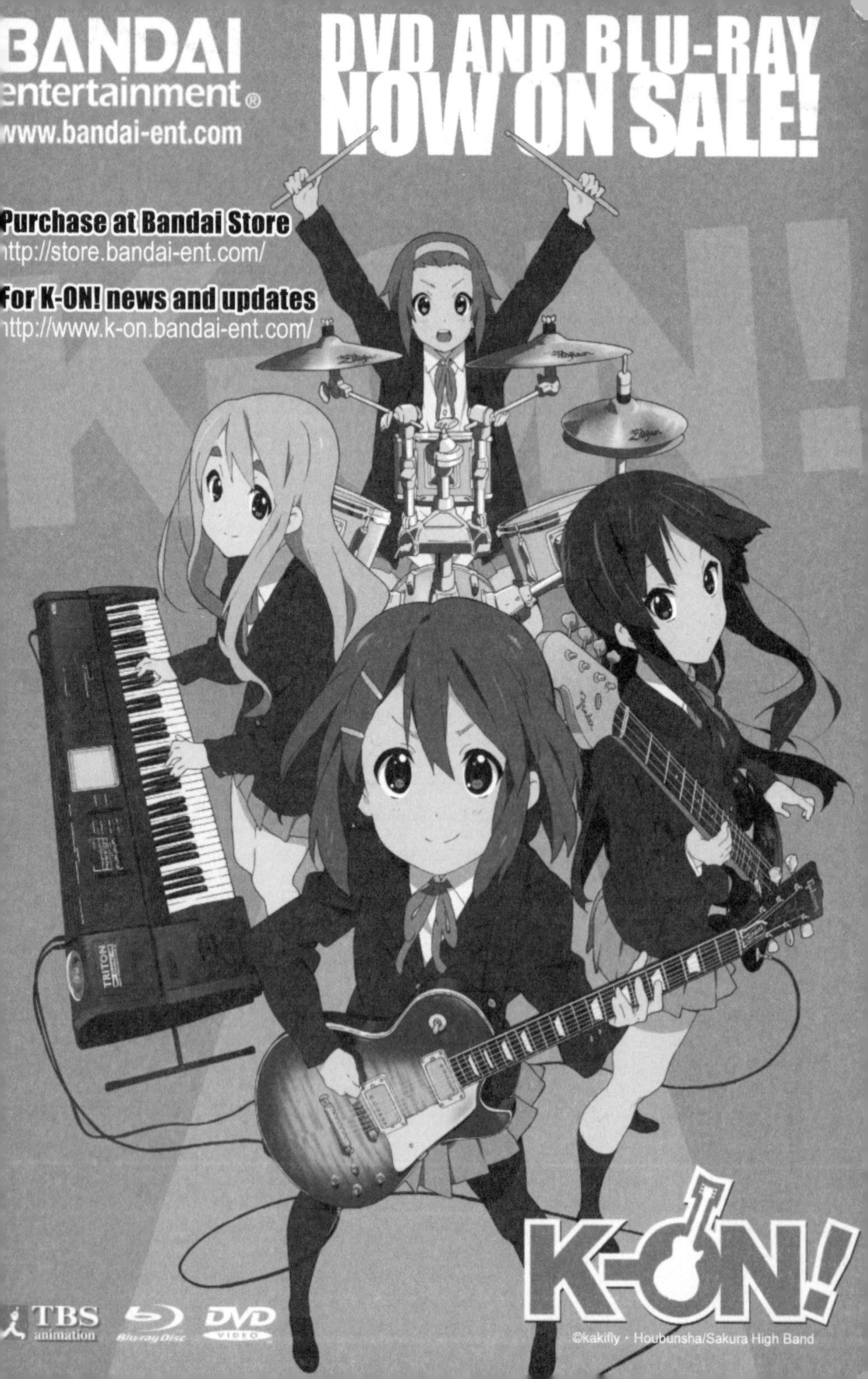
BANDAI
entertainment®
www.bandai-ent.com
DVD AND BLU-RAY
NOW ON SALE!
Purchase at Bandai Store
ttp://store.bandai-ent.com/
For K-ON! news and updates
ttp://www.k-on.bandai-ent.com/
TRITON
K-ON!
TBS animation
Blu-ray Disc
DVD VIDEO
©kakifly · Houbunsha/Sakura High Band

K-ON! ④

KAKIFLY

Translation: Jack Wiedrick

Lettering: Hope Donovan

K-ON! vol. 4 © 2010 Kakifly. All rights reserved. First published in Japan in 2010 by HOUBUNSHA CO., LTD., Tokyo. English translation rights in United States, Canada, and United Kingdom arranged with HOUBUNSHA CO., LTD through Tuttle-Mori Agency, Inc., Tokyo.

Translation © 2011 by Hachette Book Group, Inc.

Yen Press
Hachette Book Group
237 Park Avenue, New York, NY 10017

www.HachetteBookGroup.com
www.YenPress.com

Yen Press is an imprint of Hachette Book Group, Inc. The Yen Press name and logo are trademarks of Hachette Book Group, Inc.

First Yen Press Edition: December 2011

ISBN: 978-0-316-18835-7

10 9 8 7 6 5

RRD-C

Printed in the United States of America